GW00660078

Just for the Thrill

Thrill

Competitive motorcycling in
Ulster in the Seventies

Written and Compiled by Roy Harris

BALLYHAY BOOKS

Contents

Acknowledgements

Author would be the wrong word to describe me; In this book my task has been to compile information gleaned from a variety of sources and re-written, picked and re-jigged from reports published at the time.

Many of these sources were provided by Sydney Steele to whom I owe a great debt of gratitude for giving me free rein to peruse the treasure trove of memorabilia stored in his attic which was complemented by Sam McMinn and Phillip Campbell who loaned me old programmes.

For the hundreds of photographs (many previously unseen) included within these pages I owe a huge thank you to all those who dug through their collections to provide images of the sport in the Seventies and who gave me permission to use them in this book.

In particular I'd like to thank Rowland White, Frankie Corrigan, Norman Waddell and Derek McIntyre whose archives were the source of the majority of the photos in the book and whose knowledge in tracking down the images I needed was invaluable.

Thanks are also due to Kenny McKee and Dennis McBride whose photographs of off-road motorcycling added significantly to this aspect of the book as well as all those contributors who provided me with images from their own private collections including Alfie Mayrs, Trevor Armstrong, Harold Crooks, Con Law, Denis Quinn and John Smyth (for both his own pictures and others taken by the late Billy Reid).

Of course support in a project like this can be either active of passive and it would be remiss of me not to acknowledge the vital role of my wife Mary who was a rock for me through the occasional stormy periods inevitable in a project of this magnitude.

But most of all I'd like to thank all those competitors who lived, breathed and in some tragic cases died for their chosen sport and along the way gave me, and I assume you, a huge amount of pleasure in an era described by many as arguably the best there has been – I dedicate this book to them.

R Harris

Introduction

A scene that epitomises racing in the seventies with Ray McCullough leading Mervyn Robinson, Joey Dunlop and Sam McClements in a hammer and tongs battle.

As Big Ben resonated to bring 1979 to a close, it also brought an end to a decade in which the motorcycle world had been transformed with the decline of established European manufacturers in the face of a wave of new machines and technology from Japan.

Over and above this, the flare up of huge civil unrest in Ulster ensured that the change in competitive motorcycling in the Province during the decade was even greater as, in parallel with the introduction of new machinery, foreign competitors became reluctant to cross the Irish sea.

Thus the bass growl of the Norton, AJS, Triumph and Matchless machines or the howl of the MV Agusta ridden by the likes of Jack Findlay, Guyala Marsovsky and Giacomo Agostini at the beginning of the decade, had been replaced with the metallic scream of over the counter 2-strokes ridden by a generation of home grown heros such as Ray McCullough, Tom Herron and Joey Dunlop supported by a few stalwart overseas competitors including Mick Grant and Ron Haslam.

On the off-road scene a similar picture emerged as lighter and more powerful 2-strokes became the norm and, while mid-week grass track events drew in huge crowds to watch local masters of the rough stuff, Norwood, McBride, Crockard, Johnston etc. had to travel to Europe to prove that they were able to compete with the very best in various international competitions.

Of course these were not the only changes going on: the seventies also saw the arrival of superbike racing, scrambles became motocross, tarmac push starts abolished in favour of clutch starts, mass starts became group starts (following the death of Ernie Kerr during the 1968 Temple 100), the loss of world championship status for the Ulster Grand Prix and the TT and the arrival of a young William Joseph Dunlop to challenge the established star of the decade, Ray McCullough.

Yet while these dramatic changes were under way, the Ulster competitive motorcycling scene, perhaps because of the paucity of overseas competitors, retained many of the elements of competition in earlier years.

Thus while in the rest of Europe the decade saw a move away from road circuits to dedicated tracks with large run-off areas, in Ulster road racing retained its pre-eminent role. This, allied to the emergence of a raft of local talent to fill the space left by stay-away overseas competitors, ushered in a decade which is regarded by many as a golden era for motorcycle sport in Ulster and which laid the foundations for the disproportionate representation this small province has enjoyed since at the highest levels of motor cycle sport.

Unfortunately such success came with a price.

For any competitor in motorcycle sport there is a huge amount of sacrifice, skill, bravery, money and sometimes selfishness required to throw your leg over any form of motorcycle to compete in what appears to the normal human as an alien world of unbelievable speeds, impossible angles, gravity defying climbs up rock faces, breakneck charges into tight first corners handle bar to handle bar, shoulder to shoulder trying to get the hole shot and an immediate advantage over fellow competitors.

All motorcycle sport carries some element of danger, though perhaps none more so than road racing in Ireland which takes place in a corridor between hedges, ditches, walls, barbed wire fences, houses, pillars, telegraph poles and other roadside 'furniture' where the smallest mistake can have fatal consequences. Although the speeds in the seventies were lower, the circuits were certainly not as well prepared or the roadside furniture as well protected forty years ago as they would be today and the number of injuries and fatalities reflected this.

Why did (and do) they do it? That question has never fully been answered. A brief glance at the meagre prize funds shows it wasn't for the money and, with only three on a podium, for the majority of the competitors it couldn't have been for the glory.

What I do know however is that once a competitor pulls on that helmet, pulls down his visor (or goggles as it was in the seventies) they step from the hum-drum world of human existence into an alternate world of adrenalin fuelled concentration – clipping apexes, slip-streaming inches from the rear wheel of the rider in front, flying through the air over jumps, maintaining balance and control of their machines in situations that lesser mortals would regard as impossible providing an unparalleled thrill for rider and spectator alike.

Nothing stirs the emotions like racing: exhilarating to watch as a neutral; traumatic for family and friends in pit lane; an adrenalin rush like no other for the competitor; impossible to understand for the uninitiated – but a tradition in Ireland and beyond that has drawn huge crowds for generations.

Motorcycle sport feeds a hunger for thrills and excitement which seems to be built into our DNA, a need that has been about since the wheel was invented.

With nobody forcing anyone to go racing and every competitor fulfilling a dream, long may it continue – doing it *Just for the Thrill.*

The world of Motor cycle sport is not just for the riders but is a close knit family as this group of partying riders, marshalls, spectators and friends shows.

1970

The year the SDLP was formed; a loaf of bread was nine pence; pint of milk five pence and a gallon of petrol seven pence – ah those were the days.......

A wave of violence hit Belfast in 1969 as the infamous Northern Ireland 'Troubles' erupted, but through all the dark days of the decade covered in this book, motorcycle sport continued relatively unscathed.

As the decade opened the hot topic under discussion in racing circles was whether clutch starts should be introduced into motorcycle racing rather than push starts, provoking differing views – closer racing as everybody gets underway cleanly, versus the traditionalist view that push starting is an art and a part of racing.

Time shows that clutch starts won the debate.

Bob Coulter

The only Ulster competitor in a Motor Cycle News poll amongst readers for their 'Man of the Sixties' was Sammy Miller in seventh position behind winner Mike Hailwood.

Belfast's Bob Coulter, seriously injured in the 1968 Belgian Grand Prix, was convalescing at home having spent several weeks in hospital having his spine strengthened. He was soon competing in another season on the 'Continental Circus' on a brace of Yamaha's, a special 125cc and a 250TD2, he collected from Germany in April.

Ray Spence on his 750 Triumph at Maghaberry 1970

Maghaberry Airfield, now the site of Her Majesty's Prison, was the venue for short circuit racing organised by the Motorcycle Road Racing Club of Ireland (MCRRCI) at the start of the decade.

The 1½ mile circuit saw some memorable battles with the first meeting of the 1970 season providing Cecil Crawford with a double in the 350 and 500cc classes riding an Aermacchi and Norton.

In the 500cc class Tom Herron rode a Triumph to second position behind Crawford while Abe Alexander was runner-up in the 350cc race.

Eight races formed the programme that saw wins for Bobby Whyte (200cc Bultaco), Jack Wilkin (250cc Yamaha) and Ken Ferguson (Unlimited Triumph) while Joe Coxon was a double sidecar race winner on his Rumble BSA.

Campbell Gorman rode a 350cc Bridgestone to victory in the club member's race beating the 500cc machines of Jimmy Heath and Herron into second and third.

In 1970 there were no compulsory helmets in trials, just bare heads or flat caps at a time when Sammy Miller was destroying fields in the European championship while Benny Crawford was the undisputed local king of the feet-up branch of the sport.

Miller stormed around the frozen sections of the British round winning by 32 marks from 20-year old Malcolm Rathmell before making it four wins in five rounds to virtually clinch the European Championship on home soil with his 13th victory in the Hurst Cup.

Sponsored by Duckhams Oil, the Hurst Cup, no doubt helped by Secretary of the Knock Club, Stanley Scott's offer of free entries to International and National licence holders, drew a best ever entry of 95 riders who tackled six laps of a six-mile course at Clandyboye Estate with 20 observed sections on a frosty, but dry, bright day.

Another title clinched at the Hurst was the Irish Championship with Benny Crawford, who finished seventh overall in the main event claiming maximum points to secure the Irish title with three rounds remaining.

One notable entry in the Hurst was ex-road racer Ernie Lyons riding a 250cc Bultaco.

In what was a prelude to his highly successful museum in Hampshire (still well worth a visit today) it was reported that Sammy Miller had a new hobby – after collecting a fine array of ancient firearms he had switched to historic motorcycles.

Sammy Miller

L-R Drew Armstrong, Benny Crawford, Donald Fleck, Kevin Martin, Harold Crooks and Bobby Hewitt at the Slemish Trial

Tommy Robb and Ralph Bryans raced at the Daytona 200 in Florida as part of a British Team who raced factory prepared 750cc four-cylinder Hondas.

A white leathered Bryans suffered a spectacular crash in practice losing control of his machine as he swept onto the infamous Daytona banking from the infield luckily escaping injury although the Honda was burnt out.

Come race day Bryans, riding teammate Bill Smith's practice machine and Robb retired with broken camshaft-drive chains.

At Daytona Mike Hailwood rode for the first time in one of the new all-enveloping helmets and commented, "It's a bit hot in there, like sitting in a greenhouse."

A new 3-mile course at Mallusk was in the grip of ice, snow and sub-zero temperatures for the Knock Club Trophy Trial where Benny Crawford (Bultaco) and Billy McMaster jnr (Montesa) were head to head until the penultimate lap of ten observed sections tackled five times.

McMaster had his chain jump from the sprocket at the fourth section, which he had already 'cleaned' (no marks lost) three times, costing him five penalties and the trial as Crawford went on to win by four marks – 39 to 43.

Tom McBride at Kelly Cup Trial

Tom McBride won the McMaster Cup Trial having encountered a few problems along the way.

Midway through the Knock Club event at the Lead Mines, Newtownards the chain of his AJS broke, so he freewheeled to his house close to the venue where the chain was hastily repaired. Then in a rush to get back to the competition he collided with a tree in his garden causing a split in his fuel tank, a problem quickly remedied by transferring a tank from another bike in his workshop before rejoining the trial to take the premier award.

Ulster racing suffered a great loss in February with the death of Ronnie Conn, who for the past three years was instrumental in moulding the career of Brian Steenson by providing competitive machinery. Former world champion Ralph Bryans, Ray McCullough and Tom Herron were others who benefited from Conn's influence with his greatest moment coming during the 1969 Isle of Man TT races where Steenson finished second to Giacomo Agostini in the Junior TT.

Brian Steenson (left), Ronnie Conn and Son

Heavy Rain throughout the Lightweight Club Irish Trials Championship at Saintfield added to rider's difficulties, as did the new ruling that standard time would be the average time of the first six riders!

The big surprise was the return to form of ex-Irish champion Brian Lamb, who paid most attention to the new rule to win the Larkin Cup finishing without penalty on time losing 99 marks on observation while runner-up Benny Crawford lost 96 marks on observation around the 75 sections, but also seven on time, which meant he lost to Lamb by four marks 99 –103.

Robert Wilkinson was the man in form on the scrambles scene, the 20-year old taking his Husqvarna to four wins from four starts during the Ayton Trophy meeting at Killinchy and then a week later lifting the prestigious Brian Bell Memorial Trophy at Saintfield. Wilkinson may now be forced to miss a number of major Irish meetings because of University exams.

However double Irish champion Winston Norwood (AJS) won the Wills Trophy for the third successive year despite frequent snow showers at Dromore, Co Down, where Scottish visitor Norrie Lymburn (CZ) finished second after the retirement of Davy Crockard, Dennis McBride and Wilkinson.

This meeting saw the first round of the new Irish Junior championship with J. Bell winning from G. Hill and J. McCoosh.

Robert Wilkinson

Brian Steenson, on hearing that BSA were not to support production racing in 1970, burnt the midnight oil to build his own 750cc BSA-3. He started work on a Monday, had the machine ready to track test at Oulton Park on Thursday and minus a fairing raced it to sixth position in the production race at Cadwell Park on Sunday completing a treble of sixth positions at the meeting in the 350cc and 500cc races on his Seeley machines.

At the 14.2mile Nurburgring West German Grand Prix Tommy Robb (Seeley) finished third in the 500cc race behind Giacomo Agostini (MV) and Alan Barnett (Seeley) with Steenson finished fifteenth of the thirty one finishers.

Steenson's hang it all out riding style took him to a superb fifth in the 500cc French GP held on the 2.7mile Bugatti Circuit at Le Mans with Robb eleventh.

Brian Steenson on 500cc Seeley at Henry's Corner at NW200

Cecil Crawford on 500cc Norton

Steenson and partner Pat Mahoney rode a 750cc BSA-3 to overall third position in the prestigious Thruxton 500-mile race completing 208 laps of the 2.36 mile Hampshire circuit taking the class win on the way despite numerous problems along the way.

Ulster's road racing season erupted into life with the Tandragee 100, in the days of two laps practice before each race, where pint sized Cecil Crawford gave the Ryan Norton its first win in two years with victory in the 500cc race completing a double with a 350cc win on his Aermacchi.

The 1970 North West 200 held on Saturday May 23rd saw Ireland's first world champion Ralph Bryans (50cc World Champion in 1965) announce his retirement from racing after coming from the back row of the grid to win the 250cc race riding a nine year old ex-works 4-cylinder Honda borrowed from former team mate Luigi Taveri.

Another significant milestone at this particular meeting was the first international road race victory by 21-year old Tom Herron in

Ralph Bryans on his way to winning the 250cc race at the NW200

the 350cc race having diced with 35-year old Tommy Robb for four laps of seven before Robb was forced to retire at Juniper Hill after a stone entered the carburettor of his Yamaha.

A production race was introduced to the North West programme at this meeting with Cliff Carr winning the 250cc class riding a Spanish Ossa machine, Stuart Graham taking a Suzuki to victory in the 500cc class and Malcolm Uphill winning the 750cc category riding a Triumph.

This was the only year during the seventies that this particular race was run with a production race not reintroduced until 1987.

Brian Steenson rode the 500cc Seeley QUB single cylinder two-stroke in its first public appearance during practice, but a broken primary chain brought its debut to a premature end, Steenson reverting to his four-stroke Seeley for the race where again a broken primary chain sidelined him from the race lead handing victory to Peter Williams on his Matchless.

Unfortunately this was to be Steenson's last race on home soil as he was to lose his life following an accident during the TT a fortnight later.

Race day at the North West was marred by the death of English rider Andrew Manship from serious head injuries following a crash at Primrose Hill on the opening lap of the 350cc race.

Gordon Blair, Colin Seeley and John Cooper with the 500cc QUB Seeley

It was business as usual at the Cookstown 100 despite road works on the wide main street threatening the future of the course.

A battle royal developed in the 350cc race with Tom Herron (Yamaha) and Cecil Crawford (Aermacchi) as they fought wheel-to-wheel for six pulsating laps. Herron was in front for the first four laps and then Crawford nudged ahead only to lose out narrowly to Herron on the final circuit with Len Ireland in third.

The 250cc went flat after Herron and Billy Guthrie retired on the opening lap with seized engines in their Yamaha's leaving Ray McCullough to win comfortably from Alfie Mayrs and Norman Dunn.

Crawford's Ryan Norton proved too fast for Herron's 350cc Yamaha in the 500cc race where the Norton of Roy Reid snapped at Man of the Meeting Herron's back wheel throughout.

Brian Steenson on a BSA Rocket 3 at the 1970 TT

The TT races on the Isle of Man brought tragedy with the death of six competitors during practice and racing with one of Ulster's brightest young competitors Brian Steenson amongst them.

Steenson, a BSA research worker, crashed out of fourth position at the Mountain Box during the Senior TT and was rushed to hospital with multiple injuries from which he died five days later.

In addition to Steenson the others who lost their lives were Les Iles, Michael

Collins, Denis Blower, John Wetherall and Santiago Herrero.

A controversial plan to start the competitors in batches of nine at 90sec intervals in the Senior TT was dropped the day before the race.

Tom Herron was 13th in the 250cc race, his first TT, but it all went wrong in the Junior 350cc race when he crashed at Ballacraine on the first lap fracturing a thigh.

Tommy Robb finished fifth in the 125cc TT riding a Maico having stopped on the opening lap before Ballacraine with a dead engine. Luckily he carried a spare plug and once fitted he carried on although well down on time.

During the Killinchy 150 meeting at Dundrod Ray McCullough gave the 500cc single cylinder two-stroke QUB its competitive race debut. McCullough led the 500cc race and lapped at over 94mph before a cracked expansion chamber caused the machine to run weak and slow dramatically eventually to seize on the penultimate lap.

This race was the highlight of the meeting as Cecil Crawford made

Ray McCullough on the new QUB bike at Killinchy 150

a blinding start only to coast to a halt when the petrol pipe on the Ryan Norton came adrift, as McCullough, Gerry Mateer and Tommy Robb set the pace.

Having refitted the offending pipe Crawford restarted in 28th position and rode like a demon to eventually retake the race lead six laps later and win from Billy Guthrie and Mateer after Robb retired with a snapped throttle cable.

A week later McCullough gave the QUB its first ever track success at the Mourne Club short circuit at Bishopscourt winning both Unlimited races.

On his debut at the Southern 100 on the Isle of Man Billy Guthrie, a 30-year old Moira cabinetmaker easily won the Solo Championship race after a superb start that renowned Motor Cycle News correspondent Norrie Whyte described as, *"leaving the line like a Crumlin Road rocket."*

Dead heat in 500 Event

from Scotland's Charlie Dobson (Norton) and F. O'Callaghan's (Triton) Herron's average for the eight laps was 82.55 mph.

Denis Gallagher and Gerry Mateer could not be separated after 8-laps of the Temple 100 500cc race. Eight Temple Club judges of the meeting deliberated for five minutes before declaring a dead heat – the first time an Ulster event had ended in this fashion.

The Mid Antrim 150 saw Ray McCullough debut his 250cc Yamsel (a Yamaha engine in a Seeley frame), completed only the night before and race to his fourth 250cc race win at the event in four years setting a new class lap record of 79mph.

Visiting riders Scotsman Alex George, Liverpool debutant Ian Richards and Coventry's Bill Henderson claimed second, third and fourth with Albert Miller from Strabane fifth.

Cecil Crawford riding an ex-Tom Herron TR2 Yamaha for the first time rode to victory in the 350cc race following a close dice with Billy Guthrie, who came a cropper at a slow bend gathering himself up to maintain second over 20secs behind Crawford despite a new track record of 82.44mph.

Crawford doubled up with a start to finish victory in the 500cc race on the Ryan Norton well ahead of a wheel-to-wheel dice for second between Roy Graham and Gerry Mateer, which Graham won.

42nd Classic International **Ulster Grand Prix** DUNDROD 15th Aug. 1970

Official Souvenir Programme 3/-

The 42nd Classic International Ulster Grand Prix was held on Saturday August 15th still a counting round of the Federation International Motorcycling (FIM) World Championship (although the writing was on the wall) and consisted a five-race programme for 50cc, 250cc, 350cc, 500cc solo machines and a 500cc race for sidecars in the tenth of the twelve rounds.

The programme for the meeting cost 3 shillings on top of a charge levied on all vehicles entering an area defined as the 'Race Area' on race day incorporated in a windscreen label issued to cover the admission to the various car parks around the 7mile 706 yard Dundrod Circuit.

The charges were as follows; Motorcars 5 shillings; Motorcycles 2 shillings; Motor Coaches 20 shillings and Taxis 5 shillings.

Each Car Park had a designated colour and you had to follow the road signs

50cc tail enders at UGP, C M Walpole, (Garelli), A Lawn (Honda), C Geary (Honda) followed by travelling Marshal Natty Ferguson

for your particular colour to get to your chosen area e.g. to get to Leathemstown Corner you followed the Blue Route, Deers Leap / Cochranstown was Red route and Wheelers, Tornagrough and the Hairpin was the Yellow route.

Race day saw Dundrod covered in heavy cloud although the roads were in perfect dry conditions with only the final race for sidecars experiencing wet roads.

In the 50cc (Tiddlers) six-lap race, future 13 time World Champion, Angel Nieto broke away with a new 83.95mph lap record to win.

The 15-lap 250cc race saw the 'works' Yamahas of Rod Gould and Kent Andersson plus the private Yamaha of Kel Carruthers battle for the lead; Carruthers going on to win by 37secs from Gould and Paul Smart.

In the Gallaher 350cc race and Black Label 500cc 15-lap races Giacomo Agostini won as he pleased completing the 350 / 500 double for the third year running.

In the 500cc race Welshman Malcolm Uphill, in third position at the time, sustained a badly broken thigh when his Suzuki seized at Deers Leap chucking

Giacomo Agostini in his last appearance at Dundrod

him through the hedge at high speed.

Fifteen chairs lined up for the ten lap sidecar race, the final race in their world championship, with Klaus Enders winning the race with a new lap record of just over 92mph finishing some fifteen seconds clear of fellow BMW rider Siegfried Schauzu to clinch the championship.

Dan Jordan, Chairman of the UGP Supporters Club formed in 1963 when the future of the 'Prix' was in crisis, stated in the programme that the club, whose annual minimum members subscription was 5 shillings., *"contributes between £2,500 and £3,500 per year to the race."*

In the Who's Who section it was noted that Elmer McCabe, who passed away in Australia in February 2013, was making his first trip home from Australia to race in the 250cc class at the UGP on a Yamaha having emigrated to Australia from Antrim in 1951.

At the Manx Grand Prix the Coleraine Club won the team award for the second year running in the 250cc Lightweight race with Alfie Mayrs (9th), Errol McCready (18th) and Willie Galbraith (25th).

In last lap drama during a sun-baked John Donnelly scramble Cheshire's Alan Clough ousted last lap leader Jeff Smith (BSA) when the Midlander suffered a rear wheel puncture luckily hanging onto second from the fast finishing Robert Wilkinson.

Surprisingly the two Ryan Norton's of Cecil Crawford and Ian McGregor, back in the Ryan fold after a two-year absence, failed to finish the 8-lap Carrowdore 100 unlimited race handing victory to Gerry Mateer also Norton mounted, who matched the absolute lap record of 91.67mph set earlier in the day by 350cc race and Ulster championship winner Crawford.

KILLINCHY & DISTRICT MOTOR CYCLE CLUB LTD.

BRYAN WADE
DICK CLAYTON
VIC EASTWOOD
JEFF SMITH
have all won the

JOHN DONNELLY SCRAMBLE

KEITH HICKMAN
ARTHUR BROWNING   MALCOLM DAVIS
JIMMY AIRD   BRYAN GOSS
                          DAVE BICKERS
and many others must try again !

✱✱✱✱✱✱✱✱✱✱✱✱✱✱✱✱✱✱✱✱✱✱✱✱✱✱✱✱

THIS YEAR'S EVENT ON SATURDAY 5th SEPTEMBER AT KILLINCHY, Co. DOWN WILL INCLUDE THE USUAL LINE-UP OF STAR RIDERS.

Come early and see all the action—
Practice 11.00 a.m.—First Race 1.00 p.m.

Tommy Robb took Kirkistown by storm rounding off his best season of late with a superb treble, the 36-year old taking the feature King of Kirkistown ten lapper plus the 500cc and 350cc races.

In the 350cc race Cecil Crawford crashed heavily just after the start and was taken to hospital with what were reported as, 'serious head injuries'.

Dave Crockard

Rob Wilkinson, Davy Crockard and Dennis McBride kept going at a chaotic wet and muddy 250cc Trophee des Nations in Sweden to finish a creditable sixth for the Motor Cycle Union of Ireland Team.

Just four months after breaking his thigh at the TT Tom Herron won his comeback ride at Maghaberry, victorious in the 250cc race from Robin Smyth and Anthony Owens at the MCRRCI confined short circuit meeting.

Torrential rain left floodwater two-foot deep in places playing havoc with the river sections selected by the Ards Club for the Turner memorial Trial over a three-mile course at Ballyskeagh, Newtownards. Tackling fast flowing rivers that were gently flowing streams prior to the rain Billy McMaster jnr emerged victorious in the experts class.

Sammy Miller, arguably the world's greatest trials rider of all time, decided to retire from national and international events. Miller won the Hurst Cup 13-times; he won two European championships (before world championships were introduced) and was five times a winner of the Scottish Six-Day Trial, his versatility shown by winning the 250cc race on an NSU at the North West 200 in 1958 with Mike Hailwood 200-yards behind him.

Billy McMaster Jnr Turner Trial Winner

After 15-years the Walter Rusk Trophy changed hands from the mighty Sammy Miller to Belfast car salesman Billy McMaster jnr, who won the annual Boxing Day Trial at the Lead Mines.

Renowned photographer Bertie Martin (left) with Tandragee 100 officials

John Bell commentating at Bell Scramble

Brian Steenson at Carrowdore with Syd Lawton

*50cc Competitors
at 1970 UGP
including 13 time
World Champion
Angel Nieto (No.1)*

*Elmer McCabe
made his first
trip home from
Australia in 19 years
to race at the UGP*

*Campbell Gorman
and Roy Reid at an
early Bishopscourt
meeting*

*Gordon Blair (left) discussing QUB project
with frame builder Colin Seeley (centre) and
English competitor John Cooper at NW200*

*Cecil Crawford, pictured here at the
Skerries, was "flyin" in 1970*

Norman Calvin
and Dennis
McBride at
Bell Scramble

Arthur Browning John
Donnelly 360 Greeves

Terry Patterson

Brian
Clough

Derek
Stewart at
Slemish

Davy Andrews
at Kelly Cup

Derek
Russell

Dennis McBride

remembers... The Trophée des Nations

Today the The Motocross des Nations is a single event where national teams representing their countries compete in 125, 250 and 500 classes with one rider entered in each class. However, back in the seventies each class had its own competition held as a stand alone event with the 250s competing for the Trophée des Nations.

Ireland had been a regular competitor in the event since it's inception in 1961 but, given that the riders from here were competing on off-the-shelf bikes against teams riding what were effectively full works machinery, top results were hard to come by and the ninth place we had achieved in 1969 in Kester, Belgium was widely regarded as a remarkably good result given the level of the competition.

Knutstorp, Sweden

When the Irish team of Gordon Bowden (Sprite), Dave Crockard (Greeves), Winston Norwood (Husqvarna / Sprite), Robert Wilkinson (Husqvarna) and myself (Husqvarna) departed on the overnight Liverpool boat with Team Manager Sydney Steel and Jury Member Kevin Martin on the first leg of the journey to Ring Knutstorp in Sweden for the 1970 event the feeling was that if we could repeat the Kester result we'd be doing very well.

After a strenuous 17 hours journey we rolled in late on

Born and reared in Lisbane near the John Donnelly course, Dennis served his time as a mechanic, after which he progressed through various jobs in the motor industry before setting up an oil distribution company with his son Stephen.

His first attempt at racing was at the Temple Scramble in 1964 where his 350cc Royal Enfield failed scruitineering as "the wheels were falling out of it!"

In 1966 his brothers bought him a Greeves Challenger on which he won all 3 legs of the McClay Scramble only to fall off breaking his own leg two days later.

Undeterred, he raced successfully for another 10 years until family life had to take precedence although he still maintains an interest in the sport through his nephews' participation in MX.

Myself and Willie Simpson at Cambridge Scramble

Friday night to the Esso Motel, Helsingborg where we paid at a kiosk, received the keys to our rooms and headed off for a welcome night's rest. Saturday arrived bright and early and, following breakfast from a vending machine (a lifetime first for all of us), we headed of to Ring Knutstorp, a car and bike racing circuit still used today.

Although the hillside part of the track was unfamiliar to most of us, Saturday practice went well, and when the team gathered together for a team talk in one of our rooms, everyone seemed upbeat, though under no illusions as to how hard it would be to maintain the standard set the previous year.

But then nature offered a helping hand.

During Saturday night it started to rain and boy did it rain! When we arrived at the track early on Sunday for free practice and qualifying, conditions were atrocious with a track that resembled the Lead Mines in Newtownards in mid winter – grist to the mill for us lads.

The parade of countries participating started at midday, where we were resplendent in our Irish shirts, but when it came to the playing our National Anthem we all had a good laugh when Danny Boy blared out over the circuit speakers!

With the preliminaries over by one o'clock, it was down to business with forty riders lined up for the 40 minutes + two laps first leg. With a good start essential to stay out of early trouble and inevitable jams on the steep hills, nerves were stretched to breaking point and when the starter tried to hold the field too long a false start was guaranteed.

As we lined up again with tempers flaring and the continuing torrential rain it wasn't hard to predict problems on the early laps and thus Robert Wilkinson and I were hugely relieved to make cracking starts and escape most of the carnage behind us as the pack of mud-splattered riders blasted off on the restart for a grinding 50 minutes of racing in the pouring rain.

When the chequered flag at last came out we made our bedraggled way back to the pits where we set about trying to clean ourselves and the bikes. Bearing in mind we had travelled with only three cars and two trailers (hoping for some prize and starting money to pay off the expenses), there were none of the amenities offered by the race transporters of today such as power washers, shelter, a kitchen or toilets, but standing out in the pouring rain with no cover was made easier by cups of warming tea made by Peggy Martin and Sadie Steel and the buzz going around that we had finished ahead of the Swedish and British teams.

Because the best three riders results counted, nothing was confirmed until after the Jury meeting, but eventually the news filtered back that we were lying in ninth place close behind the teams ahead of us with every thing up for grabs in the second leg.

Everyone was on edge as we lined up for the second leg with a good start again being a priority, as that would probably dictate the final result and all of us aware we could be onto something good.

It was a case of heads down and backsides up hoping for the breaks that count as we slogged it out in a sea of mud that took its toll on riders and machines and such was my concentration that thankfully the fifty minutes seemed like twenty and Sydney kept giving us a thumbs up board, which I took to mean we were doing all right and on for a decent result.

After the race as we were washing down standing in basins in our underpants in the dark with the ladies supplying hot water (no mean task) my eyes started to play up. I'd always had a problem with my eyes from the dirt thrown up and that evening I ended up in the circuit hospital where they performed a delicate operation to remove the grit which left me in a temporary state of total blackout, with two black eyes for my troubles.

After we loaded everything up it was time to head for the prize giving under strict instructions from Kevin Martin to dress in grey flannels, MCUI blazers, white shirts and Ulster Grand Prix ties.

As I still couldn't see, Winston Norwood drove my car and on arrival we were presented with a smorgas board (raw fish, bread etc). Having not eaten properly all day since the vending machine breakfast

Winning the Lisburn Motocross wearing the new style of helmet sourced from USA which would take over from the old pudding basin. Lack of goggles may explain my eye problems ....

Peggy fed me all this raw stuff and with my eyes still completely closed I was able to convince myself it was just like the tinned salmon sandwiches we had at lunchtime.

The MC for the evening announced the results starting with first position which was, as expected, Belgium whose multi-world champion studded team of Roger De Coster (world champion), Joel Robert (world champion), Harry Everts (world champion), Sylvain Geboers and Jack Van Velthoven, were dominating the competition at the time. As the runner up positions were announced we were anticipating a ninth or tenth place finish which would have been a fine result.

You can thus imagine that when he came to sixth and announced Ireland, I was stunned – all the experience gained over foul wet weekends in the mud and glar at the leadmines and other venues had stood by us and I can honestly say I've never been as proud of being involved with a bunch of people who had never had the resources or, as we thought, the talent to compete in this world arena, as I was at that moment.

All the idols that I looked up to at the time were congratulating us on posting a result like this simply because of our amateur status, beating the works teams of Sweden, Britain, France and Italy was an added bonus.

Holice Czechoslovakia

The 1971 Trophée des Nations proved to be a very different experience from Ring Knutstorp but for many reasons was just as memorable.

This event was another long haul for us and the team of Robert Wilkinson, Dave Crockard, Winston Norwood, Raymond Davidson and myself accompanied again by Team Manager Sydney Steel and Jury Member Kevin Martin travelled in 3 cars and 2 trailers from Belfast to Liverpool, then down to Dover crossing over to Calais and onto Germany where we stopped overnight before embarking on the final leg of our journey.

Following the hopes and optimism of the "Prague Spring", Soviet forces had invaded Czechoslovakia in late 1968 to bring liberalisation to a halt and we weren't really sure what to expect though we had been advised that a supply of goodies to give away (such as cigarettes and ladies tights) could smooth the way. Even so we were shocked to see the high wire fences with the lookout posts with armed guards which lined the Czech border and we were made to hang around for half a day until someone decided to wave us through after liberal handing out of stickers and packets of Benson & Hedges cigarettes.

Travelling through the towns it was clear that life for the Czechs wasn't easy with long queues at shops for what to us seemed like very meagre fare. However it didn't seem to dent their friendliness and, when we arrived in the town of Pardubice around 9.30pm on Friday and couldn't find our hotel, a bus driver

Local competition in the early seventies, L-R Myself , Jack Duddy (Gallaher representative), Alan Clough and Harry McQuaid.

who was waiting on passengers realised our plight and jumped in my car and guided us to the hotel car park. (More Benson & Hedges).

On Saturday morning we all headed out for a first sight of the track and to get in some timed practice. In a total contrast to the Knutstorp rain, the heat was unbearable and where the track ran up a steep rocky hillside you could see the black rubber laid down on the surface of the rocks during practice. The heat was even more unbearable inside the army tents the organisers supplied for the pits although we received some welcome help from a local teenager who, though he didn't speak English, was happy to hang round, cleaning bikes and kit etc in return for a share in our meals. He seemed particularly fascinated by our long hair which was very much the style in western Europe but had apparently been banned along with other western 'decadences' such as pop music in the Soviet clampdown.

However, this cultural straightjacket didn't seem to dampen the Czechs' enthusiasm for motocross and on arriving at the track on Sunday morning we had a real eye opener. They had put a cordon around the entire area and armed guards directed hundreds of coaches and cars into massive stubble fields, making the estimated attendance of around 70,000 cheering spectators who were totally thrilled to be at the event.

The day passed without incident and although we couldn't emulate our previous year's success, given the advantage the works machinery had over our bikes in the dry fast conditions, we were reasonably pleased with twelfth place.

That night after a meal of fried potatoes, onions and half raw egg we were invited to a club connected to the hotel and sampled some wine, receiving a bill for each bottle we ordered. It was sometime later a man approached our table dressed in a blue blazer with a local TV company badge on his breast pocket. Willie Johnston and myself recognised him right away as the works Jawa rider Franta Šťastný, who had been commentating on the event for the local TV.

For an example of how small the world we live in is, it's worth pointing out that I'd met Franta before when he was competing at the UGP as he sometimes stayed with local trials rider and travelling Marshall, the late Natty Ferguson

František (Franta) Šťastný on 350 Jawa at Dundrod

on his farm at Island Hill. Franta would cycle into Comber to the Spar Supermarket in the Square, owned by my two brothers Everett and Wilmer to stock up on provisions for the paddock. A true gentleman, Franta had fond memories of his visits to Northern Ireland having won the 350cc UGP in 1965 and scoring a 3rd and a 6th in the 250 and 350 UGPs respectively in 1969.

After the usual introductions he asked if any of us could sing and if so would they be able to sing any Englebert Humperdink songs as his records had been banned in Czechoslovakia. None of the other boys knew any of these songs so I volunteered and was introduced to the conductor of the orchestra. We agreed on the songs and the keys and away we went, covering about six or seven songs altogether.

The craic was good but after a couple of hours we decided to head for bed as we had an early start and a long journey back home. We said goodbye to the locals and headed for the door with our wine bills to pay the cashier, when all of a sudden 5 or 6 men blocked the exit.

With the language barrier being a problem we could not understand what was happening until Franta appeared and explained to us that these men wanted us to join their table with their friends for a drink and guess what, our wine bills were wavered due to the Englebert songs.

When we eventually got outside and before there was any prospect of forty winks I was delegated to drive two young couples we had befriended in the bar back to their homes in Robert Wilkinson's car as mine was jammed in. I duly dropped them off and they gave me a piece of paper with directions back to the hotel but, given the circumstances, I got totally lost and decided the only option was to enlist some local help in the form of a big bloke who was swaying up the footpath. He clambered into the car and I gave him the directions but he proved little more adept at interpreting them than me and in short order he guided me the wrong way into a one way street. Half way up we were abruptly stopped by a police car going the right way and 2 officers approached with batons in hand. The big bloke jumped out of the car with a packet of Benson & Hedges and I

Showing off the Irish Team gear for Vesoul France 1974 where we finished 8th: L-R Sammy Stokes, me, Winston Norwood, (Missing Robert Wilkinson and Dave Crockard)

thought he had deserted me but, although drunk, he knew how things worked in Czechoslovakia and after a brief negotiation resulting in the handing over of 2 more packs of good quality cigarettes we were escorted back to my hotel. On arrival we found the door locked and my new friend hammered the door to awaken the Manager who, when he appeared, was ready to fight but for the intervention of another trusty packet of Benson and Hedges which to my mind by this stage were proving to be more useful than a squad of UN peace keepers.

Next morning Sydney Steel and Kevin Martin were livid when we told them of our experience as they had befriended Franta at the UGP and would have loved to have met him again.

Having been advised to spend all our small change or give it to the locals before we left on the Monday morning, we were caught short when we reached the border and stopped for a tea break beside a café where we noticed the truckers enjoying litres of cold beer. We thought we'd have some of that but with no money we had no hope and of course denial only made the desire stronger. Out of the universal currency of Benson & Hedges, we were at a loss until I remembered the box of tights Davy Mills had advised me to take with us (they were not available in Czechoslovakia), so I grabbed a couple of pairs and along with Winston Norwood made our way to the bar to be greeted by a very dour lady whose demeanor immediately changed when we produced the tights for which she was happy to exchange 2 litres of beer and 2 packets of their local cigarettes although I have to say when we tried the cigarettes it was immediately clear why Benson and Hedges were such a valuable commodity!

Thus ended the second of two trips, each memorable in their own way but both illustrating the joys of competition and making lifetime friends which epitomises motorcycle racing.

1971

Decimalisation introduced – 68 people died in a crush at Ibrox during a Rangers v Celtic football game – number one chart hits included Benny Hill with Ernie The Fastest Milkman in the West and Rod Stewart with Maggie May.

UGP 250 podium Jarno Saarinen, Ray McCullough and Dieter Braun

In 1971 Ulster was in the midst of chaos thanks to the ongoing Troubles leaving no sector of society untouched including motorcycling with the bombing of Grand Prix House at Dundrod and the FIM Congress being moved from Larne to Geneva simply because of the Troubles.

However for many involved in motorcycling the abiding memory of '71 was Ray McCullough winning the 250cc Ulster Grand Prix overshadowing world championship contenders Phil Read, Rod Gould and Jarno Saarinen.

The race meeting where that happened is one that everyone still talks about today, the Ulster Grand Prix when Ray McCullough gave a riding lesson to upset the world championship contenders to win his first and only world championship Grand Prix.

However there was more to this meeting, held in absolutely atrocious conditions. Despite the bombs and bullets in nearby Belfast the Ulster Grand

Ray McCullough on his way to victory in UGP

Prix went ahead with double world champion Giacomo Agostini staying away, cabling the organisers late in the day saying he simply could not travel.

McCullough's victory was sensational as he blasted a high quality field into oblivion with a masterful display of wet weather riding.

Read, the championship leader, made a faultless start, but three laps later McCullough was tucked in just ten yards behind. The crowd loved it, but Read was not happy. The pair were so far ahead of the field that Read kept waving McCullough down, his obvious intent to slow the pace and for him to score maximum points. Supermac was having none of it and took the lead.

Read dived back into the lead on lap ten in what was a titanic battle, but like the great ship his chances were sunk when firstly McCullough retook the lead and Read's Yamaha engine went sick and he eventually retired, the fault discovered to be a broken crank pin.

McCullough raced on to what was a historic victory, the last world championship Grand Prix victory by an Ulster rider at Dundrod, with second position going to Jarno Saarinen, who was a massive 1m 25secs adrift of McCullough when the chequered flag came out after 14 rain sodden laps.

Acknowledging McCullough's ride Read said, "He just put his head down and carried on sliding round the corners riding his own race."

Horst Owesle and Peter Rutterford

In the worst weather of the day works MZ rider Peter Williams came through to win the 350cc race inheriting the lead after Sarrinen crashed at the hairpin and Tommy Robb slowed with mechanical woes.

Robb bounced back with third place in the 500cc race won by Jack Findlay from Rob Bron while in what turned out to be the last world championship race to be held at Dundrod Horst Owesle and his English passenger Peter Rutterford triumphed in the sidecar race the German / English partnership, unknown at the time, becoming the last competitors to win a world championship Grand Prix at Dundrod.

Findlay, McCullough and Williams were winning their first ever Grand Prix, however the question posed in Motor Cycle the following week in a frank article was:−

Can the Ulster survive?

For three years the event has been hit by the civil unrest in Northern Ireland. Last years meeting ran at a loss and the organisers went ahead this year knowing they had to show a profit or the meeting was in real danger [remember at this time appearance money was a huge part of the bill for Grand Prix events and for major internationals]. Then came the rain. It started on Thursday and did not stop until halfway through Saturday's race programme, coupled with no public transport because of the trouble in Belfast the crowd was kept down to a conservative 20,000 estimate. The Ulster enthusiasts who run the meeting obviously face an uphill task to keep their famous Ulster Grand Prix alive.

A hint to the future came later when the proposed FIM Annual Congress, due to be held in Larne in October, was transferred to Geneva amid fears that a number of the National Federations would refuse to travel to Northern Ireland amid the mounting tide of violence. In a federation poll nine wanted the congress called off while five were willing to travel to Ulster.

Billy McMaster jnr and Derek Stewart tied on observation at the Knock Club McMaster Trophy Trial at Bells Hill, but Stewart was declared the winner on the tie-deciding last lap when he lost only four marks to McMaster's five.

An odd tale from this event was that Irish Champion Benny Crawford was reported as stopping one lap too soon and had changed out of his riding gear before discovering his error!

The first ever continental entries were among the 97 starters for the Hurst Cup held over six laps of a five mile course through Clandyboye Estate with twenty observed sections on each lap.

Persistent sleet showers and high winds made things tough although punctures were the main talking point as a mainland carve up of the top positions saw Gordon Farley losing 168 marks on observation, six clear of Malcolm Rathmell, who in turn was sixteen better than Rob Edwards.

Ray McCullough riding the first Yamsel to arrive in Ireland travelled to an early season meeting at Oulton Park and won the British Championship 250cc round, his first win on the mainland.

In light drizzle McCullough took the lead from Barry Sheene at Cascades on the second lap of eight and within a couple of laps had developed a race winning lead nine second ahead of Sheene at the chequered flag with reigning champion Steve Machin third.

Some weeks later Sheene took up the Ulster challange by racing at Bishopscourt!

Yes it did happen on 3rd April during the Temple Club's 50th Anniversary Carling Black Label sponsored short circuit. Paul Smart was to have ridden at the meeting, but was unable to do so and his future brother-in-law Sheene

Above; Barry Sheene on 250cc Yamaha at Bishopscourt and right: his 125 Suzuki

was contacted and he arrived with his ex-factory Stuart Graham 125cc Suzuki and an ex-Smart 250cc six-speed Yamaha. Davy Wood and Sheene won their respective 200cc heats, but in the 10-lap final Sheene showed his future world champion class by streaking to a 21sec victory over Richard Hewitt and Anthony Owens with Wood in sixth. Sheene led Ray McCullough in the 250cc race until, as he stated in MCN, "I could feel the gears seizing." This allowed local idol McCullough to race to a half minute victory over Sheene, who had re-grouped after the scare of almost being thrown off, with Steve Murray third. Next home runner was Ronnie McQuillan on his 250cc Greeves in sixth behind Mal Kirwan and G. Corbett. In this particular race Tom Herron fell off without injury. Herron compensated by overhauling Tommy Robb in the 350cc race the 22-year old winning comfortably from Billy Guthrie and Bill Smith after Robb was forced to quit with clutch problems. Smith comfortably won the 500cc race on his Kawasaki-3 from Robb and Brian Kemp while Ray Spence triumphed in the concurrently run over 500cc race while Lowry Burton won the invitation handicap and Dubliner Joe Coxon was the first of just four finishers in the sidecar event. This was the one and only time that Barry Sheene, one of the most popular (or maybe you found him intolerable, depending on your personal view) English racers who ever raced in Ireland.

Tom Herron leads Billy Guthrie on his way to 350cc win at Tandragee

Tom Herron had his first real road race since his 1970 TT accident with the 22-year old demonstrating at the Tandragee 100 that his broken thigh had not affected his racing skill.

During the 250cc race he lost over three minutes at the start, as his Yamaha would not fire-up, but once he got going he scythed through the field to finish second behind Ray McCullough. He went one better in the 350cc event with a lap record of 87.57mph to beat off the challenge of Billy Guthrie, Mal Kirwan and Gordon Bell.

Guthrie won the best race of the day when there were three different leaders of the unlimited race, initially Ian McGregor was to the fore before he retired the

Ryan Norton, then Wilfie Herron (750cc Norton) led for three laps before his machine slowed allowing Guthrie to the front when it mattered most – as the chequered flag went out.

One Joey Dunlop described in Motor Cycle as *"a bright new prospect on the Ulster scene"* finished second in the 200cc race riding a 196cc Suzuki behind Kells rider Jackie Robinson and his well used 125cc Honda.

Carling Black Label sponsored the Brian Bell Memorial Scramble at Saintfield where Robert Wilkinson (Husqvarna) squeezed past the similar machine of Dennis McBride on the last lap to take victory – although McBride was subsequently disqualified for changing his bike from the one he rode in his heat.

Gordon Bell, brother of the late Brian, switched from road racing at Tandragee to scrambles and finished fourth.

During the 'Pinta' sponsored Tom Henning scramble at Tinker Hill Newry Robert Wilkinson grabbed the glory with a hat trick while Davy Crockard took a commanding lead in the Irish 250cc championship.

Multi scrambles winner,
Robert Wilkinson

An interesting article by Mick Wollett Sports Editor of Motor Cycle had a headline:–

Road Racings Wet Threat.

Is it worth holding road races in the rain or should they be cancelled? Racing in heavy rain is miserable for riders, officials and spectators, speeds are cut, close dicing is nearly impossible because of the spray thrown up and retirements rocket. The event becomes damp, limp and dangerous shadow of what a race should be. When it comes to races on public highways, such as the North West 200 or the TT officials should be more prepared to cancel or curtail events than they are now. I realise the problems, riders starting money, refunds to spectators (?), but surely insurance by the national governing body could cover such contingencies. Racing should be enjoyable to all concerned and I have yet to meet a rider who genuinely enjoys competing in the rain.

– an interesting piece from 1971 when even today people question the wisdom of racing in heavy rain and events or individual races have been abandoned or curtailed in recent years.

In a storm lashed North West 200 Paul Smart won the 350cc race, but in the 250cc event Smart and Tony Rutter going at it hammer and tongs in the

Albert Miller with goggles lowered to see his way through the rain

treacherous conditions when Smart's Yamaha slid away into the path of Rutter, both crashing at high-speed at Cranagh, the fast right hand bend approaching Coleraine, just past where Coleraine Borough Council offices are today.

The cruel blow of the grim weather was a nightmare for the organisers, who had gathered together one of the best entries for years.

Steadiest and most consistent rider on the day was John Cooper who finished second in both the 250 and 350cc races before scoring a tremendous victory in the 500cc race as the aces around him slithered and skated on the ice-like soaking surface.

A small toddy was the only way to warm up after the 500cc race as Cooper passed a bottle of the local Bushmills Whiskey around the winners' enclosure!

Tony Rutter and Alan Barnett at storm lashed NW200

New central reservation in Cookstown main street.

Racing was back on the 7.7 mile Orritor Circuit for the first time in eight years for a Wednesday Cookstown 100 that saw the competitors racing down one side of the new central reservation on the ultra-wide Cookstown Main Street.

Race of the day was undoubtedly the 5-lap 500cc event dominated for three laps by Ray McCullough, who set the fastest lap of the day at 86.61 mph riding the second version of the single cylinder two-stroke QUB Seeley, before retiring with suspected broken piston rings leaving Abe Alexander, Billy McCosh and Mal Kirwan at loggerheads for the remainder of the race, the trio swapping places a number of times on the final lap with McCosh (Seeley) taking the win by a fraction from the similar machine of Alexander and the Aermacchi of Cheshire rider Kirwan.

McCullough did win the 250cc race by a country mile from Jackie Robinson and Alfie Mayrs while Gordon Bell and his Aermacchi inherited the lead of the 350cc race when Billy Guthrie went out with a broken crankshaft, Bell victorious after a good scrap with Manxman Derek Harrison with McCosh third.

Bobby Whyte easily won the 200cc race from Tom Finlay and 'impressive new boy Joe Dunlop.'

Unbeaten in every race he contested, Co Down farmer Winston Norwood (CZ) thrashed the opposition including 'star billing' former world champion Jeff Smith (BSA) during the Cambridge Trophy Scramble at Portaferry.

A huge crowd witnessed one of Norwood's best ever displays that saw him take

Derek Bowden at Cambridge Scramble

a start to finish victory in the main race; his day completed by taking maximum points from both legs of the 250cc Irish championship where Robert Wilkinson and Smith pushed him hard.

In leg one the three went into the last lap all in with a chance of winning, but with the crowd anticipating a photo finish Norwood put on a spurt to win by three seconds from Wilkinson with Smith a similar distance back in third.

Three laps from the end of leg two Norwood was baulked by a slower rider and Smith swept into the lead only for the local idol to regain the lead to win by two seconds from the factory BSA rider and Davy Crockard.

A week later and Robert Wilkinson (Husqvarna) with three-second place results became the first Ulster rider since 1966 to win an action packed Tommy Stewart Scramble at Downpatrick.

In extremely dusty conditions Norwood won the first leg while Scot Jimmy Aird won the second and third legs.

Norwood and Wilkinson went into the third leg dead level on time. Norwood grabbed the lead, but Wilky was closing fast and when the CZ started to shed rear wheel spokes, the wheel eventually collapsing, Aird went through to win from Wilkinson enough for the QUB student to win the main trophy.

Denis Gallagher (Yamsel) set the fastest lap of the day at 96.16mph during the 350cc Killinchy 150 whilst chasing race leader Billy Guthrie, who was forced out with a broken con-rod handing victory to the Scot, who had Gordon Bell and Billy McCosh follow him home.

McCosh went on to win the 10-lap 500cc race from Abe Alexander and Wilfie Herron after Ray McCullough retired the QUB Seeley with a cracked expansion chamber when in the lead.

McCullough took a runaway victory in the 250cc race riding his Yamsel finishing well clear of Jack Wilken, Jackie Robinson and Norman Dunn, while Bobby (RJ) Whyte was equally in control of the 200cc class.

Winston Norwood, dominant force in local scrambling

A broken chain three laps from the end of the 25-lap Fred Beckett Trophy scramble spelt disaster for Winston Norwood and handed a lucky victory to Robert Wilkinson over a twisty course at Ballynahinch.

With a safe 30sec lead Norwood looked a safe bet to win, but his chain jumped off the sprocket and although he was able to put it back on and re-start still in the lead cruel luck played a part with the chain snapping and the chance of a win gone, as Wilkinson fended off the challenges of firstly Harry McQuaid and then Davy Crockard to take the win.

The following week over a new venue at Portaferry the McClay Scramble produced a scorching contest between Norwood (CZ) and the Husqvarnas of

Wilkinson and Davy Crockard. Such was their pace that they lapped the entire field with Norwood snatching the victory.

Crockard second in the main race won the 250cc race from Norwood, Dennis McBride and Roy Neill (CZ). Neill of course is today the voice of motocross and a leading light in the Motorcycle Racing Association (MRA), the off-road branch of the sport in Ireland.

Ray McCullough gave the QUB Seeley 500 its first major success when he won the 10-lap unlimited race during the Skerries 100 – upping the lap record to 85.6mph.

Still on cloud nine after his UGP victory McCullough continued his 250cc roll with another comfortable victory at Kirkistown in sweltering conditions where he also took the QUB Seeley to another victory.

In that race McCullough got away mid-pack sweeping through to take the lead on lap two of ten. From the halfway mark Gerry Mateer threw down a challenge taking the lead around the outside at Fishermans only to see McCullough regain the lead a lap later with 40-yards to spare at the chequered flag with Campbell Gorman on a recently acquired Linto third.

Mickey Laverty in Lurgan Park action

Lurgan Park was the venue for the first local all-clutch start short circuit meeting promoted by the North Armagh club.

A week later just up the road at Maghaberry Airfield Coventry toolmaker Bill Henderson shattered the 1½ mile circuit lap record with a speed of 69.29mph on his way to winning the 350cc race eclipsing the 1963 record set by Ralph Bryans.

A dog fight for second between Gordon Bell Jackie Robinson, Wilfie Herron and Mickey Laverty was settled just after the halfway mark when Bell, exactly a year after switching from scrambling to tarmac, bit the dust with Herron, who broke a collarbone.

Coventry based Ulster exile Bill Henderson (he left Donegal when he was fourteen) set a searing pace in the 350cc Carrowdore 100 350cc race for the first two laps until a cylinder head cracked on his Yamaha and he coasted to a halt. Also out went Denis Gallagher his machine suffering ignition trouble and Jack Wilkin with a faulty gearbox on his Padgetts Yamaha.

Billy Guthrie streaked to a two-minute victory over Gordon Bell with the only other rider out of forty starters on the same lap as Guthrie and Bell being George Rodgers in third, as Gerry Mateer crashed out on oil and Ray McCullough retired his Wilfie Herron borrowed Yamaha with a gearbox problem.

McCullough, chasing a clean sweep of national 250cc races, was forced to retire from the Carrowdore race with a broken crank pin, but he gave the 500cc QUB Seeley its first Ulster road race win fending off Mateer, Roy Reid and Sam McClements.

As a last minute replacement for the "injured" Bryan Wade (who rode in England the next day), veteran BSA rider Jeff Smith interrupted a holiday to travel to Ulster and cruised to a brilliant start to finish victory in the Carling Black Label John Donnelly scramble at the 2-mile Killinchy course – his second success in this major event. Incidentally Smith's first Ulster appearance was at the Hurst Cup trial in 1949!

Headline in Motorcycle News:–

Bomb Blasts Ulster Race HQ

A bomb wrecked the Ulster Grand Prix administration building (Grand Prix House) situated at the start – finish area of the Dundrod Circuit on Saturday night 2nd October.

The 10-15lbs gelignite bomb destroyed two-thirds of the 6-year old building, but the part left standing suffered serious structural damage and will have to be demolished.

An UGP spokesman said, "This won't stop the race. The replacement value on the building is in the £5 -£7,000 region."

Grand Prix House

Ulster's championship racing season came to a close with a Tommy Robb hat trick including being crowned King of Kirkistown for the second successive season.

Still pushing his Yamaha from his allotted back row start as the King of Kirkistown field disappeared Robb made it into third halfway

Tommy Robb tries on the King of Kirkistown Crown presented by his wife Noreen

through the race and by the penultimate lap was on leader Sam Davis (687 Rickman) back wheel. Under pressure Davis dropped his machine on the last lap and that left Robb's defence of his crown safe – well clear of Ray Spence and Mickey Laverty.

Robb back from his final globetrotting campaign in the world championships won the 350cc and 500cc to cap a magnificent day.

Robb had finished seventh in the 500cc world championship and announced that it was to be his last season riding on the continental circus although he was planning a full Irish season in 1972.

Ten times Irish Trials champion Benny Crawford and Derek Russell, both Bultaco mounted tied on 22-penalties each at the second round of the 71/72 championship over four laps of fourteen stiff sections at Finnis in the Dromara Hills. However the outright winner of the Shaw Cup was piano tuner Crawford by virtue of his superior last lap performance.

A strange occurrence at the end of season confined short circuit meeting at Maghaberry came when officials had to drive a herd of cattle away from the circuit perimeter – twice!

Winners at the end of season finale included Ray Spence, Bobby Whyte, Robin Smyth and in the 500cc race John Cooke who won from Frank Kennedy and John Wallace, a staunch member of the MCRRCI who later lost his life in a road traffic accident making his way home from preparing the clubs Aghadowey Circuit and after whom the Wallace Hairpin was named.

Past and present members of Queens University who have excelled in sport were honoured at a distinguished presentation.

Ray McCullough received a special tankard while Mr and Mrs Alex Steenson received an award posthumously on behalf of their son Brian, a graduate of the university.

During the third round of the Irish Trials championship at the Lead Mines the second section became the focal point after the landowner blocked access on the grounds that the organising Ards Club had not sought permission to use that particular piece of ground, this after the first lap of the trial had been completed.

A group of enthusiasts then marked out an alternative section away from the disputed territory and the day was saved for the 86 starters.

A battle royal between Billy McMaster and Benny Crawford lasted

Benny Crawford

to the last section, a steep drop into a slippery bank, a tight turn and a steep climb out over rocks. Crawford took a 'five' while McMaster took a different line climbing a gigantic rock to go clear and take a winning advantage.

Pay at the Ulster Grand Prix plan:–

In an attempt to prevent extinction of the Dundrod classic, a Road Races (Amendment) N. I. Bill, which would permit charging a general spectators fee, was introduced and given a second reading at Stormont.

With the UGP due to celebrate its Golden Jubilee in 1972 it was anticipated that a modest charge of 30p per head would provide the necessary injection of financial help required to keep the meeting afloat.

*Campbell Gorman and Billy McCosh
battle it out at Kirkistown*

*Getting round Fisherman's
at Kirkistown (clockwise
from top) Abe Alexander,
Roy Reid, Ray Spence,*

Cheshire visitor Mal Kirwan at
Bells cross-roads Tandragee

Retired Ralph Bryans
in Civies still getting
a fix at Tandragee!

Tom Herron, Tandragee

Tommy Robb on his Seely
at Temple Club's 50th
anniversary meeting

19 Peter Williams;
9 Silvio Grassetti;
11. Peter Berwick; 4.
Guyala Marsovszky;
26 E C Santos ;40 A
Darlington at UGP

Mickey Laverty's 350
Yamaha, the first
to carry the British
Enkalon sponsorship

Tommy Robb leads Ray
McCullough through
Leathemstown in
the Killinchy 150

Gillie Iveston & Billy McGivern

Martin Lamkin at Hurst Cup shows how its done ...

... while Malcolm Rathmell doesn't

Alfie Mayrs

remembers the Manx ...

Originally from Coleraine now living in Antrim Alfie Mayrs spent 35 years in the motorcycle business, managing the Kawasaki Centre in Ballymena before moving to manage Hurst Motorcycle Centre in Belfast, his day job tending to spoil his hobbies – racing motorcycles and then sailing.

After retiring from racing motorbikes Alfie raced sailing boats with moderate success for many years out of Antrim Boat Club on Lough Neagh, competing in major events like Cork week (sailings equivalent of the TT). "I can get the same buzz doing 15mph in a sailing boat on a windy day as flat out down Deers Leap he says

Being originally from Coleraine and living within the Triangle area gave me an early introduction to motorcycle racing with the North West 200 taking place on our doorstep. I'm sure every schoolboy watching the racing had the same thoughts but I can remember from I was no age watching the bikes thundering round and deciding that one day I'm going to race in that.

I remember a man by the name of Stewarty Whitley, a leading light in the Coleraine Club who used to take part in the sand races held at Magilligan, taking me around the pits (which at that time were just after York Corner heading towards Henry's Corner in Portstewart) and looking around all the bikes and riders – school-boy heaven!

Thereafter I immersed myself in all things motorcycle racing – I don't think I ever missed Motor Cycle News as well as various other motorcycle magazines, reading all the Grand Prix reports, who the riders were and the bikes they rode so that by the time I ventured to the Ulster Grand Prix practice for the first time I was able to identify everybody by their helmets!

My first outing on the race track was at the Tandragee 100 in 1967 on a wee 50cc Itom that I'd bought and fixed up myself though I soon moved on to a Tiger Cub (that I'm currently restoring!).

200 class start Tandragee 1970 (I'm number 11)

My first win was at the 1970 Tandragee on a 196cc Bultaco in the 200cc class although I didn't actually own the machine. It belonged to a guy in Belfast, John Meennan, who intended to race it, but when he went for his medical he found out he was a diabetic and the authorities would only give him a license to ride on the short circuits, so he loaned me the bike for the road races.

I also rode a 250cc Greeves Silverstone before switching to a 250cc Bultaco which at the time was the thing to have (Tommy Robb was their works rider) before the Yamahas arrived, sweeping all before them.

Chasing Mickey Laverty

Road races in those days were longer, the 50 mile championship was a full 50 miles and the 100 mile races were what they were called. Today the public want to see good quick races, basically short circuits on the road.

All the road courses had their own wee quirks – Tandragee was a good circuit as were Dundrod and Carrowdore while the Temple was very, very difficult, especially as the bikes got quicker – nearly like motocross on the roads and just not suitable for racing. I remember when riding the wee 200 round there thinking as I went over went over the jumps 'my goodness what's this going to be like on the 250?'

What I thought on a 250 is not printable …

In the early seventies Ray McCullough was the man to beat and I reckon he was the best of the lot. I still think if he had gone abroad to race he would have been a world champion, but he chose to stay at home where he was virtually unbeatable as many a big name rider who visited to these shores will vouch! In my last season he was to prove to be my nemesis when I finished second to him in nearly all the national 250cc races with the notable exception of the Carrowdore 100 when his bike broke down and I won the race, a result that gave me the Irish 50 mile championship – and I have the plaque to remember it by!

In those days the accepted progression from the Irish scene was to race on the Isle of Man – definitely the place to race, no question about it. To me the North West, Dundrod and the Isle of Man are what road racing is all about and, while there is much controversy about whether road racing should or shouldn't carry on, once you ride any of those three circuits you find there is something about them that you would never, ever get on a short circuit – and once it gets in your blood it will never leave you.

Having raced at the first two, the next, and for me the ultimate, challenge was to tackle the Mountain circuit which meant either the TT or the Manx Grand Prix.

Taking it cautious over Ballagh Bridge

Having to choose between them, my thinking was that with the Manx being an Amateur event I could be in with a shout whereas there was no chance of winning a TT with all the works teams there.

Everyone prepares for the challenges of the Isle of Man in their own way and the only time I had been on the Island before I raced in the Manx was on a Young Farmers trip to see the TT – that was all I had ever seen of the circuit!

However I had discovered some time before a great a book on the Isle of Man circuit with lots comments by the likes of Mike Hailwood and by the time of my arrival I had that book pretty well studied – in fact I had nearly memorized it! After that it was a matter of driving and riding round and round trying to memorize the 37¾ mile circuit, either on the road bike I had brought with me or in an old Bedford van loaned to me by fellow racer Jim Scott.

Danger wasn't a thing you thought about to be honest. To me the biggest worry was my bike breaking down – the risk of falling off was very much a secondary consideration. My plan for riding the Mountain Course was to ride safely fast or at nine tenths – you can do it safely and quickly if you know where you are going.

Between 1968 and 1973 I competed in seven different races at the Manx for which I have five silver replicas (still proudly displayed!) with a best result of fourth in the 1973 Lightweight race, my last, averaging 93.668mph.

Among my many fond memories from those races were two magic moments at the Manx when in 1969 and 1970 myself, Errol McCready (from Kells) and Willie Galbraith (from Coleraine) won the team award for the Coleraine Club

Myself, Errol McCready and Willie Galbraith with the Bills/Hardy Trophy after winning the team award at the Manx

which had very generously given us £50 each towards team expenses.

To win this competition required a mix of speed and reliability, for if one of the team failed to finish that would be it. So you were very reliant on your help and support and in this I was well blessed with my now famous pit crew and mechanics were Eddie Johnston, who now has an MBE and Gary Anderson who became a top designer in F1 car racing.

When we came back from the Island the Coleraine Club made quite a fuss of us. They took us out for dinner and then to the Arcadia Ballroom and re-presented the cup to us in front of throngs of people (remember the Arcadia was as famous then as Kelly's is now). That was quite an event and we felt a bit like a pop stars although we almost didn't have a trophy to hand over to the club!

We were to be the first winners of the Bills / Hardy Trophy – a quite expensive Trophy – and the Manx Club didn't want it to go to Northern Ireland because of the troubles but after we made a strong protest about it they relented, although they took out extra insurance on it before they let it out of their sight.

Still reflecting on the lighter moments of the Manx I recall one year being camped in the paddock at the Manx where there was always a lot of young kids running about. Someone jokingly told them we had no milk bottles in Ireland (all used for petrol bombs), so they carried enough bottles to the paddock in two weeks to fill a Manx refuse truck!

Unfortunately that 4th place in 1973 was to be a high-water mark for me as that was the year I retired after relatively short career in racing from 1967 until 1973. Although in those seven years I'd fallen off a couple of times each season and had used up a few helmets and ripped a set of leathers or two, I had never broken a bone – but that didn't mean I was unaware of the dangers and I made an agreement with my wife that if any kids came along, I would stop racing. Lo and behold in 1973 we found ourselves in that happy position and I stuck by the agreement which I don't regret – racing is a wee bit like gambling in that sometimes you are better to quit while you are ahead!

Of course I missed the racing but I still had the memories – the great buzz of the racing, the camaraderie between riders, the huge crowds, the craic, the changing face of racing and the challenge of the Mountain Course.

Ah those were the days; enjoyed every minute of it.

Jim Atkinson

remembers…Cookstown and District Motorcycle Club

Cookstown and District Motorcycle Club first ran a road race on a Thursday in 1922 and no, I was not there – in fact of all the road races still running Cookstown is the oldest in Ireland.

Moving the clock forward the club ran the race on a Wednesday, the normal ½ day around the province when business closed and a number of national road races took the opportunity to run their particular event.

I recall the Cookstown ran on a Wednesday right up to 1974 before moving to the now traditional Saturday.

One of the features of Cookstown was that the race took in the main street, one of the widest that I know of prior to a central reservation being put in by the authorities.

Thinking back to my days in the club and the road race in particular, as the club also ran trials and scrambles, during the seventies it was so laid back, none of the endless meetings with agencies involved like we see today, no working on it from one year to the next like today.

I remember going out on the Friday night prior to the event with the Club Chairman Noel Anderson to paint a few signs indicating the corners and braking distances to said corners.

It has to be said our artistic flair was lacking, so what the signs looked like at racing speeds can only be imagined.

Remember this was when there was no Friday practice

Born in Ballymucklehcancy, Magherafelt on 18th Nov 1941 Jim's first encounter with bikes was a 250 BSA in his early teens, which he fell off on a regular basis. He had several other bikes and well remembers falling off them all at one stage or another, so, as Jim freely admits, Joey, Speedy (Brian Reid) and McCullough were never in any real danger but that didn't dent a lifetime interest in racing.

Jim began reporting on racing with 'Townland' radio and was the first to report live from the track, which coincidentally was from his local race, the Cookstown 100, and he's been reporting on road racing across the length and breadth of the country ever since.

Cookstown 100 250cc start on Main Street for the last time.

with the roads closing on a Saturday at 1pm for the racing and practice, which was two laps prior to each race – you basically turned up on a Saturday and raced the roads that normal everyday traffic had been using right up until road closing time.

There were no safety committees, little or no track preparation, a scarcity of prohibited areas, no transponders, treaded tyres (no wet or dry as one size fitted all), no elf and safety breathing down our necks and very few officials.

Cookstown I remember went from the 6.6mile Grange Circuit in 1970 to the 7.5mile Orritor track for one year in 1971 and then to the 6.4mile Sherrygroom Circuit in 1973 and unlike today there was no such thing as taking away trackside furniture, removing ditches and hedges, no run off at corners, no Recticel bales, kerb or pole protectors.

In my time the 250 and 350cc classes were the stand out races with up to eighty riders lining up in four groups A, B, C and D starting at timed intervals.

The idea of the groups as I remember was that the best riders went in group A as your ability determined what group you started in. That was the theory anyway.

Sherrygroom was a technical real rider's circuit with competitors vying for a win and very little monetary reward.

Yamaha was the choice of the majority and not for one moment do I believe that the Japanese workers or bosses ever envisaged their mass produced machines would be raced around what was mostly the bumpy, twisty 'B' roads around Stewartstown with the main road between Cookstown and Stewartstown the best of the five used.

Riders like Ray McCullough, Tom Herron and Campbell Gorman were to

Ivan Houston and Danny Shimmin power away from Sherrygroom Hairpin on the Cookstown course

the fore in the early races during the seventies at Cookstown while in the latter part of the decade it was the Armoy Armada and Dromara Destroyers who set the circuits alight with Joey Dunlop, Frank Kennedy, Jim Dunlop and Mervyn Robinson taking the battles to Brian Reid, Trevor Steele Ian McGregor and McCullough.

McCullough was dominant at Cookstown in the seventies and if my memory serves me right he won a race every year at Cookstown bar 1978 – 13 races in total seven in the 250cc class, three 350's and three 500cc events.

It was a pleasure to witness McCullough in action, his quiet no nonsense approach with immaculate prepared machines and economical style – a joy to watch.

Those were the day's; I clearly remember a titanic battle between Noel Hudson and Robert Britton that went to the very last corner when Hudson made a move inside to win by half a bike length with another half dozen riders noise to tail in their slipstream; the year I don't remember, possibly it was 1975.

Another time I remember Joey, in his early slightly rough days, coming in with quite a few scrapes on the fairing the result of an altercation with a hedge on, "the first lap two thirds of the way towards Redlands."

I was there in 1977, the day Ray McCullough and his 350cc Yamaha became the first man to lap the Sherrygroom Circuit at just over 100mph and then a year later when the track was lengthened to take in Stewartstown Hairpin Joey

Dunlop again 350cc Yamaha mounted went around at just over 100mph – unbelievable speeds to us mere mortals.

One of the highlights from the Cookstown for me was the after Race Dance in the Town Hall with the Snowdrifters Showband. It was six shillings (30p) to get in - provided you weren't intoxicated and the dance was over at 12 midnight.

Many a tale was told between the Hucklebuck and the slow waltz as to how races were won or lost, the close shaves or the mechanical woes encountered prior to the handout of the trophies.

Then the Thom family came on board and the 'do' moved to the Royal Hotel and the Reflections Showband.

People my age (a pensioner) say that the seventies saw the best years in road racing and the Cookstown 100 provided the heroic men and their flying machines the opportunity to give it their all thrilling those of us privileged to watch in awe at their skill and daring.

Ah! The seventies, what an era that sends the hairs bristling on the back of my neck just thinking about them.

1972

Troubles reach crescendo in Ulster with Bloody Friday and Bloody Sunday – road racing cancelled for the first half of the season – Watergate Scandal in USA – Mary Peters wins Gold at Munich Olympics – No.1 songs included You Wear it Well by Rod Stewart, Vincent by Don McLean and My Ding-a-Ling by Chuck Berry.

As part of Golden Jubilee Celebrations the Temple Club ran their unique 100-mile time trial and this produced only one gold medal winner – Terry Patterson, a former Ulster scrambles champion.

Silver medals were awarded to Billy McMaster jnr Jim McMahon and Billy Hutton at this 'mini-six day' event over 32 observed sections, three timed stages plus a braking and acceleration test.

Cross discipline participation!
Tommy Robb completes the braking and acceleration test on the 100 mile time trial while Gold Medal winner, Terry Patterson signals for Robb at 1971 UGP

Dubliner Gerry Scarlett (Ossa) travelled north for the seventh round of the Irish Trials Championship over a demanding course at Drumkerragh Forest near Ballynahinch and although accumulating 98 penalties he still won the Larkin Cup with the only score under one hundred. Fellow southern rider Brian Lamb finished runner-up losing 103 penalties.

An off-day by Billy McMaster jnr in sixth, and Derek Russell in tenth still saw Benny Crawford retain his championship lead by five points from Scarlett despite his worst performance of the season (mostly time penalties) finishing seventh.

Quote from Barry Sheene in Motorcycle with regard to the TT, *"I didn't enjoy the TT. The whole Isle of Man set up is a waste of time. It puts so many miles on the bike that after one TT it's rooted (done). It's like a whole season of Grand Prix races and with riders so spread out over the long lap I can't see what's in it for the spectators. I think it is over rated, under paid, dangerous and expensive. I like racing too much to risk sticking my neck out in the TT, so I suppose I'll never do well on the Island."*
Needless to say he never returned.

Constant chain problems and two punctures with his new Ossa forced favourite Davy McBride to retire from the Sandown Trophy Trial, but his younger brother Tom upheld family honour to take the main award making his first appearance at a local trial for eighteen months.

Ossa broke the stranglehold of Bultaco domination at Ulster Trials with a 1-2-3 in the McMaster Cup event won by Derek Stewart from the McBride brothers Tom and Davy.

With no signs of the civil unrest in Northern Ireland abating, questions were being asked as to whether the Ulster Grand Prix was on or off. With the FIM unable to hold its congress in Larne the previous year, would they be prepared to allow a world title round to be staged on the Dundrod Circuit near trouble torn Belfast?

Thus it was not a huge surprise when in March the MCN headline read:

North West 200 axed: Ulster at risk.

Following warnings that authorities might have to withdraw road closing orders on the day of an event the MCUI (UC) advised clubs to confirm or abandon their meetings at least a month in advance and recommend that organisers run their events on private circuits if possible.

Acting on this advice the Tandragee 100 was rescheduled as a short circuit meeting at Kirkistown and shortly thereafter both the Cookstown 100 and the North West 200 were cancelled.

Ray McCullough gave his 350cc QUB Bridgestone (powered by a basic production engine given to McCullough by Chester dealer Bill Smith that went under many modifications and tests at Queens University) a winning debut at Kirkistown on Easter Monday while 37-year old Wilfie Herron equalled the lap record on his way to winning the 750cc race.

In early April the 50th Anniversary Ulster Grand Prix was cancelled. Threatened with being scrapped for several weeks the decision to cancel was taken with the organisers now planning to run an international short circuit at Bishopscourt despite an offer to run the UGP at Oulton Park, an offer rejected by Ulster Centre Promotions.

Davy Crockard was in devastating form on the motocross scene with back-to-back hat tricks at Ardmore followed a week later by another at Tinker Hill where he won the feature Tom Henning Memorial Trophy race and the third round of the 500cc Irish championship.

Despite twenty years racing around the world 1971 was Tommy Robb's debut at Maghaberry where he won the 500cc race and finished third in the 350cc race won by Wilfie Herron, a race in which Frank Kennedy appeared on the leader board in fourth position.

No Tandragee 100 due to the ongoing security situation, so the North Armagh Club ran a short circuit meeting at Kirkistown where despite a slipping clutch on a Yamaha borrowed from Jackie Robinson, Ray McCullough was never headed in the 250cc race while Tommy Robb led the 500cc race from start to finish.

McCullough was also hot favourite for the 350cc race on his newly fettled Bridgestone and quickly opened up what seemed an unassailable lead, but with three-laps remaining an oiled plug put him out handing victory to former national champion of two decades ago Wilfie Herron, who was 15 secs ahead of Robb while Mickey Laverty came from nowhere to finish third.

Laverty won the 200cc race from Brian McComb, both Honda mounted, while Herron made it a double by winning the over 500cc event.

With precious little racing in Ulster Ray McCullough made a rare racing visit to the continent and finished ninth in the 250cc race at Tubbergen in Holland, a race in which Bob Coulter finished eleventh and Tom Herron thirteenth.

Coulter took a Maico (possibly a Yamaha engine in a Maico frame) to fifth in the 125cc race while Herron managed sixteenth in the 350cc event.

As a substitute for the North West 200 the Coleraine club, who had to shelve plans to run a shorter national road race on roads basically in the middle of the normal circuit, ran a W.D. & H. O. Wills sponsored grass track at Portstewart

Willie Johnston

with Winston Norwood winning four races. Dessie Percy (Jap) won the 350cc race and Willie Johnston the 200cc race on his Villiers.

A bleak TT for Tom Herron – no finishes, just retirement after retirement.

This was the TT that had a huge influence on the future status as a world championship event.

Italian Gilberto Parlotti, making his TT debut, was leading the 125cc race in very wet conditions, crashed at the fourth of the Verandah's right hander's. In the flat in fifth over 100mph accident Parlotti crashed into two concrete posts at the side of the track and was killed instantly.

In the aftermath of the accident 10-times world champion Giacomo Agostini, shocked by the death of his compatriot, declared that he wanted the FIM to strip the Isle of Man TT races of world championship status – *"every year riders are killed at the TT and the organisers do nothing to make the circuit safer. I certainly hope I never have to race at the TT again."*

He was backed by a number of competitors including Phil Read, John Cooper, Chas Mortimer and Rod Gould at the time.

Earlier in the week MV celebrated the 21st Anniversary of their first TT success in style with Agostini cake walking the Junior TT marking their 33rd Isle of Man victory since Cecil Sanford won the 125cc race in 1952.

Agostini was five and a half minutes ahead of second finisher Tony Rutter, who recorded lap of 100.90mph on the fifth and final lap.

Local riders did not have such a good TT with Billy McCosh (Suzuki) 11th in the Blue Riband Senior, Gerry Mateer (Norton) 16th and Abe Alexander Seeley (21st).

Following the TT Motor Cycle in an Editorial felt that:

'The TT on the Mountain Circuit seemed doomed because, in view of their current campaign for safer circuits, the FIM are highly unlikely to grant the Isle of Man classic world championship status next year. It is nonsense to demand another line of straw bales at Brands Hatch yet allow racing on a circuit lined by concrete fence posts and stone walls.'

Billy McCosh on his Yamaha at a wet NW200

The article went on to say that,

Riders will probably band together to boycott the TT, in fact some have already done so, namely Jarno Saarinen, Angel Nieto, Hideo Kanaya, Renzo Pasolini and Dieter Braun – resulting in some of the poorest TT racing for years! It is obvious the TT is a dying duck although it could linger on. On a positive note, the TT can be revived for both spectators and riders. The solution – For the Manx Authorities to build a brand new four or five-mile course with modern safety features, as the Dutch did. What other alternative is there for the Manx authorities?'

This is an abridged version of the article, however you get the drift – thankfully it never happened, yes the Grand Prix riders encouraged the demise of road circuits from world championships, but along came F1 and new breed of TT hero with the event still going strong despite of what the article intimated would happen.

During an Ulster Centre Championship Grass Track at Newtownards Willie Johnston (Villiers) and Dennis McBride (CZ) scored doubles – Johnston in the 200 and 350cc events while McBride was successful in the 500cc and expert races. Winston Norwood, who regularly cleaned up at these type of meetings had to settle for a 250cc victory and two runner-up finishes.

Dave Crockard

Meanwhile a ten strong raiding party of Irish riders ventured across the Irish Sea to Girvan in Scotland where the best of the party saw Dave Crockard notch up a couple of wins, Robert Wilkinson had a win and two second places while John Hoey managed a fourth position in the 500cc race.

In typical Dundrod weather, gale force winds and driving rain, 130 enthusiasts completed a lap of the 7.4-mile Dundrod Circuit during the UGP Supporters Club sponsored walk. Among the dedicated 'walkers' were riders Tommy Robb and Dick Creith plus Ulster Centre officials Donald Fleck, Sydney Steel and Bobby Hewitt.

Gallahers Ltd donated £30 to the first man across the finish line, Jimmy Todd from a local harriers club.

OVER 200 competitors lined-up on the starting grid at Dundrod on Saturday, not for a premature world championship round, but for the first-ever sponsored walk organised by the Ulster Grand Prix Supporters Club.

It is estimated that proceeds will amount to £1380, which will go towards the increasing promotional costs of the Ulster, which last year incurred a deficit of £1600.

With increased demands of £4000 from the GPRRA. A financial crisis is looming over the future of this Irish meeting.

Supporters club secretary Des Jardin said that although there were considerably less than the 600 cards issued, the venture was a big success and is almost certain to be repeated next year.

First to finish the course in a time 55 minutes was 14-year-old Alan McKee from Downpatrick, Co Down.

Brian Stronge, secretary of the MCUI, was among several leading officials who completed the course, watched by UGP chairman Bertie Mann.

A family of three travelled 300 miles from Cork to support the event, while others came from as far away as Londonderry and Donegal.

Picture above shows chairman of the Ulster Supporters Club, Mr Dan Jordan, flagging in Mrs Hewitt and Mrs Neill—just two of the folk who help out in the offices during race week.

Robert Wilkinson and Winston Norwood were involved in a fantastic race of the day at Comber in June when after thirty minutes of no holds barred action Wilkinson just managed to squeeze home in first position by the width of a tyre (if it had been available a photo-finish would have been required to satisfy fans of both riders, who both thought their rider had won.

The high-speed duo were well clear of third finisher Dennis McBride, who found it no easy task to shake off slow starting Davy Crockard and Harry McQuaid.

Norwood went on to win both experts races.

A glimmer of hope for pure road racing, curtailed by the civil unrest for the first half of the year, saw the Mid Antrim, Temple and Carrowdore organisers all hopeful their meetings would go ahead with the Mid Antrim circuit reduced from eight to five miles.

The first road race of 1972 was the Skerries 100, just North of Dublin, the races held over two legs with Ulster riders dominating – Ray McCullough won both 250cc races comfortably setting a new lap record of 85.18mph for the 2.92 mile course, his near neighbour Ian McGregor clinched both 350cc legs

Bill Henderson

that saw Danny Keaney and Gordon Bell collide just after the starting area whilst battling for second position in leg two, both escaping with minor injuries. Sam McClements was the overall unlimited class winner albeit by a mere six one hundredths of a second on time after two second place finishes behind leg one winner Bill Henderson and second leg victor Billy McCosh.

Henderson set an outright lap record of 87.16mph and appeared to have the second leg and overall victory sewn up only for a mechanical problem to force him to retire from the race.

Dennis McBride and Robert Wilkinson forced Winston Norwood to pull out the stops to win the Temple Club Castrol Motocross at Saintfield – Wilkinson securing second spot in the closing stages.

McBride showed a clean pair of heels to Norwood in the experts' race in which Wilkinson raced through the pack from an abysmal start to take third. Best junior was Stan Chambers who managed to stave off the constant attack from Hans Cairnduff.

At the time the Ulster Centre did not allow schoolboy scrambling, but a dozen budding competitors all under-10 using 50cc machines took part in a demonstration run around the Saintfield course, the fore-runner of Ulster Centre Youth Motocross which commenced in 1976.

In the McClay scramble promoted by the Ards Club Wilkinson had a start to finish win over McBride in the main race in which Norwood was forced out of the action on lap two with a broken exhaust when in close company with Wilkinson.

Norwood did not go home empty handed winning the 500cc race from Leslie Wright and Sammy Stokes, while Wilkinson completed a double heading home McBride and Norwood in the 250cc event.

In July Campbell Gorman riding a 'travel to work' 750cc Triumph complete with kick start stunned the star-studded opposition to win an incident packed Wills Invitation race at Maghaberry Airfield making it a double on the day by winning the Unlimited event.

The Ryan Norton with Sam McClements on board left the line like a bullet in the lucrative W D & H O Wills 15-lap feature race ,

but by lap three Gorman had reeled him in and take the lead. Coming from nowhere Tom Herron (250cc Yamaha) arrived at the front for four laps before Gorman once more took over at the front. As the race reached its conclusion Gorman made a race winning break as slow starting Ian McGregor, also Yamaha mounted carved his way through the field to snatch second from Herron.

Shivering with the flu Ray McCullough was never headed in the 350cc encounter to take the 25-mile championship on his QUB-Bridgestone, although local star Gordon Bell made several spirited attacks on the leader with his 'naked' Yamaha eventually settling for second with Herron third.

Herron won the 250cc race by three seconds from Alfie Mayrs while McClements and Gorman fought tooth and nail over 500cc honours settled in the Ryan Norton's favour when Gorman's petrol tank ran dry on the last lap coasting over the line in second.

Ian McGregor

Andrea Williams, the future Mrs Tom Herron, rode in the 250cc race, but was unplaced.

It was later learned that Andrea, who had made her road race debut at Fore, Co. Westmeath, had her entry turned down for both the Southern 100 and Manx Grand Prix.

During the Southern 100 Ray McCullough, still suffering the effects of a mystery virus, only rode in the 250cc race and finished a distant second behind the first man to clock up a hat trick of wins around the Billown Circuit, Charlie Williams a future favourite of Ulster and TT fans.

Tom Herron was third in the 250cc event and fifth in the solo championship race.

EVENT 4—250 c.c. CLASS							(5 Laps)
HEAT TWO—SCRATCH							

No.	Name				c.c.	Machine	1	2	3	4	5
68.	Miss ANDREA WILLIAMS	...	...		250	Yamaha					
75.	W. STEWART				250	Greeves					
76.	L. FREEMAN	...	...	...	250	Bultaco					
77.	N. DUNN				250	Yamaha					
78.	B. HENDERSON				250	Yamaha					
79.	S. WATSON	...	...	...	250	Yamaha					
80.	B. SIMPSON				250	Boyd-Suzuki					
81.	J. JOHNSTON				250	Bultaco					
82.	N. McKINNEY				250	Greeves					
83.	E. COATES				250	Aermacchi					
84.	R. FERGUSON				250	Yamaha					
85.	S. HARRISON				250	Greeves					
86.	S. SHEPHARD	...	...	...	250	Greeves					
87.	C. GORMAN				250	Yamaha					
88.	A. MILLER				250	Aermacchi					
89.	J. SANDS	...	...	...	250	Bultaco					
90.	H. SAVAGE				250	Greeves					
91.	P. QUINN				250	Suzuki					
92.	M. HALL	...	...	...	250	Greeves					
143.	J. FERGUSON				250	Suzuki					
144.	J. ROBINSON	...	...	...	250	Yamaha					
148.	A. MAYRS				250	Yamsel					

Mickey Laverty was best 350cc newcomer in a race that saw Bill Smith, riding McCullough's QUB computer tuned Bridgestone, shatter the all-time Southern 100 course lap record lap record setting a sensational speed of 87.23mph before a troublesome clutch forced the Chester bike dealer out of the race on the fourth lap.

Sadly in July Bertie Mann, a former President of the M.C.U.I. who steered the Ulster Grand Prix through the last three difficult years, died in hospital from bronchial pneumonia aged 55.

Bertie was a successful competitor himself in grass track where he became an Irish champion, won gold medals in International Six Day Trial, was a keen scrambler and road racer. He was also Clerk of the Course at Dundrod for eight years.

A sea of mud greeted competitors at Comber for the Irish 5-mile grass track championships, but conditions did not deter Dennis McBride from scoring a well-earned double in the 500cc National race and the invitation. In the 500cc race he lapped the entire field except for second place finisher D. Davison.

Winston Norwood clinched the 250cc title, Willie Johnston the 200cc and Eric Kean the 350cc.

Bertie Mann

The first road race of the Ulster season, the Temple 100, finally took place on the last Saturday in July.

Unfortunately the event was marred by the death of Bobby Whyte, who was fatally injured during the 250cc race having earlier finished fifth in the 200cc event.

Bobby was a former Ulster road race champion, and a brilliant all-rounder having won a Gold Medal at the International Six Day Trial in Sweden in 1966. Five years later representing Ireland at the corresponding event in the Isle of Man he claimed a silver medal.

The winner of the ill-fated 250cc race was Ray McCullough while the little Honda's of Brian (Spikey) McComb and Mickey Laverty were evenly matched in their 200cc clash. McComb led into Rectory Corner, the final bend, but the crafty Laverty nipped through on the inside to snatch a split second success.

Tom Herron took his Bass Special Yamaha to a 350cc win, his uncle Wilfie took the unlimited race honours while Billy Guthrie won the 500cc race to add to third in the 250 and fourth in the 350cc events.

Special mention to Scottish visitor Alex George finished second in the 350cc race and set a new outright lap record of 89.59mph an all the more incredible feat considering that he stopped early in the race to assist fellow Scot Roy Graham, who had crashed, before proceeding in the race.

Former works Norton rider Artie Bell, who lived on the Temple Course and winner of the 1948 Senior and 1950 Junior TT races died aged 57. His racing career had ended when he was seriously injured following a crash during the 1950 Belgian Grand Prix.

In a dream debut for the new lighter 500 QUB Ray McCullough won the 500cc Mid Antrim 150 race beating Norman Connor and Gerry Mateer into second and third.

His luck was out however in the 350cc race when the QUB Bridgestone only managed a mile of the shorter revised Rathkenny Circuit (now turning right at Adam's) before packing up.

This was the best race of the day with Tom Herron and Ian McGregor duelling throughout on their Yamahas. The dice came to an end two laps from home when they both collided and crashed as McGregor went for an inside line at Dubought Hairpin. Herron quickly remounted to win the race from Billy Guthrie while McGregor also remounted to finish third.

McCullough made it a double on the day leading home Alfie Mayrs, Jack Wilkin and Christy Clarke, who had just edged Courtney Junk out of fourth in only his second road race, in the 250cc encounter.

Richard Hewitt scored his first ever 200cc road race success in which Joey Dunlop was fifth riding a Suzuki while 'Spikey' McComb and Mickey Laverty crashed uninjured.

Andrea Williams in her Ulster road race debut fractured a collar bone and suffered concussion after crashing at the hairpin during the 350cc race.

The 19th August saw the Bishopscourt International take place, the substitute meeting for the cancelled Ulster Grand Prix.

One of the pre-meeting favourites Bill Smith was flung from his 500cc Kawasaki during morning practice breaking three toes and a bone in his left

Gerry Mateer, note sponge chin rest

foot, gashing an elbow and suffering various bumps and bruises ruling him out of the racing although even had he escaped unscathed, his machine only fit for the scrap heap after it caught fire.

The star of the show from amongst the visiting riders was a shocked Stan Woods a Cheshire electrician who in front of 10,000 spectators scored a hard-earned hat trick thanks to a stroke of luck and sheer ability

His first Irish success came as a bit of a shock in the 20-lap 250cc race that Tony Rutter led virtually all the way until he ran out of fuel close to the chequered flag handing victory to Woods and his Yamaha 3.4secs ahead of Tom Herron, Alex George, Billy Guthrie, Campbell Gorman and

Stan Woods, triple winner at Bishopscourt International

the unfortunate Rutter who pushed across the line in sixth.

Woods second and third race wins came on board Suzuki machinery in the 500cc where he held off a determined challenge from Dave Croxford (Kawasaki) and feature invitation race in which John Williams and Graeme Fish finished second and third while Ian McGregor led home Herron and Mickey Laverty in a local 350cc Yamaha 1-2-3, John Williams won the F750cc race riding a Honda, Swiss rider Rudi Kurth and his English passenger Kenny Arthur won the first sidecar race on a Crescent Monark while Mick Wortley won race two when Kurth was forced to retire the fragile Crescent..

It was a day to forget for 1971 UGP hero Ray McCullough, who crashed out of the 250cc race on the first lap, his 350cc Bridgestone cried enough during practice and the QUB developed clutch trouble on the second lap forcing his retirement although he salvaged something by finishing fourth in the invitation race.

Christy Clarke, a joiner from Dublin became the 100th rider to lose his life on the Isle of Man Mountain Course, when he crashed his 250cc Yamaha on the approach to Glen Helen during second practice for the Manx Grand Prix. The Christy Clark Memorial Trophy became a much sought after trophy at Mondello Park and has been won by many of motorcycle racing's top competitors.

In race week Sam McClements brought the Ryan Norton home in eleventh position during the Senior Manx. The only non-four-stroke inside the top twenty was the Crooks Suzuki of Keith Martin in third position – this was soon to change.

Joe Lindsay was the top Ulster rider in the Junior Manx finishing sixteenth in a race in which Mervyn Robinson riding an Aermacchi ran out of fuel in his only Mountain Course experience.

Paddy Reid was best Ulster rider finishing eighth in the Lightweight 250cc Manx.

Campbell Gorman riding a 250cc Yamaha and an ex-works 500cc Linto (two 250cc Aermacchi engines) scored two runaway victories at Lurgan Park in August.

Gorman streaked to a comfortable victory over Jim Smyth and Alfie Mayrs in the 250cc race, then riding the ex-Alberto Pagani Linto he had time to admire the park scenery pulling out a huge lead over Tommy Robb, who had last raced at the venue 15 years previous.

In the North Armagh Club promotion it was the 350cc that provided the drama with local star Gordon Bell leading for seven laps before his Yamaha went off song handing the lead to Wilfie Herron for two laps before he retired on the final lap.

Billy Guthrie could not believe his luck taking the win from Bell, who stopped, fixed a loose plug and regained second place from Norman Dunn, who was riding Ray McCullough's Bridgestone.

A rejuvenated Ian McGregor (Danfay Yamaha) scored a split second win over Billy Guthrie in a sensational 350cc race at the Carrowdore 100, a fitting climax to the curtailed Ulster road racing season. Pushed to the limit by Guthrie, McGregor set an absolute lap record of 94.20mph for the Co Down circuit, as the pair left Norman Connor well in their wake in third, however his machine ran out of fuel on the final lap handing Tommy Robb a fortunate third following a poor start.

Tommy Robb

Ray McCullough cruised to his customary victory in the 250cc race from Cambell Gorman and Connor while in the 500cc he romped home well clear of Gerry Mateer and Sam McClements.

The MCN headline read

Tom Herron Master of Maghaberry

Despite writing off a Ford Capri 3000 in a road traffic accident less than 24-hours earlier, escaping serious injury, Tom Herron was in top form in the 15-lap feature race at the airfield circuit near Moira.

For four laps his 37-year old uncle Wilfie led Campell Gorman and Tom, before the young Herron ousted his uncle for the lead a lap later leaving him to battle with Gorman over second while Roy Reid and slow starting local idol Gordon Bell were engaged in a battle for fourth.

At the chequered flag Tom won by 150yards from Gorman, who just pipped Wilfie for second with Bell fourth, Reid fifth and Eric Wilson sixth.

Tom went on to make it a double comfortably winning the 350cc race in which a terrific three-way scrap for second that went in favour of Bell, twelve seconds behind Herron, slightly ahead of Tommy Robb and Mickey Laverty, whose Yamaha developed an oil leak in the closing stages.

Robb won the 500cc race by a hundred yards from Ray McCullough, who was only able to use three gears on the QUB, with Reid third and Wilson fourth.

Gorman also completed a double winning the 250cc and Unlimited events while Jackie Robinson was victorious in the 200cc encounter, Don Carlisle the 50cc and Jim Rush the sidecar.

Double Irish champion Winston Norwood (CZ) had to fend off a determined Leslie Wright (Maico) to win the Campbell Donaghy Memorial Trophy Scramble at Limavady. Wright fought hard, but had to be content with second only a few yards clear of trials kingpin Benny Crawford (Bultaco).

Wright however did win the 250cc final from Sam McMinn (Husqvarna) with Norwood third..

Despite losing the first half of the road racing season due to the civil unrest the Ulster Centre carried through a curtailed programme of road races and the class champions were – 200cc Richard Hewitt (Suzuki), Ray McCullough (Yamaha), Billy Guthrie (Yamaha), 500cc Ray McCullough (QUB) and Unlimited Wilfie Herron (Norton). The Ralph Rensen Trophy went to McCullough.

A modified 48-seater coach was used by a team of Ulster enthusiasts to travel to the International Six Day Trial in Czechoslovakia.

Entered on 250cc Bultaco Matadors by Belfast agent Albert Clarke the five-man team was Derek Hamilton, Gerry Scarlett, Jackie Shepherd, Winston Buchanan and Davy Mills – all five retired from the event.

The Irish Championship Shaw Cup trial was staged over rugged mountain terrain near Dromara and due to the severity of the course and a tight time limit there were a host of retirement ranging from broken forks, punctures or rider fatigue. Defending champion Benny Crawford took his Bultaco through five arduous laps of fifteen observed sections for a loss of 56 penalty marks eleven clear of runner-up Derek Stewart. Crawford still harboured a personal ambition to win the Hurst Cup an event he had finished runner-up in eight times!

During the FIM Congress in London in October the number of World Championship Races were reduced from fourteen to twelve the two losers being the East German Grand Prix and significantly the Ulster Grand Prix, however both would remain on the calendar for 1973 as International events.

After just three years on the committee that directs world championship sport (CSI) Billy McMaster lost his position at the same congress a move described by Norrie Whyte in MCN as 'the disgusting dismissal from the CSI. He had committed the cardinal sin in the eyes of his weak fellow FIM delegates, he had become too strong and too outspoken. He made the fatal mistake of pushing too hard the worthwhile claims of, in particular, the road racers as a professional group.'

It was announced in November that the 11.2mile North West 200 circuit was to undergo a change with racing no longer allowed along Portstewart Promenade on security grounds.

The circuit would now turn left at York Corner along the Cromore Road to Shell Hill Bridge thus casting Henry's Corner, Milburn Corner and the Boulevard into the history books although the circuit would still omit the Metropole and turn in at Glenvale, as it did from 1968 –1974.

Derek Russell
'72 Hurst

Mr All-rounder, Billy Hutton riding in '72 Hurst Cup
where he was also at various times clerk of the course,
and served on the organising committee. He also rode
as a travelling Marshall on road races throughout the
seventies and was a prominent Ulster centre official.

*Dennis McBride
winner Inter Cities
Scramble, Cork*

*Dennis McBride
winner at Ayton
Scramble Killinchy*

*Robert Wilkinson at
John Donnelly*

*Mickey
Laverty &
Tommy
Robb at
Kirkistown*

*John Williams
on 750 cc
Honda at
Bishopscourt
UGP
substitute
meeting*

*A pensive Billy
McCosh awaiting
a race start*

*Raymond
Davidson needing
a shower after
the Temple Trial*

*Mick Andrews (above) and Peter
Gaunt (right) display varying
interpretations of how to protect their
heads during the 72 Hurst Cup*

Mickey Laverty

remembers…Racing and Tom Herron

From Toomebridge Mickey started racing on a Triumph Cub, moved to 200cc Bultaco and Honda machines before concentrating on the 350cc class riding a McClean Yamaha.

Racing against the best racers of arguably the best period of racing in Ulster Mickey was well able to hold his own with the best.

Following his career he turned his attention to being mechanic, sponsor and official cheer leader for his 3 boys and today the Laverty name is synonymous with motorcycle racing with Michael, John and Eugene having plied their trade from schoolboy motocross ranks right through to the highest class of two-wheeled sport, Moto GP.

Although I started racing prior to the seventies, my memories of that time are a bit hazy although one thing that sticks out clearly is winning the first ever Race of The South at Fore in 1973 on a 350cc Yamaha the same day I believe Bill Henderson won the 250cc race.

Another abiding memory from that time was being a good friend of Tom Herron's when he came on the scene.

When he decided to make the break from home racing and go on the continental Grand Prix trail he actually tried to persuade me to go with him and why I didn't, I still ponder to this day. I think I would have enjoyed it, but I suppose you could say I was a home bird. I had a good job and a decent set up at that time and was not prepared to take the gamble he did.

Tom jumped straight in at the deep end, going from homeland racing to world championship and international events at 26-years of age, sacrificing everything to go racing and I felt I simply could not afford to go with him even if the £15000 that Tom would·have spent on a year's racing seems pitifully small beer by today's standards. No one was standing offering a fistful of dollars to buy your way into a team. Everything Tom achieved was hard earned and few from here were prepared to follow in his wheel tracks at that particular time.

Tom and wife Andrea, (sister of Peter Williams and a racer herself until she sold her bike to help finance some of their early meetings abroad) became the equivalent of desert nomads, travelling from venue to venue across Europe in search of world championship points and just as important the start money from non-championship meetings that was essential to keep the wheels turning and put a meal on the table.

It has to be remembered that there were no motor-homes, hotels, major sponsors, entourage of technicians, etc etc that you see in today's pit garages – in fact there were no pit garages.

When Tom and Andrea headed to Europe in 1974 they

The full GP team:– Tom and Andrea Herron with mechanic Peter Kelly on grid at UGP

were living, sleeping and eating from the back a of Transit van – a caravan was added for 1975, a comparative luxury for eight months of the year.

Of course this was their choice, no one forced them to go racing on a shoestring budget, but this was exactly what the 'Continental Circus' was like in the decade when race paddocks were more friendly with everyone mucking in to help each other out – the paddock became a small village where wives and girlfriends multi-tasked, as the riders put their life on the line for 'the love of the sport' criss-crossing Europe just making ends meet.

Andrea was the organiser looking after entry forms, letter writing with spares to order, ferries to book, pit boards to hang out and phone calls to make while Tom looked after machine preparation and earning a crust racing against the best in the business.

The usual pattern would have been to arrive at a circuit, unpack, rebuild bikes in readiness for Thursday, Friday and Saturday practice and qualifying, race on

Sunday, pack everything away and then travel anything up to 1000 miles to the next race and the whole process begins again.

So just why did Tom and Andrea do it? Simply because it was and still is the best sport in the world and everyone who competes aspires to be a world champion one day or at least reach the highest level possible.

After a couple of years learning the scene I reckon he was the best to come out of Northern Ireland and was really coming good on the short circuits when Jim Finlay and other sponsors came on the scene after 1976 and that was the beginning of Tom going on to become one of the top privateers in world championship racing eventually getting the break he deserved - a 'factory' ride with Suzuki in 500cc Grand Prix alongside Steve Parrish and Barry Sheene. Unfortunately as we all know it wasn't to be as he lost his life at the North West in 1979.

Mickey Laverty leads William Watt and Bobby Whyte in 200cc Bultaco action at Kirkistown 1970

I suppose the furthest I would have ventured with Tom was Oulton Park in Cheshire where I remember out-qualifying him one meeting – things like that are hard to forget!

At the time I was riding Charlie McLean's 350cc Yamaha and British Enkalon in Antrim, where we both worked, were my main sponsors, paying my entry fees.

At that time, a few years before Enkalon Motorcycle Club was formed, the

Mickey Laverty flat on the tank of Charlie McClean's Yamaha

factory workshop carried out a lot of 'homers' for a number of racers, Tom Herron included. This was all done supposedly on the 'QT' and although the Enkalon management knew fine well what was going on, a blind eye was turned as long as you had all their factory jobs carried out and the homers were 'kept below the radar' which meant that getting parts in and out could be a problem.

The owner of my bike, Charlie McClean had had a bad motorcycle accident outside Antrim and had lost a leg when a car drove straight into him. But it didn't dent his enthusiasm for racing – in fact when I went to see him in hospital he whispered into my ear, "we'll be able to buy a good bike when the money for this comes through!" When he returned to work his misfortune turned out to be a boon for local racers as he was allowed his car through security, often with undeclared racing parts in the boot or, if particularly critical, inside his prosthetic leg.

The other main man on the roads in my day was Raymond McCullough, but he was a bad traveller – he was a wizard on a motorbike, a one off and had all the talent to make it abroad but could not be tempted, which meant here at home the rest of us were mostly dicing for second or third place, with Billy Guthrie, Alfie Mayrs, Bill Henderson and Courtney Junk to name a few. The grids were packed with good riders in the seventies and top three places were not easy earned – you had to ride hard to even be in the top six or seven.

I remember winning a 200cc race riding an 182cc Honda at the Temple (1969) after a great last lap dice with Spikey (Brian) McComb. That place would have scared the life out of you. I was out on the 350cc Yamaha later that day and it broke down on the first lap. I was never as glad to hear the thing stopping to be quite honest – no point telling any lies about it, the 200 was more than enough for me over those jumps which just shows that sometimes even a non finish can be a result – in fact one of my most satisfying races was holding onto fourth place going onto the last lap of a 350cc Ulster Grand Prix race, but the bike packed in going into Leathemstown and that was that.

To sum up the seventies, everybody from GP riders like Tom Herron to local scratchers raced for the fun and enjoyment rather than for prize money, working all hours and ploughing every penny we earned into racing.

It was a terrific time to go racing, great friendships were made, there was great dicing on the roads and short circuits with crowds of people just feet away from the action and hardly any animosity between riders. Good times indeed!

Harold Crooks

remembers... Commentating

My formal involvement with motorcycle sport began when I came back home in 1957 to a teaching post in Clough Primary School and shortly thereafter joined the Mid Antrim Motor Club when founder member Herbie Harper, who worked in his father's family garage at the top of Thomas Street in the town, got me involved with the race as a flag marshal.

The club was 12 years old at that stage having been formed in 1945, by a bunch of like minded members of the Transport Platoon of the Second Antrim Battalion of the Ulster Home Guard (Dad's Army) with Lieut-Col. Arthur O'Neill Chichester of Galgorm Castle as the founding President.

The first race they'd organised was held on Wednesday afternoon, the 24h July, 1946, with a 3.00pm start on the basis that Wednesday was the 'half day' in Ballymena. The race was run over a six mile course, called the Ballygarvey circuit, and raced in an anti-clockwise clockwise direction or left hand in.

In subsequent years the race was run over a number of courses in the area including the 10.4 mile Ballygarvey Course which was run in a clockwise direction from 1948 to 1954, when the direction was reversed. I well remember spectating at the 90 degree right-hander half-way between McGregor's Corner, (where Turtle's Showroom is now),

Harold's day job may have been Principal of Broughshane Primary School but he is likely better known for his role in the motorcycle world as a reporter for the Ballymena Guardian (Hi Cam), Sunday Life, Downtown Radio, and BBC Radio Ulster.

As race commentator at the NW200 and Mid Antrim 150, as well as various short circuits and grass tracks, Harold's dulcet tones were instantly recognisable to racing fans across the province.

Today his time is spent looking after his classic cars and taking them out on many vintage runs throughout the summer.

Spectating at the Temple with Wilfred Dickey (left) and Ray McCullough (centre)

and Broughshane watching in awe the speed of Mickey Roche going through on his twin-cylinder Grand Prix Triumph, similar to the one on which Kildare ace Ernie Lyons won the mist covered Manx Grand Prix in 1947. When the direction was changed I moved to Hugh Keery's garden at Moattown, just after the Ballygarvey Hairpin where we could revel in the sight and sounds of the machines going up through the trees, particularly Wilfie Herron's sweet sounding 500 single.

Being in the right or wrong place at a specific time (depending on your point of view!) has been the underlying common factor in all my connections with the sport which has dominated my casual life for over forty years. One such happy coincidence occurred around 1962 when I was attending a Grass Track meeting in Crumlin during their Civic Week and the guy who was supposed to be commentating failed to turn up. With the position needing filled and me probably being the most vocal member of the motorcycling committee, I got the job. I must have done it without upsetting too many people for I was asked back to do it at various other grass track meetings where there was tremendous rivalry amongst very skilled riders like Billy Hutton of road racing travelling marshal fame, on the Matchless, Arthur Clarke, and Bertie Mann, who rode his machines on both the grass and tarmac, at Bangor Castle and Lurgan Park.

In a case of one happy coincidence leading to another, in 1965 the Mid Antrim 150 moved to the Rathkenny circuit and commentator Jack McCann, a local solicitor, decided it would be a good time to hang up the mike and the organisers reckoned that, with my experience of blathering away at grass track meetings, I would be just the man for the job.

Around this time I'd started writing the Hi-cam column in the Ballymena Guardian for the late Maurice O'Neill and this, together with commentating, opened many unbelievable doors for me in the ensuing years with the opportunity to work alongside outstanding colleagues such as Tom Steele, Wilfred Dickey and Jimmy Walker. Along the way I got the opportunity at various stages to be the motorcycle sport reporter for Sunday Life, Downtown radio, BBC radio and television, Ulster Television and even Radio Trent at the British Grand Prix!

At some events like the NW200 where, alongside Alan Drysdale and George McCann I had over 20 years on the mike, I would be commentating live to the spectators at the track while at others it would be to a radio audience over the airwaves. For such events I'd roll up in the 'Downtown Radio Car' (actually a Ford Fiesta Van) and try to get a good vantage point from which I'd try to convey to my audience the excitement of events – not an easy task at places like the Temple 100, where the racing was so fast and furious over the famous jumps (where to my eye the best 'jumper' was Billy Guthrie) that even the great Joey Dunlop was moved to state after a particularly epic tussle with Ray McCullough "I'll never do that again!".

However looking back I think my favourite has to be the NW200. It was there that I saw some of the best and closest racing, with legends like Bushmills farmer Dick Creith on the Ryan Nortons, the unbeatable Phillip McCallen in 1992, and of course the Dunlop brothers, Joey and Robert who, with Frank Kennedy and Mervyn Robinson, made up the Armoy Armada whose battles with the Dromara Destroyers, Ray McCullough, Brian Reid, Ian McGregor and Trevor Steele, were something else. Close finishes were not uncommon and I remember two in particular. In 1973, Tony Rutter beat John Williams by the narrowest of margins in the 250 race, and in 1977 Tony Rutter, again and Ray McCullough were inseparable and were credited with a dead heat finish.

Memories like these convince me that I have been privileged to have been involved with what I believe is the greatest sport in the world (including the much acclaimed Formula One car racing). Everyone talks about the good times they have had, and I have had more than my fair share. Motorcycle sport has been very good to me, and hopefully I have given something back in return.

To finish off on a lighter note I've asked the publisher to include the following piece written in 1961 by Noel Graham for that years race program. Noel was the Mid Antrim Club's race secretary at the time but also a dab hand with a pen and I hope the piece will bring as broad a smile to your face as it did to mine.

MOTOR CYCLE NEWS by **Hi-Cam**

RECORD-BREAKING TRIPLE FOR McCALLEN

FROM THREE starts, Phillip McCallen had three wins at the Carrowdore '100' road races, where Islandmagee rider Iain Gibson was fatally injured on the last lap of the 350 race.

Gibson, a 27 year-old after-sales manager with Toyota dealers Neville Johnston, had been racing for six years, and was one of the most respected riders in the sport. He had competed earlier in the day in the Regal 600 race, but had been forced to retire through engine problems.

An eye-witness said, "He seemed to be in difficulties coming into Cardy Corner, as he struck the bales on the inside of the bend, before crashing into those on the outside, where his bike trapped him against the fence."

McCallen then made sure of the McBrides Fashions Irish 250 title, with another convincing record-shattering win over the 1990 Champion, Fran Morrison and Alan Irwin.

Joey dunlop set the pace for the first two laps before an expansion box on the Honda went bang, and he lost power. As Dunlop slowed, McCallen in contrast turned up the wick, pushing the lap speed up to a record 110.27 mph.

As Dunlop's problems continued, Morrison, Irwin, Dave Leach, Ian Lougher and Derek Young all went past him, demoting him to seventh place. McCallen's winning average of 108.45 was

Hi-cam featured in the Ballymena Gaurdian for over 40 years

THE CHARIOT RACE

by Norman Graham

1. In the days when Thomas the Slattite ruled over the children of MAMC, James, son of William the Sassenach, spake unto his father saying, "Would that I had a chariot, that I might send an entry unto the children of MAMC, for they have need of them".

2. William answered his son, saying, "Thou art my first-born; thou shalt have a chariot". And he called his servants and said unto them, "Bring me a 7R". His servants trembled and answered him, saying, "Master, 7Rs do not grow upon trees".

3. And William the Sassenach spake wrathfully upon them saying, "Have I not many acres, and a Ferguson withal? Go, now, even unto Malcolm of the Temple, and bring unto me a 7R". And there was brought unto him a 7R, richly dight with chromium, from the place which is called Broadway. And he brought it unto his son, even unto his first-born, and said unto him, Go.

4. Then James, the son of William the Sassenach, girded his loins, and clothed himself with the skin of the young calf, and put a helmet upon his head, and goggles withal, and departed thence to the place which is called Rathkenny. And there was gathered together a great multitude of the people, and the daughters of the children of MAMC moved among the people, saying, "Buy a programme, for we have need of the brass".

5. And many there were who bought a programme, yea, even they that dwelt in the valley of the Braid, for they were wont to support the children of MAMC in their misguided efforts.

6. Now there was on the grid that day one Harold the Crosscannonite, and he spake unto James saying, "Wind her". And James answered him not, for his knees were knocking one against the other.

7. And it came to pass that in the fullness of time the flag dropped, and they that were left on the grid lifted up their voices and cried unto their servants in the pits, saying, "Bring me a plug, that I may yet win a trophy".

8. But the servants heard them not, for the heavens were filled with the roar of megaphones. And they that were left wheeled their chariots away, saying, "We have lost our threeten". And there was weeping and gnashing of teeth.

9. And James gazed upon his rev counter and remembered the words of Harold the Crosscannonite, and he wound her, and behold, he was out in front, yea, even before Bill the Ballymenaite, and Len the Crosscannonite, and Richard the Bushmillsite, and all they that came after.

10. Now the children of MAMC had made signs upon the ground with their staves, so that they that drove the chariots might not end up in Boughshane St., but rather that they might turn safely for the place which is called Bally- garvey. But James heeded them not, neither got he down a couple of cogs.

11. And behold, the marshals were scattered even as chaff before the wind, and they were sore afraid. Yet none was so afraid as James the son of William the Sassenach, and he pulled up at the place where Adam sold Regent. And they that stood by said unto him, "Have another go", and he did, saying unto himself, "I must roll it off a whit".

12. And when all was over, the children of MAMC came unto him and spake saying, "Thou hast won a trophy, and a cheque withal" And he went his way rejoicing.

Note--All persons contemplating litigation as a result of the publication of this article should proceed to the Clarence Hotel where Jimmy Henry is willing to be called to the bar.

Len the Crosscannonite AKA Len Ireland

1973

Value Added Tax (VAT) introduced at 10% as UK joins the European Economic Community – Concorde made its first non-stop crossing of the Atlantic – Sunningdale Agreement signed – No 1 hits included Blockbuster by Sweet, Can the Can by Suzi Quatro and I'm the leader of the gang by Gary Glitter – MCN and Motorcycle were 7p.

In the world of Ulster motorcycle sport *'Campbell Gorman dominated virtually everything demoralising the opposition with wins from most starts'* – stated Motorcycle in a candid interview.

He was crowned 'King of Lurgan' with an unbeaten five victories at Maghaberry Airfield and took six titles; short circuit 250/350cc double champion, Irish 25-mile 350 and 500cc double champion, pocketed a £135 cheque as Embassy champion and was the unlimited class road race champion.

Two new classes were introduced to the local short circuit and road race championships namely 50cc and sidecars.

Robert Wilkinson, now in his last year of engineering studies at Queens University, rode his new 250cc CZ and a borrowed 400cc Maico to two wins in the Experts and second 500cc races (Sam McMinn had triumphed in the first) and a second place in the first 250cc race after a tough battle with eventual winner Dennis McBride, at a wind-swept Magilligan Point.

Wilkinson went on to secure double success in the 3-round Foyle Club series winning the 500cc and Experts classes with McBride clinching the 250cc challenge.

Martin Lampkin, the youngest of three competing brothers, won the Duckhams sponsored European Championship Hurst Cup Trial at a snowy Clandyboye Estate.

The promoting Knock Club attracted a record 112 starters, a proud achievement in the wake of the continuing civil strife in the province.

The top three Ulster competitors were Tom McBride, Billy McMaster jnr and Benny Crawford, who clinched the Irish Trials Championship for the twelfth time in eighteen years.

The winning club team was the Knock team of Billy Hutton, Billy McMaster jnr and Derek Russell.

Ulster short circuit racing received a timely boost, as a new six-round Embassy Championship sponsored by W. D. and H. O. Wills with £100 going to the winner of the final at Kirkistown in October following five qualifying meetings at Maghaberry organised by the Road Racing Club and Belfast and District meetings at Kirkistown – the top 25 points scorers who have ridden at both venues in at least three meetings will contest the final.

During 1973 Wills expected to contribute in excess of £1000 to Ulster motorcycle sport.

Meanwhile the Tandragee 100 Road Race, for the first time in its 15-year history, was to receive financial support from Esso Petroleum for the 350cc cash prizes and trophies, Tayto add their name to the 250cc race while Golden Cow Butter support the 500cc event.

Ulster rider Bob Coulter celebrates his tenth season of continental racing with rides on F750 and production Commando's loaned by the Belgian Norton importer, plus continuing in the 125 and 250cc classes.

Story in Motor Cycle News –

Ulster Grand Prix returns to Dundrod

Following last year's cancellation of the Ulster Grand Prix and the subsequent running of a substitute event at Bishopscourt due to the ongoing security situation and the bombing of Grand Prix House, not rebuilt yet, The Ulster Grand Prix is set to return to the 7½mile Dundrod Circuit.

Also announced that the North West 200 is also to go ahead after a year out, but will not use the Portstewart Promenade to Coleraine part of the circuit, instead turning sharp left at York Hairpin and along Station Road to Shell Hill Bridge with a new start and finish area close to the golf course at Primrose Hill.

Robert Wilkinson (CZ) was never headed on his way to a double success in the Wills Trophy event that commenced the Ulster Scrambles season at Dromore, while double Irish champion Winston Norwood choose CZ ahead of Bultaco for the defence of his titles, as the 325cc Bultaco he received does not comply with Irish championship regulations of 351cc to 500cc.

A switch from a faithless Ossa for another trustworthy Ossa (it was all in the head) did the trick for Davy McBride at the Slemish Trial, the final

Dennis McBride heads Jimmy Aird at Leapoughs, Dromore

round of the Ulster Championship, as he left the rest of the field for dead over five laps of fifteen sections on the slopes of the famous mountain.

His season of heartbreak with his Spanish machine suddenly changed and he won by twenty-five marks losing seventy in total with runner-up Gerry Scarlett dropping ninety-five, one better than Derek Stewart with Benny Crawford a further mark down in fourth.

A practice prang failed to dampen the enthusiasm of Belfast newspaper sales representative Abe Alexander (350cc Yamaha), who created his own little bit of history as he stormed to victory ahead of Mickey Laverty and Tom Herron in the first qualifying round for the new Embassy championship during the wind-swept meeting at Maghaberry in front of a near record crowd.

On a damp and greasy track Laverty overhauled early leader Gordon Bell to comfortably win the 350cc race, while Wilfie Herron won the 250cc race having his first ride aboard a 250cc Yamaha leading Jackie Hughes and Ivan Porter home.

Other winners at the opening meeting of the season were Courtney Junk (200cc Honda), Sam McClements (500cc Norton), Campbell Gorman (Unlimited Triumph), Norman Taylor (sidecar scratch) and Wallace Coates the sidecar handicap.

Continuing his winning start to the season Robert Wilkinson took time out from his final year studies to chalk up a brilliant double at the Ayton Trophy scramble at a blustery Killinchy course winning the main race by 25secs from Dennis McBride with Davy Crockard a lonely third, Wilkinson completing his double in the 500cc race.

Winston Norwood was the initial leader of the feature race, but by lap three Wilkinson was in front with visitor Pete Mathia pressuring Norwood.

Leslie Wright, Robert Wilkinson, Dennis McBride at Championship grasstrack races at Ballyalloly Rd, Comber

Dennis McBride from a poor start was flying and overtook Mathia and Norwood to take second before Norwood crashed taking Mathia down with him, Mathia quitting with a bent bike and a sore neck.

Wilkinson won by 25secs from McBride with Davy Crockard taking advantage of the crash to claim third.

Mathia went on to win the 250cc race while the most disappointed rider of the day had to be Ulster-exile Gordon Bowden, who broke the frame of his Sprite in half.

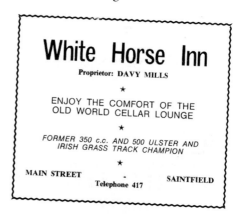

A week later at Magilligan Point a cool calculated ride by Crockard (Suzuki) saw him overhaul early race leaders Norwood and Terry Patterson to win the 250cc Irish Scrambles Championship race to tie BNR Suzuki team mate McBride at the top of the series after two rounds.

Easter Monday at Kirkistown was a Herron benefit as Tom stormed to a brilliant win in the second round of the Embassy Championship on his 350cc Yamaha also taking a 250cc victory while uncle Wilfie won the over 500cc race on his Norton.

However in the 350cc final Mickey Laverty got the better of Tom to take the chequered flag first.

An interested spectator at Kirkistown was Tommy Robb, having his first Easter Monday off in 22-years racing, but due to compete at the forthcoming Tandragee 100 on a 250cc Danfay Yamaha.

At a damp Tandragee 100, back on track after a year's lapse, Ray McCullough (QUB) beat Sam McClements (Ryan Norton) by a second in a thrilling Golden Cow 500cc race. The result went down to the last lap with the QUB winning the drag from the final bend just taking the chequered flag a bike length in front. McCullough made it a double convincingly beating Wilfie and nephew Tom Herron in the 250cc event.

Gerry Mateer was in devastating form on his brand spanking new 350cc Yamaha in the Esso Petroleum 350cc race inflicting defeat on the Bass Special Yamaha of Tom Herron with Gordon Bell, Joe McArdle, Drew Alexander and Joey Dunlop (Aermacchi) completing the top six.

Jackie Robinson set a new class lap record of 73.70mph on his way

Wilfie (5) and Tom (3) Herron at a wet Tandragee.

to victory in the 200cc race after a heart-stopping battle with Courtney Junk and Richard Hewitt, who eventually crashed out while Campbell Gorman lapped the entire field to win the Knox 750cc class on his Triumph.

Headline MCN 2nd May –

Act now to save the TT

When entries closed for this years TT so ended its claim as the world's most important road race as for the first time no solo world champions will be competing.

The questions asked by MCN were – Can it survive as a world championship event without the best riders and can it survive as a crowd-pulling week of speed without world stars and works machines?

Forty years on and yes the TT has changed, but still attracts factory-supported machines, top road racers (no Grand Prix stars) and is as popular with fans as it ever was.

Leslie Wright scored a quick-fire double at the East Antrim grass-track meeting at Lylehill on Easter Tuesday in the 250cc and 500cc classes, repeating the feat four days later at Six Road Ends, just outside Bangor.

Millisle 275   Phone   Donaghadee 3307

L. T. WRIGHT

CONTRACTORS PLANT
ROAD TRANSPORT
SALES AND SERVICE

◆

"BRAEVILLE," GRANGEE, MILLISLE

The big motorcycling story of May was the news of a tragedy at Monza in Italy where Finnish star Jarno Saarinen and Italian Renzo Pasolini were killed after a first lap 120mph accident in the 250cc Italian Grand Prix race.

The North West was back after the compulsory one-year absence and it was all change – a new circuit mentioned earlier, new men at the helm with Tom Steele Clerk of the Course and Billy Nutt Race Secretary, the event was of national status and all classes counted for the Ulster Road Racing Championships for the first and only time.

'The fastest road racer in Britain' said the headlines, after Tony Rutter covered the new 9.73mile North West 200 circuit in a stunning 5m 11secs setting a lap speed of 112.44mph on his way to winning the 350cc race on his Bob Priest Yamaha.

Rutter made it a double by taking the 250cc honours after an epic scrap with John Williams, while Billy Guthrie (Yamaha) was an easy 500cc winner after Billy McCosh retired his Suzuki having led for two and a half laps.

Geoff Barry (Oakley Norsel) won the 750cc race from the Norton of Wilfie

200 cc Start NW200, 8 Billy Redmond, 5 Race Winner Jackie Robinson, 27 Hugh McCartney, 46 Raymond Campbell, 23 David Morton in the only ever 200cc race at NW200

Herron after John Cooper (Triumph 3) ran out of fuel when leading a few miles from home after a great battle with Barry.

Kells rider Jackie Robinson dominated the 200cc race on his 12-year old ex-Bill Smith 182cc Honda – the one and only time a 200cc race was ran at the North West 200.

Practice had been marred by the death of 32-year old Graham Fish from Stockport, who was killed instantly after crashing at Station Corner on only his third lap.

Four days after the North West Ray McCullough put his disasters there behind him with a 250 / 500cc double at the Cookstown 100.

Tom Herron won the 350cc race, was second in the 250cc and third in the 500cc race plus he set the fastest lap of the day at 90.39mph for the Sherrygroom – Stewartstown 6.4mile circuit being used for the first time since 1929 after the traditional circuit that took in Cookstown Main Street was not available for security reasons. In fact like most towns across the province Cookstown is sealed off by permanent security barriers, which would have made it impossible to run the races on the traditional circuit that ran right down the main street.

Herron's fastest lap came as he chased down McCullough (QUB) and Mal Kirwan (Aermacchi) having slowed with ignition trouble at one stage of the race.

McCullough whittled away at Herron's 250cc lead eventually catching and passing him on the fifth and final lap to win by a whisker.

When it came to the 350cc race Herron made no mistakes clearing off from a race long scrap for second that eventually went to Mickey Laverty from Campbell Gorman, who won the 750cc race easily and Kirwan.

Sammy Dempster won the 200cc race on his little Honda from the Suzuki of Billy Redmond and the 125cc Maico of Davy Morton.

It was reported that a worldwide shortage of castor oil, caused by a disastrous groundnut crop is affecting 4-stroke racers. Castrol R is in short supply, clearly the spectators would be affected badly if the aroma of said product was lost!

Tommy Robb at Ballough Bridge, 125TT

Tommy Robb won his first ever TT after 15-years and 42 races in the Isle of Man, the 38-year old riding his Danfay Yamaha to a 125cc success and thinking of his fellow competitors by keeping his speed down to let as many as possible win replicas.

Gerry Mateer (12th) and Robb (16th) were the only Ulster riders in the top twenty of the 350cc Junior TT earning silver replicas while Tom Herron (9th) and Mateer (16th) were similar replica winners in the 250cc event.

Billy Guthrie (350cc Yamaha) was the only local rider to finish the F750cc race in 11th position.

In torrential rain popular Scot Jimmy Aird's consistency and ability to stay upright earned him the Henderson Trophy and a victory in the 500cc Irish championship race at Mallusk.

Main talking point apart from the weather, was that Wigan's Dick Clayton led the 500cc race for seventeen of the eighteen laps before his Husqvarna's chain jumped the sprocket letting Aird, despite a broken gear lever on his Maico through to take the win.

Three top Ulster riders Ray McCullough, Tom Herron and Ian McGregor gave the Kirkistown meeting a miss because they were not happy with the prize money. Herron in particular wanted the top award of £10 doubled!

This left the way clear for others and Abe Alexander on his 350cc water-cooled Yamaha scorched to a first ever King of Kirkistown victory making it a double by winning the 350cc race.

Ryan Norton team mates Cecil Crawford and Sam McClements finished 1-2 in the 500cc race while Campbell took his usual victory in the 750cc class while Jim McCoosh with Winston Lyons as ballast were victorious in the sidecar scratch race.

Best action of the day saw a titanic 200cc battle between Richard Hewitt, David Wood, Robert Hanna, Bill Simpson and Courtney Junk, who emerged victorious in the end for his third success of the season.

After a lapse of almost two years racing returned to Dundrod with the Killinchy 150 meeting that saw an Army helicopter hover overhead throughout, security placed at strategic points and a search of the entire circuit carried out prior to Friday practice.

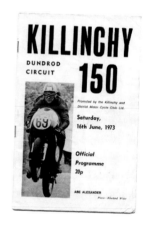

Racing saw the magical 100mph barrier at national level obliterated in a hectic 350cc race.

Ian McGregor was first to top the ton at 100.12mph powering through to take the lead at half distance with Abe Alexander right in his wheel tracks. Two laps later, just before the rain came down, Alexander clocked 100.51mph but McGregor on a dampening track started to ease ahead winning by 15secs from 'Big Abe.'

A three-way 250cc tussle between Tom Herron, his uncle Wilfie (who won the 500cc race at the very first Killinchy in 1956) and Tommy Robb was eventually settled two laps from home when Tom opened the taps to draw clear and win his first Dundrod race by 14secs from Wilfie and Robb.

Herron made it a double by winning the 500cc race while Courtney Junk scored his first open road race victory in the 200cc race.

Three wins in three classes on three different machines for Campbell Gorman at Maghaberry, but the opportunity for a four-timer disappeared when he collided with another competitor and crashed pushing off from the start of the 4th qualifying round of the Embassy series.

Gorman won the 350cc, 500cc and unlimited races on his Yamaha, Linto and Triumph machines.

In the Embassy Tom Herron and Abe Alexander disputed the lead of the 15-lapper before Alexander powered away over the closing three laps.

Herron also lost out in the 250cc class after Alfie Mayrs snatched victory after a ding-dong battle.

Abe Alexander at the Temple 100

Less than a fortnight later Herron, a 24-year old truck driver, came from seventh position to snatch victory from under the nose of Roger Sutcliffe on the sprint from Castletown Corner to the finish line to win the solo championship at the Southern 100 on the Isle of Man.

Ray McCullough raced to a record breaking double at Ireland's oldest road race, the Temple 100 on his 250cc Yamaha and 500cc QUB, however it was Tom Herron who hurtled around the 5½mile Saintfield circuit at a speed of 90.41mph to set a new absolute track record on his way to winning the 350cc class.

Tommy Robb made his first Temple appearance for twelve years and rode to fifth place in the 250cc race and third in the 200cc event where he rode an ex-works 125cc Honda.

Norman Dunn (Yamaha) clinched his first major success when he won a scintillating 350cc race at the Gallaher Mid Antrim 150 overtaking local publican Campbell Gorman with a last bend manoeuvre to win by a second and setting an absolute lap record of 84.37mph for the 6-mile Rathkenny circuit.

Tom Herron had made a lightning start, but slid off on the opening lap aggravating an old thigh injury.

A split fuel tank forced Ray McCullough to relinquish the lead of the 500cc race on the third lap leaving Abe Alexander and Gorman locked in battle, Gorman winning after Alexander made a last lap error that dropped him to third behind Gerry Mateer.

McCullough comfortably won the 250cc event ahead of a fierce scrap that eventually saw Alexander secure the runner-up spot ahead of Alfie Mayrs.

Top six finishers in the Sovereign 200cc race were Courtney Junk, Jackie Robinson, Sam Dempster, Jim Farlow, Ian McGregor and the only non-Honda John Lennon on his Bultaco.

Campbell Gorman at Mid Antrim

The Ulster Grand Prix, now a non-world championship event, saw a first ever hat trick completed by Cheshire rider John Williams, who averaged over 100mph in all three victories in the 250, 350 and 500cc races.

Williams won a dramatic 350cc race by 3/5 sec from Tony Rutter after gearbox gremlins saw him surrender a nineteen second lead, just holding on by the slimmest of margins to hold off the charging Rutter.

Not making life easy Williams won the 250cc race by five seconds from Ray McCullough after scything through the field from eighteenth position at the end of the first lap.

The 500cc victory was somewhat easier running away with the twelve-lap race

Denis Keen / Dave Houghton Sidecar UGP winner

on his 382cc Yamaha winning by almost two minutes from Billy Guthrie.

Denis Kneen and Dave Houghton (500cc Konig) won the sidecar race by over half a minute.

RAFSA (Royal Air Force Sports Association) was emblazoned on the Yamaha of Paddy Reid from Muckamore, outside Antrim, as he sped to victory in the Senior Manx Grand Prix.

The RAF employee took the lead of the six lap race on lap four and with the retirement of Don Padgett from second position on the last lap Reid cruised home to win by 3m 6secs from Joe Thornton with John Goodall third from a field of 107 starters.

In the Lightweight Manx Reid finished second to Dave Arnold while Alfie Mayrs from Coleraine was fourth.

Drama at Leitrim after Winston Norwood was excluded from the final results following a protest that he rode two different machines handing the 'Lord of Leitrim' overall victory to Dennis McBride (Suzuki).

Norwood broke his Maico's frame in the first of two 20minute legs, but still finished runner-up to Davy Crockard, then in race two he scored second place behind McBride on a borrowed machine to take what he thought was a nine second overall victory, however the rule book had been broken and he was excluded.

The Irish team of Robert Wilkinson, Dennis McBride, John Foley and Davy Crockard finished intact in both legs to claim a creditable sixth in the Trophee des Nations motocross at Dodington Park, Gloustershire.

Five wins from five starts including victory in the final qualifying round of the Embassy was what Campbell Gorman served up at Maghaberry despite tough competition from Abe Alexander, who fell uninjured when leading the Embassy race, Sam McClements, Alfie Mayrs, Wilfie Herron and the rapidly improving Mervyn Robinson.

Gorman, on the crest of a wave was scoring his 13th win at the venue in the four meetings this year.

Winston Norwood gave the Queens University built 500cc URM (Ulster Racing Motorcycle) three wins on its competitive debut during the Temple grass track leading each race from start to finish.

Jimmy Aird (CCM) from Scotland won all three legs of the John Donnelly International Motocross at Killinchy – the event backed for the eighth consecutive year by Bass Charington.

Of the continental riders making their first Donnelly appearance Swede Lars Axelsson (Husqvarna) followed Aird home in each race.

The John Donnelly Trophy is awarded to the best overall Irish competitor in the three legs being won in 1973 by Killinchy Club

Andres Lindforrs, one of the many Swedes to compete at the John Donnelly during the 70s

member Sam McMinn (CCM) who finished with a fifth and two sixth place results.

To cap what was a remarkable season for Ballymena publican Campbell Gorman he blew away the opposition with a start to finish win in the 15-lap Embassy final at Kirkistown to collect the £135 cheque.

Completing only two laps practice following his late arrival at the circuit after his transporter broke down on-route Gorman raced into an early 50yard lead and eventual victory over Tom Herron and Abe Alexander, as Mervyn Robinson and Gerry Mateer collided at the hairpin.

Gorman also won the unlimited race and 350cc final to complete a memorable hat trick in his best ever season.

Tommy Robb won the 500cc race in what could well turn out to be one of his final races, while Tom Herron clinched the 350cc win.

A six-year famine for John Lennon ended at the confined closed to club members meeting at a wet and slippery Maghaberry when he scored his first ever-Irish victory in the 200cc class on his faithful Bultaco.

Newcomer Con Law (Greeves) snatched a surprise second place from experienced Alfie Mayrs in the 250cc race won by Wilfie Herron, while local man Gordon Bell claimed the 350cc win from Joey Dunlop with Harry Dagger (Aermacchi) the only other finisher.

The trials scene was in full swing with Derek Stewart winning his second trial in seven days when he beat Benny Crawford by one mark to claim the Lightweight Club Autumn Trial at Wolfhill.

Sammy Miller 'Mr Trials' clinched his third successive win in the Jersey 2-day trial riding a 325cc Bultaco on the weekend he celebrated his 40th Birthday.

Dubliner Michael Orr scooped a first time Yamaha victory of the National Trials Championship Terry Hill Trophy at Saintfield dropping 13 marks four fewer than runner-up Stewart.

Archie Lappin showing the wear and tear of a hard day's trialling – yes the same Archie Lappin who owned the Tornamona which sank in Strangford Lough while carrying Joey Dunlop and his bikes to the 1985 TT.

Yorkshire rider Clive Smith (Montesa) came to Ireland for the first time with the 20-year old fending off the challenge of Ulster riders Davy McBride and Benny Crawford to win the Irish Experts Trial by thirty-six marks. – Smith lost a total of 133, McBride 169 and Crawford 183.

It was reported in MCN that Sammy Miller was to be released by the Bultaco factory eight months early after nearly nine years with the Spanish manufacturer. Miller's plan after correspondence with the Honda factory in Japan is to help with the development of a future Honda trials bike.

*L-R Terry Boyd,
Maurice Russell,
Dennis McBride*

*Derek Stewart
at Hurst Cup*

*Harris
Healey,
Paul Cott
and Mickey
Laverty
at UGP*

*Rudi Kurth /Miss Dane Rowe
in their low set outfit ...*

*.. contrasting with the more traditional
Eric Bragazzi/Jimmy Creer*

*Tommy Robb
250cc race Mid
Antrim 150*

*L-R Tommy
Graham,
Jimmy Walker
and Harrie
Palmer at Mid
Antrim 150*

*Ken Turner
Killinchy 150,
recovering at
Leathemstown*

NW 350cc Start; Mervyn Robinson (40), Billy Guthrie (14), Tony Rutter (1), John Williams (2), Campbell Gorman (6), Charlie Williams (4) and Tom Herron (8)

*Mervyn Robinson
NW pushed by
Tony Harvey - today
the Ulster centre
Incident Officer*

*Tony Rutter became
the fastest road racer
in the UK at NW200*

NW 250 Start; Ray McCullough (2), Tony Rutter (3) and Wilfie Herron (8)

Jackie Robinson

Ray McCullough

remembers... Racing

From Carnew near Dromara in Co. Down 'Supermac' as he became widely known had a career spanning 24 seasons during which he scored 109 Irish road race victories, won 14 Ulster road race championships (11 of those in the 250cc class), won the premier Embassy short circuit championship twice in 1975 and 1976 with the high point of his career the historic victory in the 1971 250cc UGP victory over world renowned riders .

After retirement from racing and work Raymond helped fettle various riders machines and still 'tinkers a bit' with engines while enjoying outings in various parade laps at meetings and touring around the country on his road bike.

It is amazing when you are asked to remember things that happened forty or more years ago how a number of incidents stick in your mind as if they were yesterday while with others it is only when you are reminded of them that vague recollections stir.

In my young days I ran about with Ian McGregor who lived just down the road from me and was into motorbikes from an early age. He had a 125cc Royal Enfield and I would have been his pillion passenger – I was about 16 at the time – before I ended up getting a bike of my own, a Francis Barnett, which was soon changed for a 350cc Matchless and then a Norton Dominator.

At the time I'd been working for a man who owned a garage in Banbridge but after I'd got the Dominator I moved to another garage he had in Portadown and I'll always remember travelling to and from work, riding that Dominator as hard as the bloody thing would go to the point where a couple of people used to come out to watch me going round some of the big sweeping bends near Gilford!

I recall one evening a couple of young lads from Portadown I'd have known, who also had Dominators, were waiting on me for an unofficial race back to Banbridge. I rode that road every day and knew it well – especially one big long straight over the brow of a hill into a long right hand bend that had a tricky off-set camber on it. Coming up to it I was in front, but as I eased off to steady the bike the two boys passed me over the brow of the hill and, as they tipped into the bend, the next thing I knew they both went down, their footrests having caught on the ground. Luckily neither of the two of them were hurt!

At this time I would have been going to watch all the 100 mile road races with my father and was fancying having a go myself but didn't have a suitable bike until my brother bought a new Triumph Sports Cub which he agreed to swap for the 600cc Norton.

I soon got the wee Cub all tuned up to race but it was very fragile with a big end no thicker than your finger and poor lubrication. We used to test it on the Gall Bog Road down at Brian Reid's (a big long straight with no roads coming onto it so nothing was going to drive out in front of you) but I can't remember riding that wee Cub up and down that road more than two or three times before it would blow up.

In 1960 I entered the 200cc race at Tandragee – and broke down; went to the Cookstown – and broke down; the Temple – and I won!

My third road race – I was hooked!

After that Tommy Graham from the Temple gave me a 350 Manx Norton to ride. It was a great bike (Ralph Bryans was about at the time and he had 350 and 500 Manx Norton's) but, despite riding it right through to about '68, I never won a race on the roads on it. I had plenty of seconds and thirds but the only race I did win on was at Lurgan Park just before the Yamahas came on the scene and started to dominate.

By this time I was working in Chambers Garage in Belfast alongside Ralph and Hector Neill. Hector was some character – the best man that I knew to take a scrap car, clean it up and make it look like new although I remember one day he was lucky to keep his job.

We had a wee BSA in that had been wrecked but was all fixed up ready for giving back to the owner and Jack Anderson the Manager said to Hector, "The man's coming this evenin' to pick it up so would you take her out and give her a wee spin to make sure she's going all right.'

Hector went out onto the main street and all of a sudden this van belonging to F S Herron, Tom's father, shot out of a side street and Hector hit it right in the door and pushed the forks right to the back of the wee bike. Jack near 'blew a valve.' when Hector come back into the garage and told him that "ye may ring that man and tell him not to come for that bike, it's lying in a heap down the road there – wrecked".

I remember there always being some sort of fun going on in the workshop, usually with Hector in the thick of it. There was a chip shop round the corner and at dinner time everybody would send out for a chip. Hector always went for them and we all thought what we got was straight from the shop until one day Hector wasn't able to go for the order. Somebody else went and when they came back with these big bags of chips the penny dropped and we all realized that Hector had been nibbling on his way back and all we were getting was about half a chip. He was a case!

Towards the end of the sixties a job came up as a Technician in Queens University which I applied for. Initially I didn't get it but a couple of months later I got a phone call and was offered the job in 1969.

It was a great place to work. I was running the mechanical engineering labs for the students and this became closely tied in with my racing throughout the seventies.

One of the projects was of course the 500 QUB – it started out as an engineering project for the students but then Prof. Blair, who was interested in racing, got Colin Seeley to make a frame.

The first setup featured a separate engine with a primary chain driving the gearbox but it didn't work very well as the primary chain kept breaking. Brian Steenson rode it until he unfortunately lost his life at the TT and after that I took over the riding duties. The bike was very light and quick enough, but not reliable until we combined the engine and gearbox in a single casing after which it never gave any more trouble. I think I rode it in nineteen races and won seventeen before

Gordon Blair checking my bike at Killinchy

the 351cc Yamahas came on the scene and proved too quick for the QUB.

The 351 Yamaha was just a 350 with a modified crank pin but there was very little difference – I remember at the time you just got a pin with a wee bit of a bump on it to off-set it and take it up a couple of thou' to give that extra 1 or 2 cc. So similar were the two models that, other than the colour of the competition numbers you could hardly tell them apart ….

Queens were also involved with a motocross bike at that time which Robert Wilkinson, Winston Norwood and Dennis McBride would have ridden. The URM bike had an engine identical to the road racing bike slotted, I think, into a Maico frame and is still sitting in the University.

I rode a great variety of machines throughout the seventies; a 350cc Bridgestone which came from Bill Smith to Queens as a project to be worked on (it was a disc valve and went well, but was not as reliable as a Yamaha); many 250 and 350 Yamaha's in various guises, air cooled, water cooled, cantilever, 350 3-cylinder, 4-cylinder 750; a 250cc Harley Davidson and Hector's RG 500 Suzuki (although I rode it only once at Kirkistown before I got sacked when I fell off it through Debtors – I blamed a bad tyre on it but Hector wasn't amused!).

Of all of them, the Yamahas were the bikes to have. With the 250 and 350s, you could buy and win on them straight out of the crate apart from the Bridgestone tyres they came with which most people swapped for Dunlop's. Having said that I often rode a Seeley frame simply because it was a lot lighter than the Yamaha frame.

In terms of racing highlights the 1971 Ulster GP had to be the biggest race win of my career, winning a world championship race at Dundrod, my favorite race track, beating Jarno Saarinen and Dieter Braun after a battle with Phil Read, who

Top: Hector Neill's Suzuki, One Race, one crash and 'sacked'!
Below: Astride the fragile 250 Harley Davidson at the Mid-Antrim

Famous UGP victory in 1971

was chasing maximum championship points, on a soaking wet track. Yes, it is true that Read waved to try and get me to slow down and he did say to me "if you are as good as people say you are, why not race in all the world championships and we'll see how you go then", but I was having none of that and anyway it didn't matter as he retired before the end. I was out to win the race simple as that and the wet conditions that day suited me perfectly. If it had been dry things might have been different, but they weren't and I was the last Irish rider to win a Grand Prix World Championship race at Dundrod.

But there were other great races in the seventies and one that I remember particularly would be a 250cc race with Bob Jackson at the Ulster (in 1979 I think) where we flew past the chequered flag so close that we were credited with the same time although I got the verdict. Then there was the North West in 1977 that I thought I had

Hi flying ahead of Joey Dunlop at the Temple

won and Tony Rutter thought he had won before it was finally declared a dead heat

Another one that sticks out was a 250cc race at the Temple with Joey. We had fought tooth and nail, passing and repassing each other flying over the jumps. It all came down to the last corner, Rectory Hairpin where I was leading and the next I knew Joey flew past me, never going to get stopped – I think he was nearly in Saintfield before he got pulled up!

Joey was a terrific rider, a bit rough and ready in his early days, but racing with him you always felt safe. A lot of boys would be pushing you out of the way but there was none of that from Joey, when he went past he always left plenty of room.

During the time of the Dromara Destroyers versus the Armoy Armada Joey and me had some great battles but after the race was over we could sit down and talk about it afterwards with no ill-will whatsoever. The press hyped it all up, but we just got on with it and the crowds loved it. You know I could never understand that crash that claimed Joey's life.

The Temple was a brilliant wee circuit, more like a motocross with all the jumps on it. I remember Tom Herron and me neck and neck one year and every time we came down to the big jump at Prices Demense I would take the lead as Tom loved jumping way off the ground while, never that keen in jumping up high, I took the jump with the throttle shut off and the back wheel still driving and would pass below him back into the lead.

I also recall another dice with Tom when he had come back from Grand Prix duty to ride at the Ulster. I got a terrible start and was way down the field but kept plugging away and caught John Williams and Jon Ekerold who were dicing for second. At Wheelers I dived below both for second and set off after Tom who at that stage was going into Tornagrough – the first time I had seen him in the race. I rode hard to try and make inroads into Tom's lead and by the last lap he was going out of the Hairpin as I was going into it. Tom was good in those days and, looking back, despite riding as hard as I could I was never going to catch him.

At the time you never thought much about the dangers, but when I look back now there were a lot of good riders that I knew well who lost their lives racing but I had a close knit team around me in the seventies such as Prof Blair, Mick Mooney, Derek Moffitt, Hubert Gibson and Robert Fleck and I just went from meeting to meeting as a way of life, be it roads or short circuits, immune from what could happen.

I have particularly fond memories of Mick Mooney who was an absolute gentleman. As a businessman he would have took no nonsense but he never put any pressure whatsoever on me to win races or anything like that and if I said I needed something it would have been got immediately.

You could say luck was on my side; all I ever had was a couple of bumps and bruises despite a couple of big 'offs' at the North West, one of which I walked away from unscathed and one where I did a bit of damage to an ankle and foot.

Mick Mooney

The first one in 1976 on a very, very wet day – I had just won the 350cc race and was in front on the first lap of the 250 and thought I could take the bend in the road before Carnalridge School flat in top 140mph. Turned out I couldn't and the thing just aqua-planed and I was ejected straight down the middle of the road, fortunately on my back, sliding for yards on the wet track. I got up ran to the machine lifted the tank that had went on fire and bucked it over the hedge into a field.

Then I probably had my biggest ever crash off the 750c Yamaha that I never

A rare outing on the 750 Yamaha at St. Angelo

really got on with. It was at the bend before Station when one minute I was on the bike and the next flying through the air. To this day I don't know what happened to make me crash. I remember thinking this is going to hurt and when I hit the road all I could think of was not getting run over and hobbled to the side of the road. I ended up in hospital and one of the first people to visit me was Joey Dunlop, leathers still on him. We were rivals on track, but off he was a shy, quiet man who would have done anything for you.

People keep reminding me that I never rode at the TT or much across the water and I sometimes wonder myself why I didn't race more outside Ireland. I was going to enter the TT in 1966, but there was a boat strike and the event was postponed to August, but by that time the notion was off me and I never bothered. To be honest I just thought there was too much hassle with the TT although I liked going to the Southern 100 even though it was a rough wee place with stone walls all the way round; much the same as it is today.

The furthest I ever went to race was when Tom Herron managed to get me to go to a race meeting in Tubbergen, in Holland in 1972 when a mate of his organized everything for us. I rode the Bridgestone at that race and some of the studs on the cylinder head broke and a big lad, a well-known racer at the time, Theo Bult, who worked in a local university took the studs and made me a new batch so I could race.

I suppose in a way that trip summed up a lot about the seventies. While money was tight, racing was affordable then, not like now when you need tens of thousands of pounds to buy your way into a team. The grids were full of 250 or 350 Yamahas all much the same (at a short circuit you maybe had seventy or eighty riders in three heats to find 36 for a final) running on treaded tyres that would last two or three races (not laps) and rider ability was the main reason races were won or lost.

Racing was more laid back, the friendship and craic was mighty, and to my mind, probably the best period of racing we'll ever see.

1974

Oil embargo by OPEC ended March 1974 with average price of a gallon of petrol 49.6p – Ulster Workers Council strike ended power sharing Assembly – Abba won Eurovision song contest with song Waterloo – Lord Lucan disappeared – First McDonalds opened in London – Phil Read retained 500cc World championship riding an MV Agusta and yes there was a global recession with MCN and Motorcycle increased to 8p.

Winter winds howled, the lights were dimmed by the energy crisis, but already thoughts were turning towards the 1974-racing season with Ray McCullough the first competitor in Ulster to take delivery of a new water-cooled Yamaha.

Bertie Mann Award first presented – the recipient being Don Cormican, a Customs Officer, for his road racing exploits in 1973.

The ACU banned racing until March because of the fuel difficulties.

Novice competitor 15-year old Colin Bell (Bultaco) not only won his class, but thrashed the semi-expert entry in the Larkin Cup Trial at Saintfield and reported in MCN as a 'bright prospect for the future.'

Don Cormican, 1st winner of Bertie Mann Award

In February it was announced that the fuel crisis ban on Manx Motorsport would definitely be lifted to allow TT and Manx Grand Prix to go ahead, while Tom Herron hoped to take over the mantle of retired Tommy Robb and compete in Grand Prix racing to keep Ireland at the top of the international scene.

Cruel conditions of blinding rain and wind did not deter a titanic struggle between Derek Stewart and Benny Crawford in the Presidents Trophy trial organised by the Killinchy Club at Ballygowan.

Both ended the tough event having incurred 26 penalties, but on the tiebreaker Stewart was declared the winner with a superior last lap for his second successive victory in the Irish championship.

Top road racing teams made a bid to axe the TT from the list of world championship events at a meeting with FIM officials in Geneva.

Phil Read stated at the time, "I refuse to race in the TT because the circuit does not measure up to present day safety standards. The ACU made me a tempting offer to ride, but while the race remains on the Mountain Circuit I will not compete on it – it is no use being a dead millionaire. I don't like the course and I don't like racing against the clock." Fast forward to 1977 when Read returned to race at the TT.

A re-buff from Mike Hailwood who commented, "Riders are employed to race- not to sit around whinging. If I was getting the money Ago and Read are I'd be happy to ride anywhere. Why is it that this pair have suddenly discovered the course is dangerous? They both rode there for years quite happily, but last year it suddenly became dangerous."

Again fast forward to 1978 and Hailwood returned to the TT.

A sleepless night suffering aching limbs strapped after a crash three weeks previous did not deter Rob Edwards (Montesa) from winning the Gamble Simms backed Hurst Cup Trial after a three-hour battle over the 5-lap twenty section course at the Lead Mines.

Edwards lost 53.6penalties while the best Ulster rider was Davy McBride, who lost 135.4 marks to put the difficulty of the Knock Club event into context.

Come in four-strokes, your time is up – across all classes 50cc to 1000cc two-strokes are ruling the roost with Yamaha, Suzuki and Kawasaki machines.

Ulster following the world trend as Aermacchi, Norton and Triumphs are being ditched in favour of the Japanese strokers.

Winston Norwood, Ulster's top scrambler, now Maico mounted is on the crest of a wave and added the Wills Trophy to his continuing winning way, racing to a treble at Dromore.

In the 30-minute plus one lap 500cc championship race he bolted into a commanding lead, as John Hoey, Sam McMinn and Ray Spence finished second, third and fourth after a no quarter asked or given battle for second.

Norwood led the feature race from start to finish winning by over a minute from a tremendous 4-man battle for second with Hans Cairnduff heading Terry Patterson, Sam Stokes and Raymond Davison across the line, as Stan Chambers retired.

John Hoey

Norwood completed his hat trick in the 250cc race while James Peake (AJS) was the junior championship winner.

A new 650cc Norton Wasp outfit saw the Campbell brothers take the sidecar honours ahead of Willie Stewart with Wilson McKibben in third.

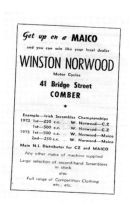

Get up on a **MAICO**
and you can win like your local dealer

WINSTON NORWOOD
Motor Cycles

4⅓ Bridge Street
COMBER

*

Example—Irish Scrambles Championships
1972 1st—250 c.c. ... W. Norwood—C.Z.
    1st—500 c.c. ... W. Norwood—C.Z
1973 1st—500 c.c. ... W. Norwood—Maico
    2nd—250 c.c. ... W. Norwood—Maico

Main N.I. Distributor for CZ and MAICO

Any other make of machine supplied
Large selection of second-hand Scramblers
in stock
also
Full range of Competition Clothing
etc., etc.

In 1972 Sammy Miller, the world's greatest trials rider, had turned down a tempting three-year contract to develop a 360cc Yamaha for trials – the offer coming too late, as he had just renewed a 3-year deal with Bultaco.

Now two years later, the 37-year old negotiated to terminate his Bultaco contract and signed a two-year contract with Honda, his brief to produce a trials machine and run a team of riders in top class events with his own personal goal being to win his 800th trial on a Honda – his total currently 794.

Still on the trials scene it was widely reported that Ulster would soon see big-time show jumping style indoor trials with man-made sections that fans are more likely to take their family to rather than a bleak outdoor event that is held on a mountain.

Thirty years later indoor trials has a world championship and here locally events have been held in the Odyssey Arena.

John Lewis (400cc Suzuki) won the opening round of the Strongbow scrambles championship at Killinchy after a spectacular second leg crash ended the hopes of rival John Hoey (400cc Husqvarna).

Hoey led the first 15 minute plus two-lap leg from start to finish with Lewis managing to hold off Alan Garrett and Sammy Stokes after a tight battle for second three seconds adrift of the winner.

On the first lap of the second leg Hoey came off heavily on the very fast, bone hard surface, fortunately escaping injury and able to remount after straightening his bent machine although no longer in race winning contention.

Lewis took until the last lap to get ahead of Garrett to take not only the leg victory. But also the overall win.

At the same meeting Winston Norwood won all three legs to collect the Henry R Ayton Trophy.

A twenty-foot high jump cost Belfast student Robert Wilkinson (Bultaco) a treble at the Henderson Trophy scramble held on a dry demanding Mallusk course.

Wilkinson's dramatic spill came during the 250cc Irish championship third round in which he had a thirty-second lead, but at the halfway point of the race he hit a deep hole and he and his machine were catapulted high into the air and out of the race sustaining heavy bruising with Winston Norwood taking the race win by six seconds from Pete Mathia.

Earlier in the day Wilkinson had scored a double in the 500cc race and Henderson Trophy event.

Campbell Gorman at Bishopscourt

Motor Cycle headline:–

Gorman shines in Ulster opener.

Pub proprietor Campbell Gorman (McBurney Yamaha) zoomed home to take two major wins at the Tandragee 100 in the 350 and 500cc races his job made easier by the retirement of main rivals rivals Ray McCullough, Ian McGregor and Billy Guthrie.

The best scrap of the day was for second place in the nine-lap 350cc race between Abe Alexander, Mal Kirwan and Mervyn Robinson finishing in that order although so close throughout that any one of the three could have been runner-up.

Mal Kirwan

McCullough destroyed the 250cc field streaking to the chequered flag 71secs ahead of Manxman Danny Shimmin and John Holmes.

Shimmin also finished third in the 500cc race behind Gorman and Gerry Mateer while John McNaul from Bangor on his 749 BRS lying in third throughout the unlimited class found himself presented with the win when race leader Eric Wilson retired and second place Trevor Bussell fell.

Winston Norwood at a muddy Bell Scramble

Filling in between University exams and setting out to compete in continental scrambles Robert Wilkinson beat Dennis McBride, both Bultaco mounted, by 78secs to lift the Brian Bell Memorial Trophy at Saintfield.

Wilkinson went on to make it a treble by winning the 250cc Irish championship race and the 500cc event with McBride again second although a loose ignition wire hampered his 250cc race progress.

Limping from a hefty practice crash Winston Norwood was fourth in the 500cc race riding the QUB URM 400cc engine machine in a Maico frame.

John Williams lapped the 9.7mile North West 200 circuit at an incredible 115.80mph on his Gerald Brown 385cc Yamaha on his way to the first ever hat trick at the North West in its 45-year history.

Williams won the 350cc race in skating rink conditions and then with the circuit having dried he added the 7-lap 500cc race with race and lap records.

It was on his way to the 750cc race win that he set the new outright lap record to cap a memorable day for the Cheshire rider and fans favourite.

John Williams and Mary Law, Miss NW 1974

However in the 250cc race he had to settle for second, starting from the back of the grid, behind local hero Ray McCullough, who was recording his first North West win which gave him a unique record of having won a race at every Irish circuit he had ever raced on.

In the soaking wet 350cc race Phil Haslam crashed through the hedge at Mathers Cross and was taken to hospital with a broken leg and pelvis. Tom Herron also crashed out unhurt when his Yamaha spun out from below him on a straight piece of road while Campbell Gorman was another faller at Black Hill escaping with cuts and bruises.

In a footnote to the North West, Manx garage owner and TT competitor Denis Brew was seriously injured when the light plane he was flying crashed in Northern Ireland. Brew and three companions had headed to Belfast, but in deteriorating weather they overshot Belfast Airport runway and search parties searched for them all night. It was dawn before the Army and police rescue teams found the wreckage and the four seriously hurt survivors.

May 29th Motorcycle headline:

Racing goes on in strife-torn Ulster

Despite being confronted by the Ulster Workers Council strike the Cookstown 100 went ahead on its traditional Wednesday date with Tom Herron disappointed with his North West 200 performances striking better fortune at Cookstown.

A new joint course record of 94.08mph was set by 350cc and 500cc race winner Herron and Ian McGregor during their 500cc duel from which McGregor retired with a misfire in his Yamaha.

Abe Alexander was the early leader of the 350cc race, but a clutch problem forced him out leaving Norman Connor, a security dog handler from Enniskillen, and Herron locked in a titanic struggle at the front, Herron eventually winning by two seconds with a class lap record in the process.

Campbell Gorman and Mervyn Robinson swept under the chequered flag as one in the same race both credited with the same race time, Gorman judged fractionally ahead in third position.

Herron and McGregor were inseparable for the first three laps of the 500cc race and both upped the absolute lap record to 94.08mph for the 6.4mile Co Tyrone venue before McGregor was sidelined with ignition troubles, Herron winning by four seconds from brothers in law Mervyn Robinson and Joey Dunlop.

Ray McCullough predictably won the 250cc race leading from start to finish with 200cc race winner Courtney Junk in second position.

Billy Guthrie takes it steady at a wet TT

It was just as well the Cookstown was held on the Wednesday, as a fuel shortage caused all forms of motorsport to be cancelled or postponed that weekend.

The dominant feature of the TT was the weather, which caused a lot of re-scheduling but despite this the week saw Ulster riders Gerry Mateer and Billy Guthrie get their first official ton-up laps.

In fact of the seventy-nine 100mph plus laps at the TT forty-eight of those were set in the 350cc, the only good weather race of the week.

Tom Herron finished third in the last 125cc TT at that time riding a Henstocks Yamaha for

Tom Herron 125cc Yamaha

the first time and fourth in the 250cc race also Yamaha mounted joining Gerry Mateer, eighth and Abe Alexander nineteenth as silver replica winners.

In the 250cc race Herron was not in the top twelve at the end of lap one of six. On lap two he was 10th with a lap speed of 102.49mph, lap three seventh

Norman Dunn

(102.49mph), lap four up to fourth (99.66mph including fuel stop) which he consolidated on lap five with a speed of 103.40mph.

In a wet and windy Senior TT Norman Dunn was reportedly blown off his bike at, of all places, Windy Corner. He remounted, but later retired at the pits saying, 'the bike just leapt across the road, went onto the grass and I fell off.'

In practice one of the meeting favourites John Williams crashed in the Kerrowmoar section when the twist grip came off his Boyer Triumph 3 and he was flung through a hedge into a garden and then taken to hospital by helicopter requiring an operation on an injured foot.

Sammy Miller's June debut on the 250cc prototype Honda at the Heath Trial in England was interrupted by stops to replenish an empty fuel tank and then to tighten loose sprocket nuts and bolts, which cost him the premier award.

Later in December Miller was excluded from Portsmouth time and observation trial for giving a female observer a lift from the first section to her section halfway around the course; deemed by the Clerk of the Course as examining other sections on his bike, which was against the organisers wishes.

After a windswept 12-laps of Kirkistown Abe Alexander clinched the King of Kirkistown title powering past early leaders Mervyn Robinson and Ian McGregor, after a slow start, at the halfway point increasing his winning margin to 10secs at the chequered flag.

Abe Alexander Kirkistown 74

Another slow starter was Campbell Gorman, who zipped past Robinson and McGregor to claim second in the closing stages.

In a rare Grand Prix outing Dennis McBride finished 19th in the opening leg and 14th in the second leg of the 250cc British Grand Prix held at Ladies Mile, Chalton in Hampshire.

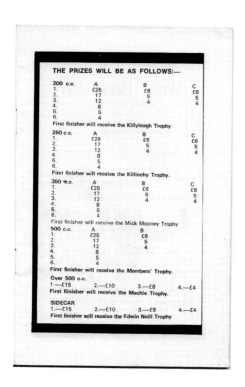

THE PRIZES WILL BE AS FOLLOWS:—

200 c.c.	A	B	C
1.	£25	£6	£6
2.	17	5	5
3.	12	4	4
4.	8		
5.	5		
6.	4		

First finisher will receive the Killyleagh Trophy

250 c.c.	A	B	C
1.	£25	£6	£6
2.	17	5	5
3.	12	4	4
4.	8		
5.	5		
6.	4		

First finisher will receive the Killinchy Trophy.

350 c.c.	A	B	C
1.	£25	£6	£6
2.	17	5	5
3.	12	4	4
4.	8		
5.	5		
6.	4		

First finisher will receive the Mick Mooney Trophy.

500 c.c.	A	B
1.	£25	£6
2.	17	5
3.	12	4
4.	8	
5.	5	
6.	4	

First finisher will receive the Members' Trophy.

Over 500 c.c.
1.—£15   2.—£10   3.—£8   4.—£4
First finisher will receive the Machie Trophy.

SIDECAR
1.—£15   2.—£10   3.—£8   4.—£4
First finisher will receive the Edwin Neill Trophy

Jimmy Walker wrote in Motorcycle – *'At a sun-soaked Killinchy 150 at Dundrod it was the Abe Alexander / Ian McGregor show'*.

In the 350cc race Alexander won his first open road race victory in a photo finish with McGregor after nine pulsating laps.

The Dromara man led for seven of those laps, but relentless progress by the tall Alexander slashed McGregor's lead to 1.4secs with two laps to go, taking a wafer thin lead onto the final circuit. As the pair flashed into sight around the final bend McGregor was marginally ahead, but Alexander found a hidden burst of power to scorch past and win on the line with a record lap of 105.03mph.

The same pair dominated the 500cc class, which Alexander again won after McGregor suffered a loss of power dropping to a minute behind at the chequered flag.

Practice the previous evening for the Killinchy was marred by the death of Enniskillen rider Norman Connor.

Dennis McBride (Bultaco) ended his success famine with a start to finish win in the McClay Memorial scramble over a new course at Craigantlet.

In the 500cc Irish championship race McBride lost out to Winston Norwood while Davy Crockard won the 250cc race on his Ossa.

Robert Wilkinson, Ulster's only professional motocross rider graduated from Queens

Irish Team, Trophee Des Nations 1974 L-R Sammy Stokes, Winston Norwood, Willie Johnston, Dennis McBride, Sydney Steel (mgr), Robin Cambell (sponsor) Missing Robert Wilkinson and Dave Crockard

University Belfast with a Bachelor of Science degree. He joined Sammy Stokes, Dennis McBride and Winston Norwood in the Trophee des Nations Team.

In a tragic accident during the first morning practice session for the Southern 100 23-year old Jim Farlow from Belfast crashed his 250cc Yamaha heavily at Church Bends and died later in Nobles Hospital.

Ray McCullough and Ian McGregor were reported as having missed the morning session as both had slept in! It did neither any harm; as McCullough went on to win the 250cc race and McGregor was best newcomer in the 350cc race finishing in sixth position.

Riders queuing for scruitineering at Maghaberry

An explosive Embassy championship race at Maghaberry saw a nail biting duel between early leader Campbell Gorman, Mervyn Robinson, Joey Dunlop and Abe Alexander.

On the fourth lap Alexander burst through to take the lead and by lap nine was 150yards ahead while Moira rider Gordon Bell joined in the scrap for second.

Dunlop bit the dust and was taken to hospital with a suspected broken collar bone while Alexander raced to a seven second victory ahead of Gorman, Bell Robinson, Norman Dunn and Ernie Coates – all Yamaha mounted.

Supporting races saw first time wins for Ballymoney's George McQuitty (500cc), and Larne rider Raymond McComb (250cc) while Brendan Ryan transferred road race winning form Cookstown and Tandragee to the short circuit on his road going Honda.

Paddock at the Temple 100 in 1974

Ireland's oldest road race, the Temple 100 benefited from almost £500 in sponsorship provided by a local businessman.

Billy Guthrie scored his first open road race success of the season in a record-breaking 350cc race at an action packed Temple meeting.

Hoisting Tom Herron's year old record from 90.41mph to 92.52mph Guthrie won a thrilling race that saw four different leaders in the 7-lap race around the notorious bumpy road course once described as a 'tarmac motocross circuit' due to the jumps on the five-mile roller coaster Saintfield circuit.

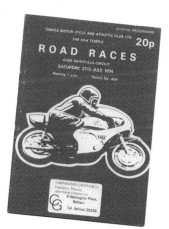

McGregor set the pace, but was forced to retire leading Alexander, Norman Dunn and Mervyn Robinson with Guthrie from a pathetic start jumping into third at the end of the second lap.

Dunn held a flimsy lead on lap five before the Moira cabinet maker edged ahead on the penultimate lap to hold off Dunn by two seconds at the chequered flag with Alexander third.

Lowry Burton, future TT sidecar winner, won the 750cc race from John McNaul after McNaul's BRS machine struck trouble on the last lap whilst leading.

Stanley Junk at Mid Antrim 150

Brendan Ryan

Records were broken in all five races at a sun-kissed Gallaher Mid Antrim 150 where Abe Alexander clinched the 350cc Ulster Road Race championship with a relatively easy first time win over the 6-mile Rathkenny Circuit outside Ballymena, where even a loose seat and a seeping gearbox did not hamper his progress finishing sixteen seconds clear of arch rival Ian McGregor, who set an absolute lap record of 86.75mph for the six-mile Rathkenny Circuit outside Ballymena in his pursuit of Alexander.

Campbell Gorman, who had a few weeks earlier said that he was taking the rest of the season off, was tempted back on track and promptly won the 750cc race on his Triumph ahead of new sensation Brendan Ryan.

Norrie Whyte described in MCN how Ray McCullough lost a chance of going through the Ulster 250cc season undefeated suffering a 20mph crash at the Ulster Grand Prix.

After ten of the twelve lap race McCullough had built up a 40sec lead, then on the penultimate lap disaster struck his Irish Racing Motorcycle Yamaha at Wheelers Corner when a tiny ignition wire broke and he 'toured' on one cylinder the two miles back towards his pit still in the lead. As he braked for his pit stop he locked his front wheel and quick as a flash he was unceremoniously dumped at 20mph head first over the handlebars in a heap on the road.

A minute and a half later after repairs he rejoined the fray in seventh spot only picking up one place on the final lap to finish 1m 15secs behind surprise winner Austin Hockley, McCullough's winning streak ended.

At the same meeting, after five years of failures and near misses over the Dundrod Circuit, Tony Rutter raced to a sizzling double in the 350 and 500cc races setting lap records in both.

Courtney Junk (182cc Honda) became the first rider to lap any Irish Circuit at more than 90mph in a 200cc national race recording a speed of 90.84mph on his way to beating hot favourite Neil Tuxworth (125cc Yamaha).

Tom Herron gave his home meeting a miss riding in the Dutch International meeting at Hengelo instead finishing eighth in both the 350 and 500cc races.

Apparently Steve Goodrum, who crashed at Ireland's Corner and broke an ankle during the 'Prix', was none too pleased about circuit fire arrangements reporting no fire extinguishers in the area when his Yamaha burst into flames and he had to wait until a travelling marshal arrived with one strapped to his back! His 4-week old Yamaha was a wreck.

When 100mph laps were the target at the Manx Grand Prix (today it is 120mph) Manxman Danny Shimmin was the first 250cc rider to top the ton during practice. Bertie Mann Award winner, Don Cormican (Yamaha), was the top Ulster rider in the wet 250cc Lightweight race finishing sixth with 'Spikey' McComb 9th and Jim Scott 13th Ulster's only replica winners.

Joe Lindsay was the only local replica winner in the Senior Manx finishing seventh while Sam McClements climbed the leader board from 12th on lap one to finish fifth in the 350cc race with Lindsay in seventh, the only local replica winners.

Answering critics of the machine Ray McCullough powered the 500cc QUB machine to a race win at Carrowdore Road Races setting the fastest lap of the race on his way to beating North Antrim duo Mervyn Robinson and Frank Kennedy into second and third positions.

Bringing the Ulster road racing season to a close McCullough completed a double with his customary 250cc win, but it was the 350cc event that had the huge crowd spell-bound as Mervyn Robinson held off all the attacks thrown at him by Billy Guthrie to flash past the chequered flag outside the White Horse Inn with a wafer-thin winning margin to record his first victory at Carrowdore, both were credited with the fastest lap of the day on what was a dramatic last lap.

Courtney Junk triumphed in the 200cc race to go through the season unbeaten in the class.

Rain before the showpiece final of the Wills Embassy Championship at Kirkistown turned what was billed as Ulster's race of the season into a one-man show with Mervyn Robinson revelling in the conditions leading the 15-lap race from start to finish.

Robinson picked up a £1 for each lap led and £125 for winning the race.

Despite nursing a broken finger from a crash a month earlier Abe Alexander finished in second spot with Ian McGregor, following an atrocious start, working his way up to third, but could make no inroads on the leading duo.

Above,and right Meghaberry 1974

The curtain came down on racing at Maghaberry Airfield with the Road Racing Club confined to members only meeting, the venue earmarked for development of a new prison.

One of Maghaberry's leading competitors over the twelve years of racing on the circuit was Campbell Gorman and he signed off with a 750cc victory on his Triumph.

Gordon Bell

The man who had the distinction of winning the last race at Maghaberry was local rider Gordon Bell who won the 'Devil Take The Hindmost' race, the last rider each lap flagged off until there was only one left on track.

1975 saw the Road Racing Club move to a new circuit at Aghadowey between Kilrea and Coleraine.

Stuart Nunn (CZ) from Cambridge came and conquered the Carling Black Label sponsored international John Donnelly Motocross in front of 4,000 sun-soaked spectators.

Level on points with Jimmy Aird and Lars Axelsson after the first two legs, Nunn was untouchable in the third and final leg lapping the entire field in the third leg with a powerhouse display of riding to finish ahead of Ulster star Dennis McBride and Swedish visitor Kent Ohlin in the overall result.

Cheshire rider Pete Mathia only managed three laps of practice, as he was struck down by a flu virus and collapsed, spending the afternoon in the back of an ambulance – sleeping!

Sam McMinn at John Donnelly

Competing on virtually his own doorstep at the Lead Mines schoolteacher Davy McBride (Ossa) upset the form book to win the Turner Memorial Trophy trial incurring 17penalties, three fewer than Stephen Pyper with Tom McBride in third having lost 21 marks.

Rising star Colin Bell won Grade 'B' and Bryson Perry Grade 'C'.

MCN headline:

Green Light for URM;

Financial backing for the commercial production of a URM motocross engine was announced by the Local Enterprise Development Unit in Belfast.

The two-stroke engine is the result of extensive research carried out by the engineering department of Queens University headed by Dr Gordon Blair.

The decision by LEDU to inject cash into the project follows intensive market research, which indicates demand for a home produced scrambler in the Irish market.

Ulster's first motorcycle factory was expected to provide up to fifty jobs when the engine goes into production.

The URM (Ulster Racing Motorcycle) two-stroke engine was the result of extensive research carried out by the engineering department of Queens University headed by Dr Gordon Blair.

Whatever happened to that project?

Dennis McBride testing the 400cc URM (developed by Queens University) at Tyrella,

Ray Pyper, a 20-year old Belfast plumber, came out on top of a selected 16-man field when he won a tough Irish Experts Trial over five laps of a demanding rock covered mountain and forest course containing 20 punishing observed sections at the Batt Estate, Rostrevor.

Pyper using a 325cc Bultaco engine in a frame of his own design and construction lost 90marks, eight fewer than Lightweight club mate and former Experts winner Benny Crawford.

This year saw Lightweight back protectors now being accepted by competitors as a sensible part of their race-wear.

Announced in the winter of this year that Ray McCullough was to make a surprise switch from his all conquering 250cc Yamaha to the locally untried Harley Davidson for the 1975 season.

A ten-lap Tourist Trophy race for Production machines will start 1975 TT week and will have three classes – 250cc, 500cc and 1000cc and starting Le Mans style

Mick Chatterton

unlike the normal TT races where riders start in pairs on a time trial basis.

Each machine will have two riders with no one doing more than three laps at a time followed by a rest period while his co-rider competes a minimum two laps.

How TT prize money increased during the first five years of the decade was shown in a table as – 1970 £5,430, '71 £10,755, '72 £11,292, '73 £13,298, '74 £13,623 with an increase to £15,650 in 1975.

Compare these figures with 1947 £2,085, 1957 £2,810 and 1967 £4,055.

Still on the TT and the debate about a major short circuit being built on the Isle of Man road race competitor Mick Chatterton from Barnsley in Yorkshire claimed in a letter to MCN that,

> "Without doubt the TT would die within two years if not ran over the Mountain Circuit. This alone draws the competitors and the thousands of enthusiasts, in spite of the absence of certain riders, the expense and the terrible weather at times. The sheer length and changes of character within one lap make the Mountain Circuit unique, making it the most respected and famous event in the world. Having been to every TT for the last 20-years I think I know what makes the TT tick – and my views are shared by all present day competitors. As for the suggestion of running a world championship meeting at Silverstone – surely they cannot be serious."

Well Mick they were serious, however the TT is still going as strong as ever as we all know, there is no major short circuit on the Isle of Man although Jurby Airfield is frequently used for racing and we now have Grand Prix and World Superbike racing held at Silverstone and Donington Park.

Colin Wickstead getting back on course at Mid Antrim 150

Billy Guthrie on 700cc Yamaha at NW200

Frank Kennedy At York corner

Sidecar duel at Kirkistown

Dennis McBride, Winston Norwood Harry McQuaid Temple Scramble 1974

Tony Rutter leads the way at Quarry Hill

*Hugh McCartney
on locally built
Kinnaird at York
Corner NW*

Ronnie (RD) McQuillan and Norman McKinney

Kenny McKee

remembers... Trials

Motorcycle trials is a specialised branch of sport which, until the advent of stadium events in recent years, did not perhaps generate the same levels of glamour and following that other racing focussed branches of the sport did. However it's fair to say that folks from Northern Ireland and particularly the North Down area (which for many years was the heartland of trials riding in Ulster) made a contribution to the sport which was far larger than their numbers would have implied.

The local trials scene can be traced back to dispatch riders for the War Department returning from the Second World War who wanted to keep up their rough riding skills by competing with each other at places like the Lead Mines or the tank testing ground at Carrick over sections of rough terrain, along river beds, over rocks, steep climbs etc. which they would try to ride through without putting their feet down.

Initially the machines of choice were ex-army dispatch rider bikes but soon there was a desire for more specialised machinery. The first trials Norton was built in Belfast by a man called Dick Chamberlin, who took an ex-WD bike cut its rear end, shortened the front forks and changed the fork angle.

At that time Cromie McCandless was building frames for Norton and, seeing that Chamberlin's bike was starting

For Kenny McKee, motor bikes were always part of life with his earliest memories being of heading off to races packed into the sidecar of his father's Norton 16H with his sister, his mother sitting side saddle on the passenger seat to keep an eye on them.

He started competing in trials on a 250 Ossa in the late 60s, competing until the early eighties when his sons took up the baton with Kenny becoming team manager and main sponsor – although he could still be seen riding on classic events such as the pre-'65 Scottish.

Today he spends his time restoring classic bikes and, with his wife Blossom, spectating at events around the country, supporting their sons who are still leading competitors on the local scene.

135

to win events, he took the design to Norton and the first 500T sold by Norton as a trials bike was the result.

At the time nobody knew exactly what a trials bike should be like and it was Millisle man Bill Nicholson, an employee of BSA at the time, who laid the ground work.

He was a frequent visitor with his machine, a hacksaw and adjustable clamps to the Lead Mines where, if he found the bike would not do what he felt it should, he would cut out the offending part, clamped things back together again and continue until he achieved something that looked and worked the way he felt a trials machine should. While his methods may seem primitive, the modern machines as ridden by multi-world champions like Toni Bou, Dougie Lampkin and Jordi Tarres still have their origins in Nicholson's measurements of fork angles etc.

Wading on my trusty 250 Ossa at Glenshane

My own involvement in Trials began as a spectator, following my brother Bobby who competed on a 1952 Norton before I joined the fray in the late 60s on a 250 Ossa.

Trials in Northern Ireland in the seventies was still a specialized sport mainly based in North Down and the top dogs were Sammy Miller and Benny Crawford – I always remember Sammy Miller's saying when he finished a trial, 'boy's it is great to be able to get my feet down!'

If Sammy didn't win Benny did and vice versa but who was the best?

On pure results Sammy would obviously be well ahead but people tend to forget that Benny, 16 times an Irish Trials champion, after riding a trial had to return to work on Monday morning with little chance of practice until the next event whereas Sammy's day job at the Ariel factory in England meant that when he finished a trial, he went straight back to the factory stripping, rebuilding the bike and practice, practice, practice until the next event.

No wonder he won 11 successive British Trial Championships, 2 European titles, won the Hurst Cup 11 times, the Scottish 5 times as well as winning a host of smaller events – they do say, 'practice makes perfect.'

As the seventies rolled through on the local scene there was Billy McMaster junior, the McBrides, Davy and Tom, Mark Curry and the Pypers while Colin Bell also burst onto the scene, although he did a lot of his riding in England.

For myself, I competed in trials through the late sixties through the seventies and into the eighties and was witness to many changes in the sport.

In the early days there were First and Second Class awards i.e. the field was split into groups and everybody rode the same trial but over time trials changed to a graded system – Experts riding the toughest sections, semi-experts taking a slightly easier route and easier still Grades 'C' and 'D' all riders graded by an MCUI(UC) committee.

On the Scottish Six Day, one of my favourite events

Most trials were over four laps of ten sections, but there were some notable exceptions such as the Boxing Day Trial which would have started at the Lead Mines, down the Ballybarnes Road, along to Ballyrogan School, two sections at Scrabo and back to the Mines via the Quarry followed by lunch and ride the same sections only in the reverse direction, which was usually more difficult as some riders preferred riding up steep sections rather than down them.

The local Trials scene was blossoming and European championships and then World Rounds came to the Province with only a select few from here (you even had to qualify for these events at one stage) being able to ride against the top riders in the world.

The European competitors were not happy, complaining about having to ride through Irish muck, as they were used to riding over dry rocks in Spain which is notably lacking in slippery, clinging mud!.

For me the Patland at Sugarloaf in the Wicklow Mountains was one event I thoroughly enjoyed – it was and still is an 'old school' trial with a long lap (in my early rides it was a 45 mile lap), sections for a keen amateur like myself, not too difficult. We would have left Newtownards at 5.30am in an old Sherpa van or car and trailer to get to the start in time – remember no motorway in the seventies.

In fact the Sherpa took us to the Scottish Six Day Trial (the pinnacle for any trials rider) where just finishing was a result in itself such as the time Jim

McMahon collided with a tree smashing the front of his Montesa, so they removed the front end from Noel Rollson's bike, who had quit the trial earlier and put it into Jims and he went on to finish. It didn't matter how many marks he was down – it was the finish that counted.

Competitions such as the Hurst Cup wax and wane. Starting off as a trade trial (you got free Dunlop tyres, Renold chains or clutch re-alignments) in the

L-R: Jeff Snyth, Ken Dundee, Philip Hanlon, Sammy Miller and Terence McKee at the presentation of The Hurst Cup team award

seventies it grew to become a European and then a World round where only the elite of local riders like Sammy, Benny, Gordon Raine or Davy McBride only to fade again in the years since. Having said that, when my son Warren won the Hurst and had his name on the trophy alongside Miller, Mick Andrew, Martin Lampkin, Yrjo Vesterinen or Dougie Lampkin, I couldn't have been more proud!

A lifetime's involvement in and around the trials scene has given me a treasure trove of memories to savor, great friendships and the chance to rub shoulders with riders whose skills, though different, would rival any elbow-sliding GP rider. It maybe wasn't in the seventies, but I once witnessed Eddy Lejeune tackling a section at Clandyboye and on the first attempt finding he could not get out of the end gate. In a feat of almost impossible skill, without putting a foot down he reversed the whole way back to the start of the section, selected a higher gear and sped up and out with no trouble whatsoever. It may have technically been a 'five' for going backwards, but he deserved a 'clean' for the ability to go backwards through the section 'feet up' – great memories indeed!

Drew Armstrong

remembers... Lightweight Motor Cycle Club (Ulster) Ltd.

Founded in 1949, our club celebrated its 21st year in 1970 with a dinner dance and prize distribution in the Stormont hotel, Belfast. Tickets were a heady £1-10s and although members numbered only 50, the club's strength and popularity was demonstrated by the attendance of over 200, including Mr Kevin Martin, President of the MCUI, Ulster Centre and Mr John Pollock, Managing Director of Carreras, the main club sponsor at the time.

During that year, under the chairmanship of Bobbie Hewitt, the club had organised grass-track races at Purdysburn, Dromara and Dundonald; trials at Wolfhill, Movilla and Saintfield as well as social events including treasure hunts, timed runs, films shows every other week, and even a fishing trip from Donaghadee followed by supper at Maxie and Nessie McQueen's cottage.

Many of the committee meetings in the early days, were held in Maxie and Nessie's home, and to this day her muffins are often talked about! Maxie was a well known character and a staunch clubman who was a great help to our trials team, for many years transporting them to and from events the South. He kept an interest in the club even in his later years until his passing in 2013 at the age of 94.

In 1971 I succeeded Bobbie Hewitt as chairman when he stepped down having been elected Chairman of the

A member of the Lightweight club since 1952 Drew was elected chairman in 1971 and President in 1977, a post which he still holds.

1978 saw Drew elected Vice Chairman of the Ulster Centre followed a year later with his elevation to President.

He became President of the MCUI in 1992, and the following year was elected to the trial Commission of the FIM..

Ulster Centre. Bobbie was later to become President of the Union in 1982 and, on the death of Billy McMaster in 1987, he was voted onto the Road Race Commission of the FIM, a post he held for 11 years, being made a Honorary Life Member when he retired.

By 1971 Carreras had become a regular sponsor of the club and their sponsorship had risen from £50 in 1969, to £120 and this helped the club to invite Jeff Smith, ex World Moto Cross champion in 1964 and 1965, over to compete in the Stock Cup scramble (now held at Dunmore mountain and renamed the Cambridge scramble). The event was held at Moneyreagh and a large crowd were entertained to a great days racing, especially as local man Winston Norwood beat Jeff to take the main award.

Jimmy Aird

Over the years this event continued to attract a healthy contingent of overseas riders and among the cross channel riders to compete were: Jimmy Aird, winner in 1974 and 1975, Bob Wright winner in 1977, Arthur Browning and Neil Hudson.

In 1972 the club and motor cycling lost a great friend, with the death of their Vice President W. R. Mann, better known to all as Bertie, who had been a great help to the club in earlier days. His funeral took place on the day of the Oxford Street bus station bombing.

1974, the Silver Jubilee of the club, saw Benny Crawford as Chairman. The same year the club, for the first time, organised and ran the Irish Experts trial in the Batt estate at Rostrevor, the winner being club member Raymond Pyper. Sponsorship was provided by Mazda cars, with the help of Mr Terry Hill. Later in the year a Dinner Dance and prize distribution was held in the new extension of the Millbrook Lodge Hotel, Ballynahinch. Over 250 people attended the function, which included office bearers of the Ulster Centre, and members of affiliated clubs. The hotel owner, Mr Jim Scott, presented the Millbrook Lodge trophy to the club, and it is still competed for to this day.

In 1975 the club joined forces with the Hillsborough club to promote a short circuit event at St. Angelo airport, near Enniskillen, and an entry of over 130 took part. Also the same year punch cards were introduced by the club at a trial at Wolfhill, near Belfast.

Drew presenting Lightweight Club's Miller Cup to James Dickson

1976 saw the end of an era for the club, with the death of our founder President Mr Fred Stock. It was at a Beetle drive at Fred's premises, on the Sandown Road, Belfast, that the club was founded, and he accepted the post of President. A quiet spoken man who had competed in road racing in his earlier days, he always maintained an interest in the club affairs, and each year conducted the election of officers at the Annual general meetings. In his memory the Stock Cup memorial trophy was presented to the Ulster Centre, for the grade A winner of the Ulster Trials championship.

The same year Mr Jimmy McRobb, presented the Dundela trophy to the club, to be awarded to the best under 16 years old competitor in the club's summer trial series, the first winner being Stephen Pyper, younger brother of Raymond. It was a sign of times to come, as Stephen went on to become Ulster trials champion, and also rode successfully for the club's trial team.

Sponsorship from Carreras continued to rise and more visitors competed in the Cambridge Scramble, such as Bob Wright, Andy Dykes, Willie Simpson and Norman Barrow to mention a few.

To celebrate 30 years of the club in 1979 a short circuit was held at

Stephen Pyper

Kirkistown and again Carreras sponsorship enabled the club to invite well known names from England to the event including, Tony Rutter, fresh from his hat trick of wins at the North West 200, TT winner Charlie Williams, James Whitham, Ian Newton, Derek, and Mike Chatterton. A large crowd saw a great days racing, with our own Joey Dunlop, beating all the visitors, and ending up with four wins. So another era of the club had passed, with the short circuit replacing the Scramble. The club continued to run short circuits until 2003.

Over the years the club has had the honour of its club members becoming World, European, British, Irish and Ulster champions. Ralph Bryans was 50cc World Road race Champion in 1965; Sammy Miller with over 1500 wins in trails, twice European and 11 times British champion; Benny Crawford 16 times an Irish champion and a member of the works Ariel team in the Scottish Six Days trial; Harold Crawford (no relation) 3 Irish , 5 Irish Experts, 1 win at the Manx 2 day trial, and scored points on 5 occasions at the World series. In later years the name Crawford again came to the fore in trials, with Benny's son Robert. He became British schoolboy champion and was the youngest rider to score points in the World trial, he also won the Irish Experts. Billy Rodgers was another successful club member to be an Irish champion, in his early days winning the 5 and 10 mile Irish grass track championship.

Away from the competition side of the sport, many club members held positions in the Ulster Centre, and at Motor Cycle Union of Ireland level, including members of various committees, timekeepers, stewards, chairmen of Ulster, and Presidents of the MCUI, delegates to, and members of FIM commissions. As previously mentioned Bob finished up as a Hon. Life member of the FIM. I was the Irish Jury member at 11 World Six Days Enduros, President of the MCUI in 1992, and the following year was elected to the trial Commission of the FIM. Billy Rodgers for a long numbers of years, was the team manager of the Ulster and Irish trials teams competing in the trial Des Nations, served as president of the MCUI and was elected to the Trial Commission of the FIM. Billy's son David is a member of the trial commission, and at present he is in charge at all indoor World indoor championships. Thus, four club members have, and are still serving at the FIM, the highest level of motor cycling in the world. Another long standing member of the club, Maurice Little who has given long service to the sport, has served as Chairman, and President of the Ulster centre, and at present is convenor of the finance committee of the Ulster centre. The club have organised 4 outdoor, and 2 indoor World Championship trials. Not a bad record for a club started at a Beetle drive back in 1949!!

1975

Margaret Thatcher became leader of Conservative Party – Government Budget saw Car Tax rise to £40, Motorcycles go up to £4 for machines up to 150cc, £8 for up to 250cc and £16 for over 250cc – the disposable razor was introduced – Queen was No. 1 with Bohemian Rhapsody for nine weeks

The first official World Trial Championship round was the Hurst Cup held at Clandyboye Estate and leading trials rider Malcolm Rathmell considered the three hour time allowance too little saying, "I fear we will end up in a race fighting with 70 riders on a short course with the introduction of the punch card system almost certain to cause delays, queue jumping and frayed tempers".

The Hurst Cup was run over five-laps of 20 sections organised by the Knock Club. The event was won by Dave Thorpe who lost 9 marks on his Bultaco, half that of runner up Benny Sellman from Sweden.

Malcolm Rathmell

Only three marks separated the top five finishers in the ninth round of the 1974/75 Irish Trials Championship, The Larkin Cup, held over four laps of fifteen observed sections.

Jim McMahon was best performer losing 29 marks on his Bultaco while second position went in favour of Benny Crawford (Bultaco) who secured runner-up from Gerry Scarlett (Bultaco) with a superior last lap as both had lost 30 marks while Norman Colin was fourth having lost 31 and Tom McBride fifth with 32 marks lost.

It was reported in March through Motor Cycle News that the Ulster Grand Prix sidecar race was to be dropped from the race programme in August in favour of a 1000cc solo race, a move that enraged Irish sidecar enthusiasts.

Ray McCullough Oulton Park

Irish hero Ray McCullough (Yamaha) made a rare excursion to the mainland circuit of Oulton Park and spurred on by an array of local fans in his first meeting of the season recorded a fine second place two seconds down on winner Bob Heath after a titanic scrap with Alan North, Pete McKinley and Steve Manship in the 350cc race.

Also in March, following a three-year absence, Harry McQuaid (Husqvarna) returned to the Hillsborough Club Dromore Course and deservedly won the Irish Senior Motocross Round and with it the Wills Trophy while Davy Crockard came out of retirement to finish in second position with defending Irish Champion Winston Norwood struggling into sixth.

Robert Wilkinson was out of luck at the opening round of the 500cc World Motocross Championship in Switzerland. He collected a brand new 360cc Bultaco from the Spanish factory four days prior to the event only for it to seize three times in practice and racing with jetting problems.

Back from his Oulton Park trip Ray McCullough drew his first blank for many years at an Ulster meeting when he failed to score any wins from three starts at Aghadowey. This was the first meeting at Ulster's newest circuit with the Road Racing Club, who had been forced to move from Maghaberry, offering a record £650 prize fund.

On his debut on the new 250cc Harley Davidson the radiator burst on the second lap while local up and coming star Mervyn Robinson won the 350cc and 500cc races.

Moving to a sun-kissed Kirkistown on Easter Monday McCullough bounced back with a double success in the Embassy and 350cc races.

Ray McCullough on Harley Davidson debut

Into May and the Henderson Scramble at Mallusk was won by visiting rider Stuart Nunn (400cc CZ) who took victory in both legs.

Another English visitor Geoff Mayes, also CZ mounted won the Irish Senior Championship race from Winston Norwood and Harry McQuaid.

A week later and McQuaid (360cc Bultaco), who had won the Ayton Cup Scramble at Killinchy, continued his fine form, becoming overall winner of the Brian Bell Trophy the main event at the Temple Club event near Saintfield, but when it came to the Irish Senior Championship race Norwood was the victor from Dennis McBride and McQuaid.

Campbell Gorman leading at Tandragee

Top Ulster rider Campbell Gorman (700cc Yamaha) suffered serious spinal injuries after crashing out of the lead of the 750cc race at the Tandragee 100 road race, injuries that left the Ballymena publican paralysed and wheel chair bound for the rest of his life.

Ray McCullough became the first man to break the 90mph barrier around the Co. Armagh circuit with a lap of 90.51mph on his way to winning the 350cc race.

The North West 200 saw the re-introduction of the Metropole Corner section of the course for the first time since 1968 and the works Kawasaki Team of Mick Grant and Barry Ditchburn was a feather in the cap for the organisers. Grant duly won both the 500cc and 750cc classes setting a new absolute lap record of an

NW200 in early seventies when it was routed through Glenvale avoiding the Metropole section

astonishing 122.62 mph in the 750 cc event. Wins for Derek Chatterton (250cc) and Charlie Williams (350cc) meant no local winners.

The 6½ mile Sherrygroom Circuit saw Courtney Junk and Ray McCullough race to doubles at a dry and sunny Cookstown 100.

Junk won the 200cc and 250cc races while the first 'Man of the Meeting' award worth £100 went to McCullough, who set a new track record of 96.40mph on his way to a 500cc win followed by victory in the 6-lap 350cc encounter.

June saw rank outsider Joey Dunlop (350cc Yamaha) stun his rivals, as well as the Ulster pundits, when he won the 'King of Kirkistown' title after red hot favourite Ray McCullough failed to qualify. Dunlop took the lead on lap two of twelve and went on to beat defending champion Abe Alexander into second with Sam McClements third.

A report gleaned from Motor Cycle News stated that

Ulster riders Gerry Mateer and Norman Dunn were the heroes in a Douglas hotel fire during the TT. They smelled smoke, the proprietor investigated downstairs and a fire was discovered.

Mateer started to clear the building while Dunn tackled the blaze with of all things a soda siphon to quell the flames until the fire brigade arrived!

During the TT Tom Herron (3rd), Billy Guthrie (6th) and Mateer (7th) received Silver replicas in the 350cc Junior race; Moira rider Guthrie earned a second silver replica by finishing fourth in the Senior

TT in a week that saw Mike Hailwood's outright lap record set eight years previously broken by Mick Grant (750cc Kawasaki) with a lap, including slowing for a pit stop to refuel, at 109.82mph.

Guthrie partnered by Chas Mortimer (250cc

Tom Herron at Ramsey Hairpin

Ridden in the 10 lap production TT by Alex George and Dave Croxford, Slippery Sam in IOM pits

Yamaha) finished runners-up in the 10-lap Production TT.

After four hours of racing (but with one lap less than the 500cc and 750cc machines to complete) the Yamaha pair finished 2½ minutes behind Dave Croxford and Alex George who were riding 'Slippery Sam' the famous Triumph Trident which won consecutive production TT races five years running from 1971 through 1975.

Despite setting a new national lap record of 105.28mph for the Dundrod Course during the Killinchy 150 350cc race Courtney Junk retired three times – twice when leading- his only finish coming with fifth position in the 250cc race.

Robert Hanna (Suzuki) won his first 200cc open road race at the same meeting.

Eric Lyons, who crashed heavily at the Killinchy broke his back confining him to a wheel-chair for the rest of his life.

Ray McCullough made the short trip across the Irish Sea to the Southern 100 on the Isle of Man and became the first rider to break through the 90mph barrier for the 4.25mile Billown Circuit close to Castletown when he scorched round at 91.20mph on his way to winning the Solo Championship Race on his trusty 350cc Yamaha. For good measure McCullough also won the 250cc race.

During the July fourth round of the Embassy championship brothers-in-law Mervyn Robinson and Joey Dunlop scooped the honours as they raced to three wins, two second places and a third at their home circuit Aghadowey. Robinson won the Embassy qualifier from Dunlop, who was victorious in the 350cc and 500cc races revelling in the wet conditions that prevailed.

Hi-Cam in the Ballymena Guardian stated that:

In ideal weather in front of a very large crowd the 'speed aces' gave the record book a new look at the Mid Antrim 150 with all class lap records being broken, as was the absolute lap record now in the hands of Joey Dunlop who set a scorching lap of 91.14mph on his way to a 500cc class win.

Mid Antrim 150: 250cc grid front row L-R Steven Cull, Ian McGregor, Courtney Junk, Ray McCullough

In the five-race programme there were five different winners, apart from Dunlop with Courtney Junk (200cc), Ian McGregor (250cc), Ray McCullough (350cc) and Steven Cull (750cc) all being victorious.

Jimmy Walker reporting on the Ulster Grand Prix for the Irelands Saturday Night (The Pink) had the headline-

108mph Rocket Ray McCullough shatters them.

Breathtaking – that's the only way to describe the record shattering performance of Ulster Motorcycling 'king pin' Ray McCullough on his all-conquering Mick Mooney backed Yamsel as he beat compatriot Tom Herron into second place in the 350cc Ulster Grand Prix.

The race saw future road star Joey Dunlop break his collarbone following a spill at the Hairpin when he came off his Rea Yamaha on lap four when in fifth position.

Mervyn Robinson won 500 UGP on 351 Yamaha

Mervyn Robinson (Yamsel) took an out of the blue victory over red-hot favourite Tony Rutter in the 500cc race while Percy Tait won the first ever 1000cc race at a canter on his 750cc Yamaha with Roger Marshall second and Herron third.

An electrical fault on the penultimate lap of the 250cc race almost certainly robbed Herron of victory in the 250cc race after an epic battle with Tony Rutter.

Templepatrick joiner Courtney Junk said goodbye to the 200cc class – going out in style winning by 45secs on his little Honda.

Percy Tait on 500 Suzuki

Sam McClements won the Senior Manx Grand Prix at a record race speed riding the Crawford 350cc Yamaha and set a new senior lap record of 103.10mph. The Bangor man also finished third in the Junior Manx in which Jimmy Heath from Belfast finished seventeenth while Joe Lindsay crashed at Quarter Bridge and was taken to Nobles Hospital for a check up.

Drew Alexander in tenth position was the top Ulster rider to finish in the Lightweight 250cc Manx.

Joey Dunlop and Steven Cull scored doubles at the Carrowdore 100 where Ray McCullough hoisted the outright lap record to 101.25mph before retiring from the 350cc race while a 'sick' Harley Davidson saw him finish sixth in the 250cc race.

The Carrowdore finalised the inaugural Irish Road Race Championships with the class winners being; Sam Dempster (200cc), Courtney Junk (250cc), Ray McCullough (350cc), Gerry Mateer (500cc), Steven Cull (750cc) and Ronnie McConnell (sidecar).

Congested 200cc starting grid at Carrowdore with No. 16 in difficulty

Leading privateer and Ulster Grand Prix and TT winner Jack Findlay stated in an interview in Motor Cycle, "Inflation, doubling of petrol prices, the rocketing cost of machines and spares is a cash crisis that threatens the whole structure of racing for a privateer competing in Grand Prix. I would estimate that it cost me £12,000 this year and I could well be looking at £15,000 next year."

On the verge of graduating to the Adult ranks 16-year old Stephen Russell rattled off five wins from five starts in the expert class at the Northern Ireland Junior Motorcycle Club grass track meeting at Saintfield then at the final round of the championship held at Dundonald there were wins a-piece for David Watson, Alan Magee and William Burgees.

In the Experts class Watson (Suzuki) beat two of the favourites Stephen Russell (Suzuki) and Lawrence Spence (Aspes).

A punctured tyre didn't stop 'ace' Benny Crawford (Bultaco) winning the Autumn Trophy Trial at Wolfhill, north of Belfast. Four laps of the quarry course saw Crawford drop only five penalty marks for his third Ulster trial win in a row.

At the Federation of International Motorcycling (FIM) in Berlin it was announced that the second World Trial Championship would commence in Northern Ireland staged by the Knock Club on February 14th 1976.

Also passed at the conference was that the TT was to keep World Championship status for 1976 and slick tyres were approved for racing, but only in the 350cc, 500cc and Formula 750 classes.

For the first time since anyone can remember two riders finished without losing any penalty points in a major Ulster Trial, it was reported in Motor Cycle. Benny Crawford and teenager Colin Bell, both Bultaco mounted, tied for first place and will hold the Iveagh Cup jointly.

During the Inter- Centre Conference of the Ulster and Southern Centres it was decided to establish a new-look Irish Motocross Championship for 1976 with a first ever cash injection.

The number of events will be halved from sixteen rounds to eight and all-promoting clubs to donate £10 to the prize fund.

The championship will be split into two sections – April to June and July to September – with four rounds, two in the North and two in the south, in each section and the six best performances – three from each half determining the winner of the championship.

*Steven Cull Ducati,
Mid Antrim 150*

*Courtney Junk,
leading the pack at
Mid Antrim 150*

*Stanley Junk shares
a quick smoke
on the grid prior
to 250cc race
at Mid Antrim*

Ronnie (RD) McQuillan

Billy
Guthrie
at
Temple,
100

Sammy Dempster,

Stanley
McKee,

Graham
Young,

Abe Alexander
& Jackie Hughes,
Cookstoxn 100

David Wood leads
Graham Young,
Joey Dunlop, Billy
Redmond, Courtney
Junk and Gordon Bell
at Cookstown 100

Jim Dunlop chasing
Donny Robinson on the
Sherrygroom Circuit

Brian McComb
and Courtney Junk,
Tandragee 100 as Billy
Hutton looks on.

Donal
Cormican at
Mid Antrim
150

Ken Moody,
Aghadowey

Geoff Barry
exits Wheelers
Corner Dundrod

Davy McBride

Tom McBride

John Smyth

remembers... Racing and fablon Cranks

My interest in bikes and racing goes back a long way – back to when I started Ballymena Technical College and became pally with a certain young class mate from Cullybackey who went by the name of Donny Robinson.

Donny (or "Don" as he became known to me, and the 20-odd other boys in our class) introduced me to the joys of Motor Cycle News and my growing interest in bikes and bike racing was born.

My first bike, a 125cc Royal Enfield was purchased shortly after, purely for riding round the fields of my uncle's farm. I also started attending local races throughout Northern Ireland with a few older friends who could drive), and my heroes of that time were Brian Steenson, Tom Herron, Mervyn Robinson, and Campbell Gorman – William Joseph Dunlop was virtually unnoticed in the early 70s until John Rea came along and got him some good bikes!

I suppose my ambitions to race were formed in those early days, but they were really fuelled after I read the biography of Mike Hailwood by Daily Mirror Sports writer Ted Macauley and, after devouring it two or three times, I was determined to race!

After the little Enfield I had purchased a few small bikes from local Suzuki dealer John Boyd, always going for ones in rough shape, which could be 'done up' and sold for a profit. By the time I was sixteen I had worked my way up to a 175cc Honda Benley, which I used for transport

After retiring from racing at the end of '79 John, alongside running his Autospray car body repair shop, managed Neil Robinson's blossoming racing career until Neil lost his life in 1986 during practice at Oliver's Mount.

In the 90s John became a full-time events promoter, organising successful Truck shows at Nutts Corner and Ballymena Showgrounds, as well as running the N. I. branch of Lakeside Helicopters, a Scottish-based Helicopter hire company.

John married his wife Lorna in 1991 and they have a 16 year old daughter Orla. In 1999 he qualified as a Driving Instructor and has been operating his successful Checkerflag Driving School since then.

and, with the experience I had gained, I began attending races as mechanic and helper for Ivan Houston, a car mechanic, who raced a home-tuned 250cc Suzuki whilst, in the garage at home, I worked on a 200cc Suzuki gradually getting it converted from road bike to racer.

I eventually got my racing licence in 1973 and was entered for my first race, the 200cc class at the North West 200 but unfortunately I never got to race the Suzuki as my Dad, who had been ill, passed away and his funeral was on the race day.

With money tight, I had to sell the Suzuki but shortly there after I got a steady job in the local Elastic Knitting factory and thoughts once again turned to racing and soon I'd bought my first racing bike, a Billy Guthrie built 350cc Bridgestone, from Willie McBurney, a local racer from Ballymena.

My first race on it made for a rather unfortunate debut at Maghaberry on April 20th 1974. Wearing a second-hand set of black leathers and a helmet borrowed from Mickey Laverty, I lost the front on the second lap of practice and crashed, wiping out one of the side-mounted Mikuni carbs in the process. Having gained a considerable amount of 'gravel rash' on my back Ivan Houston transported me to the Moat Bar, (Campbell Gorman's pub) that evening, and I can still see the mischievous grin on Campbell's face as he helped to null the pain with copious amounts of Carling Black Label. Next outing on the Bridgestone was at a sunny and windy Kirkistown where I at least managed to finish, albeit in last place!

My pure roads debut was later in July '74 at the Temple 100. The Bridgestone, with its disc-valve engine bolted solidly into the frame, had a serious vibration

problem and I can vividly remember my vision being blurred as it vibrated and bounced over the Temple bumps – perhaps it was a blessing in disguise that the bike stopped on the first lap but what an introduction to road racing!

As the '74 season rolled on I continued to experience bike problems and by

350cc Bridgestone

October Local businessman Bobby Allen had helped me buy a TZ350A Yamaha from another of my heroes, Frank Kennedy.

The 1975 season started on a brighter note as I picked up finishers' awards

Being shadowed by Con Law at Mondello Park

and prize money at Tandragee (£4.00!) and Kirkistown (£3.00!) but by June the gremlins had returned and at the Killinchy 150 I had to pull out when the frame broke, a common fault on the early TZ Yamahas. This was followed by the appearance at the Leinster 100 of a very annoying ignition problem. Some new Yamahas came with Hitachi ignition and some were fitted with a cheaper Spanish Femsatronic ignition which was prone to a problem whereby the bike would start and run perfectly initially but then, when the ignition 'warmed up', it started to break down, causing a misfire. This misfire was to plague the bike until the 'Race of the South' at Fore in Westmeath where a new ignition box saw the problem finally cured.

Around this time Dickie Martin joined our team. An employee of Bass Brewery, he visited every pub and hostelry in Northern Ireland by day, and never took a drink himself! Ivan Houston travelled to the races in my van and we shared the expenses as we got to know all the characters in the paddock. It was a great time to be racing because everyone shared and helped each other out with the loan of parts, sprockets or whatever else we didn't have! No off-bike rivalry in those days.

This spirit of camaraderie was to be put to the test in the following off season when I saw in MCN that Tom Herron had converted one of his Yamahas to cantilever suspension and reckoned this was just what I needed. I contacted an old mate, Charlie McLean from Antrim, who offered to introduce me to Tom, who of course was one of my heroes, so I was a bit nervous about meeting him for the first time at his home on Pond Park Road in Lisburn. I needn't have worried for Tom answered all my questions about the cantilever conversion, from where to obtain the DeCarbon shock to letting me take measurements from his bike. I became good friends with Tom and Andrea, and had many visits to their home that winter, as I set about building my own cantilever conversion for the TZ. One of my former school teachers, Alfie Johnston, who taught us metalwork at the Tech, was also a big fan of bike racing and I managed to persuade him to help me convert my bike. I had to travel across to Blackburn in England to buy the Renolds tubing which Alfie bent, welded and fashioned into a swing-arm, and after many late nights in the workshop we bolted together Alfie's monoshock conversion in time to debut at the Easter Monday Race at Kirkistown.

Me riding Mervyn Robinson's UGP winning Yamaha on a parade lap at the Mid Antrim 150 (engine cc unknown!)

Although the bike handled much better I had a bad day, getting a poor start in the 350cc race where I ended up 13th and then, when lying 10th in the Embassy race running out of fuel! To add insult to injury the exhaust tailpipe fell off.

Around this time a few of us with 350cc bikes opted to ride in the 500cc class. To make the bikes legal the Yamaha cranks had to be fitted with off-set crank pins, which upped the capacity to 351cc. Most of us never bothered to modify the engines, and just changed the fairing or number plates from blue (350cc) to yellow (500cc) – a strategy known as running a fablon crank! Of course the rule-makers hated it, threatening to measure engines at virtually every event, and the one rider they suspected of 'cheating' more than anyone was Mervyn Robinson, 'the Robbo'!

It all came to a head in August at the Mid-Antrim 150 where the organisers had been keeping an eye on Robbo's bike throughout the day. After finishing the 350cc race they saw he had just swapped the fairing to the same bike for the 500cc race (which he won) and they were sure they had him! When it was mentioned that they were going to measure the bike he told the Clerk of Course Tom Steele to go ahead, and then the truth dawned.... it had been 351cc all day!

My Ulster Grand Prix was one to forget although I did manage to get round at 100mph, but it was a memorable one for Robbo who won the 500cc race on his Rent-A-skip bike from Tony Rutter. The race organisers and MCUI officials suspected that Robbo's bike probably wasn't legal at Dundrod, as it was rumoured that although he had two bikes he only had one engine, but after the debacle at the Mid-Antrim they didn't dare measure his engine!

By the final road race of '76, the Carrowdore 100, things were looking up and I got 4th in the 500cc race collecting £4.00 for my efforts! Shortly thereafter Mondello Park was to be the venue for my first win at the Christy Clarke Memorial meeting, where I got a good start and after 2 laps led to the end winning £15.00 and a trophy! I finished 4th in the Christy Clarke race and for once had an upbeat weekend! This was followed up by good dice with Frank Kennedy on his Sparton at the final outing of 1976 at Aghadowey where I ended the day and the year with 3rd in the 500cc class.

The beginning of the 77 season saw a mixed bag of results but by the NW200 I had obtained a cylinder head, block and pistons from Joey Dunlop and the wee bike was really going well. Race-day dawned warm and sunny, and in the 500cc race I had a dice with Jack Wilkin and managed to beat him to the flag to claim 5th place, first twin cylinder bike behind four RG500s! The race was won by John Williams from Steve Parrish, with George Fogarty (Carl's dad) third and Alan Jackson fourth. That was the year that Ray McCullough and Tony Rutter went over the finish line so close together in the 350cc race that it was declared a dead heat, and they were both credited with the same time, equal first at 114.086mph!

The other highlight of that NW200 was when I got to meet my all-time hero, Mike Hailwood. Although he wasn't racing, Country singer and ace bike racing fanatic Brian Coll brought 'Mike the Bike' over for a look round, and as I was standing on the footpath waiting for one of the races to start who came walking along but the great man himself! As I had my leathers on he stopped with me and asked me about my racing, and of course I was nearly dumbstruck at meeting my hero! I finally managed to 'borrow' a page from someone's autograph book and got his signature, which I still have to this day, a memorable North West for me!

The summer of 77 brought a wonderful spell of weather but you can always get too much of a good thing and I recall a meeting at St. Angelo in hot, sunny conditions with the track covered in loose gravel from a recent tar-spraying operation. After practice most riders were complaining about the loose stones, which made slip-streaming very tricky as it was a bit like riding behind a machine-gun with the stones flying up from the bike in front. Sore knuckles were the order of the day and some bikes even had their screens smashed by the flying stones! There were a lot of crashes but I took it steady to finish 3rd in the 500cc class. As far as I can recall that was the day when Mervyn Robinson had a big crash and ended up with bad concussion which affected him for a long time afterwards.

It was around this time that the local Peugeot dealer Mervyn Turtle asked me to ride his Yamaha TZ350 E, and of course I jumped at the chance. Two bikes, just what I always wanted! I made my debut on the sweet-handling bike at the Temple 100 in July, finishing 5th in the 500cc race. Unusually Joey Dunlop didn't win any races at that meeting and, in a poor day for him, nearly crashed the 750cc over the big roller-coaster when his foot came off the footrest and his leg went under the fairing and the back wheel ran over his boot!

Following a crash at East Fortune races in Scotland where I had badly injured my thumb I couldn't race at the Ulster Grand Prix but I was there, and witnessed an amusing incident at the end of a very close-fought 250cc race between Tom Herron and South African Alan North who had raced wheel to wheel from half

Dundrod on the home-built Spondon 350

distance, swopping places at nearly every corner. There was no electronic timing in those days and the organisers employed several Judges who stood at the finish line and whose job it was to make a decision in the event of a close finish. Belfast Telegraph's sports editor Jimmy Walker was also present and as the two riders exited the Quarry bends side by side in the dash to the finish Jimmy shouted "Its Herron!" as they crossed the line and the elderly Judges all agreed which suited Jimmy just fine as he had already written his copy for the Telegraph and he was able to rush immediately into Grand Prix House to telephone it in! Most people reckoned it should have been a draw but Jimmy declared otherwise – wonderful!

Towards the end of the season my right hand, although recovered, was still very painful when braking, and the results at the Monarch of Mondello (8th in 1000cc Final) and Kirkistown (9th place) reflected the situation. The Enniskillen Club event at Aghadowey was wet and after a surprisingly good start I finished 5th in the 500cc class, followed up by a 4th at the penultimate event of '77, the Christy Clarke at Mondello. The Embassy Final was a disaster as the Turtle bike seized in the second practice, when a flywheel burst, splitting the crankcases. What an end to the year!

At the new year 1978 I had no bikes and no sponsors, so I decided to build a TZ350 with a new Spondon frame and a new engine from Ernie Coates, and of course it took a bit of time (and money) to build the bike, so my first outing was the North West 200. Practice 1 was cold, but bright, and as I changed into 6th gear at the top of the hill going into Portrush the engine seized, scaring the wits out of me! Practice 2 was another disaster and the bike finally stopped, out of petrol!

Race day dawned warm and sunny and I finally managed a finish in the 500cc race, getting round at 111.5mph.

The rest of the season was a very up and down affair with some decent results interspersed with numerous machinery problems including among other things, five seizures.

For the '79 season I had two bikes again as Tom Herron's brother Peter lent me his 250cc Yamaha for a few races. I got 5th place at the 2-day Mondello Park meeting before Easter in the 500cc races on both Saturday and Sunday. The next weekend, Easter Monday at Kirkistown I got a 2nd in the 350cc heat, and finished 5th in the final. At the 78 North West 200 I had breakdowns in both 250cc and 350cc classes and finished 10th in the Killinchy 150, before travelling down to Mondello where I got two more 5th places and finished first 250cc bike in each case.

At Kirkistown on June 30th I made a bad start and crashed out at the hairpin and, although unhurt, I felt the writing was on the wall and made the decision to quit racing. I did the Mid-Antrim because it was my home race, but it didn't go

A Proud moment. Receiving my Classic Parade Lap award at the IOM TT from the legendary Geoff Duke OBE. Speechless!

well and my heart wasn't in it, so my final outing in '79 was at Mondello Park where I finished 4th and, when the bike refused to start for the next race, I called it a day.

Looking back, the seventies was a great time to be racing. At home here nobody had any money, as we put all we had (and more) into our racing. We shared, borrowed, lent parts and we were all mates, with all the rivalry being sorted out on the track. If you could scrape up a few quid you could buy a TZ Yamaha and go racing and, if the talent was there, you could go right to the top!

The seventies saw the introduction of individual sponsors to the sport, with John Rea and his brothers Barry and Martin helping riders including Joey and Jim Dunlop. John in particular was an infectious character and with his personality he encouraged other businessmen into the sport, Francis Neill, Joe Millar, Trevor Turkington and Ken Dundee among others.

It was a great time in bike racing, but there was a down side too, as a lot of good friends lost their lives racing – Tom Herron, Joe Lindsay, George McQuitty, John Williams to name but a few, but for those of us who took part the thought was "It'll never be me" always someone else ....

1976

Apple was formed by Steve Jobs and Steve Wozniak a year after Microsoft – First commercial Concorde flights – Worst drought on record in the UK – Founder of Chinese Communist Party Mao Tse-Tung died – Abba dominated the charts with number one hit records Mama Mia (2 weeks), Fernando (4 weeks) and Dancing Queen (6 weeks)

Early January reports indicated that Ulster's top continental circus performer Tom Herron was to race at the Daytona 200 meeting in Florida for the first time – but only in the 250cc class where his machine had special expansion chambers made by Dr Gordon Blair at Queens University.

Things did not go well for Herron at Daytona when it was later reported in MCN that a spark plug broke and dropped inside the barrel during his qualifying race. He managed to get a start from the reserve spot at the back of the race grid finishing the race in 24th position.

Freezing sleet and gale force winds were encountered by the 66 starters in the Temple Club marathon trial over a 120mile course in South Down on New Year's Day.

Belfast scrambler Raymond Davidson riding a Bultaco battled through the atrocious conditions losing 210 penalties to finish in front of retired scrambler Hector Neill, today owner of the Tyco BSB and road race team, who lost 290 marks followed in third by champion scrambler Winston Norwood on 360 penalties – the only three to win gold medals based on the system used in the ISDT.

Teenage University student Colin Bell (Bultaco) rode superbly to win his first national event, the Tom Stanley Memorial Trophy Irish Championship Trial at Pine Forest, Co Dublin, beating another teenager Trevor Callaghan by six marks.

Bell continued his fine form by winning the Jim Boyle Cup event at Ballycarry totalling 23 penalty points, nine fewer than runner-up John Whyte.

However Bell dropped to fourth on a 'sick' Bultaco during the Larkin Cup held at a snow-capped Dunmore Mountain where Benny Crawford started the second half of the Irish championship season with a convincing victory.

Crawford then took a major step towards the championship by winning the Killinchy Club President Trophy event held over three frozen laps of a treacherous course at Slieve Meelberg, Bryansford losing 43marks in sub-zero conditions.

Road racer Mick Grant was a welcome addition to the event and won Grade 'C'.

Motor Cycle (12p) reported in a February article that the Manx Motorcycle Club Chairman Mr G P Bridge stated that *"costs to run the Manx Grand Prix were rising and that in 1970 the running costs to promote the event were £6,205, rising to £13,732 in 1975"*.

Billy Hutton

The opening round of the World Trial Championship, the Hurst Cup, was held on Valentine's Day and won by Finnish competitor Yrjo Vesterinen – the first foreign rider to win a trial in the UK.

17-year old Colin Bell made a promising international debut being best Irish competitor in 20th position ahead of fellow Ulster man Benny Crawford.

Billy Hutton, who first competed in the Hurst ten years before Bell was born, doubled up as Clerk of the Course and competitor, the 47-year old finishing as top veteran.

Former Irish Junior scrambles champion John Lewis (Suzuki) landed two morale boosting wins in the 250cc and Experts races at the Foyle Club confined event at Magilligan where John Hoey won the 500cc race.

Top schoolboy at the meeting was 15-year old Laurence Spence who put one over on another 15-year old Dave Watson.

Noted in the results of the Ards Club Sandown Trophy Trial that George McCann (Bultaco) was the best Novice competitor - George would of course later become better known as a commentator at road races and short circuit events, affectionately known as the 'two metre man' simply because of his height.

Piano tuner Benny Crawford bagged his 15th Irish Trials championship with two rounds remaining despite dropping to third behind Tom McBride and Colin Bell in the McMaster Trophy event at Crossgar.

John Lewis

George McCann

In the first round of the new Ulster Scramble championship at Dromore Winston Norwood (400cc Maico) had to fight off a fierce challenge from the 370cc Suzuki of John Lewis and the discomfort of mud-filled eyes after discarding his clogged up goggles before winning.

When it came to the feature Wills Trophy race Norwood had to settle for second position behind Harry McQuaid (360cc Husqvarna) despite leading the race at one stage.

The big news reported by Motor Cycle in April was that:–

"the Isle of Man TT was to be stripped of its world championship status- but would pioneer a new world series next year exclusively for pure road circuits.

In an unexpected move the ACU was commissioned to decide the format, based on production machines that will see the 1977 TT a stand alone specialized world championship for the new formula with the aim to bring together other road race circuits from 1978."

This would split racing into two championships – genuine racing bikes contesting the Grand Prix series on purpose built tracks and the bikes conforming to the new ACU driven rules contesting the TT championship, mostly on what many of the new breed of competitors felt were outdated and dangerous road circuits.

Ray McCullough won three Embassy Championship races in the space of nine days winning first at St Angelo Airfield and then Aghadowey and Kirkistown on Easter Saturday and Easter Monday.

MCN (14p) in a report from the Easter Saturday meeting at Aghadowey stated that:–

Ray McCullough (Yamaha) got his season off to a flier with a double, including taking maximum points in the second round of the Embassy championship.

His fiercest rival Mervyn Robinson, who had never lost an Embassy race at the venue, was detained in hospital for observation following a practice pile up.

Joey Dunlop and Steven Cull, second and third in the Embassy were the 500cc and 250cc winners respectively with local man George McQuitty taking the 750cc class.

The action moved to Kirkistown on Easter Monday with McCullough continuing his winning ways with his third successive Embassy victory.

A reported 20,000 bumper crowd saw McCullough set a record lap of 87.27mph as he caught and passed Dunlop to take the victory.

Ian McGregor won the 250cc race while Dunlop triumphed in the 350 and 500cc events to add to his growing number of successes.

Teenager Alan Garrett (250cc Maico) produced the biggest shock of the Ulster scrambles season when he won the Henderson Trophy at Mallusk.

Scoring his first major success against the 'big guns' of local scrambling Winston Norwood, Davy Crockard and Robert Wilkinson, who was on a visit home from his continental campaign.

Garrett won the first leg after early leaders Norwood and Crockard retired their 400cc Maico's with front suspension problems and a puncture.

Crockard won the second leg from Wilkinson with Garrett third, enough to give him the overall victory.

A year after being seriously injured Campbell Gorman returned in a wheelchair to the Tandragee 100 where he acted as starter for the 750cc race, while Eric Lyons, also confined to a wheelchair following a Killinchy 150 accident acted as starter for the sidecar race, which he also sponsored.

Lethal track conditions at the rain lashed event failed to curb the enthusiasm of Joey Dunlop and his Rea Yamahas, winning both the 350 and 500cc races.

Early pressure from Ray McCullough in the 350cc event eased when McCullough (the runaway 250cc winner) was forced out with a sticking throttle, but Billy Guthrie took up the challenge and at one stage was level pegging with Dunlop before easing his pace, blinded by his rivals spray, settling for a close second – Frank Kennedy got the better of Courteny Junk for third.

Frank Kennedy takes delivery of his new Sparton at his home in Armoy

Dunlop led the processional 500cc race demoralising his rivals by clearing off from the drop of the flag. A surprise second place went to Belfast's Jimmy Heath with Frank Kennedy riding his new Sparton again in third position.

The finale of the sidecar race was pure excitement, as Bill Regan (Yamaha) won by half a wheel from Jim Rush (BSA). Regan, seemingly cruising to victory, had been forced to take to a slip road on the penultimate lap allowing Rush to lead onto the final lap, but Regan was not to be denied victory and despite Rush leading out of the final bend Regan was closing hand over fist passing the BSA a couple of yards from the finish line.

Bill Simpson beat English visitor Roy Garnett and Davy Gordon in the 200cc event.

Tom Herron put in two scintillating performances during the Italian Grand Prix at Mugello finishing seventh in the 250cc race and fifth in the 350cc, just edged on the line for fourth.

In the 250cc race he was last off the line – the rest of the field had disappeared round the first bend – but turned in a classic performance to scythe his way through the filed of world class riders to seventh at the chequered flag.

Writing in MCN prior to the North West 200 legendary reporter Norrie Whyte stated,

> "There is no doubt that despite their troubles, the Irish still know how to enjoy themselves – and for me – the North West 200 is the year's best event. The North West is both a social gathering and a good race meeting on a super fast public road circuit."

Torrential rain and bitterly cold winds kept speeds down at the North West 200 from anticipated 120mph averages to around 100mph.

Riders also had to contend with a new roundabout at Ballysally, between Shell Hill Bridge and Mathers Cross, to be taken the wrong way round.

Despite the conditions it was a meeting of a few spills although the winner of the 350cc race Ray McCullough crashed his 250cc Yamaha on the flat out section close to Carnalridge School after it aqua-planed. It was reported he skidded 150 yards down the middle of the road escaping with cuts and bruises.

Ian Richards eventually won what was a race of attrition getting the better of Tony Rutter by a fraction of a second with Joey Dunlop third.

The 500cc race was a Sparton tussle between Martin Sharpe and local rider Frank Kennedy, who swapped the lead four or five times after Stan Woods Suzuki nipped up when he was 22secs in front.

Near the end Kennedy's machine went onto two cylinders intermittently forcing him to surrender the chance of a first pure road race win, as English visitor Sharpe raced to a three-second victory over the Armoy man.

The freezing and soaking crowd were kept entertained when only a few yards separated Tony Rutter and Percy Tait for the entire 750cc 8-lap race.

Stan Woods again led a race, but was forced to pit to refuel his thirsty Suzuki with Tait taking the chequered flag 1.6secs ahead of Rutter after 80 miles of torture.

Ian Richards winning 250cc class at NW200

Irish eyes smiled when McCullough led the 350cc race from start to finish, his only challenge coming from the up and coming Joey Dunlop until his Yamaha expired approaching Coleraine.

A week later and McCullough, none the worse for his North West 200 spill, racked up a historic treble plus an absolute lap record at the Cookstown 100, which netted him almost £300.

By winning the 250, 350 and 500cc races McCullough was believed to be the first Ulsterman to score a hat trick on the local road race scene.

Man of the Meeting McCullough trailed Joey Dunlop for the opening laps of the 350cc race, but with that record lap of 99.78mph for the Sherrygroom

500 c.c. RACE (6 Laps)

No.	Name Address	Machine	1	2	3	4	5	6	Rt
1	R. McCullough, Dromara	346 Yamaha							
2	J. Rea, Templepatrick	347 Rea Yamsel							
3	C. Junk, Newtownabbey	348 Yamaha							
4	F. Kennedy, Armoy	470 Sparton							
5	B. Guthrie, Moira	354 Danfay Yamaha							
6	M. Robinson, Ballymoney	352 Shaw Yamsel							
7	J. Heath, Belfast	348 Yamaha							
8	G. Bell, Moira	351 Yamaha							
9	G. Maizer, Belfast	352 Yamaha							
10	S. McClements, Banger	499 Norton							
11	J. Scott, Coleraine	346 Anderson Yamaha							
12	J. Lindsay, Belfast	347 Yamaha							
14	W. Johnston, Lisburn	347 Yamaha							
15	D. Cormican, Belfast	346 Yamaha							
16	B. Ryan, Dublin	347 D.M.G. Yamaha							
17	R. McKee, Newtownards	347 Yamaha							
18	T. Shaw, Keady	499 Norton							
19	M. R. Coombes, Oxford	492 Suzuki							
20	J. Dunlop, Ballymoney	347 Yamaha							
21	H. Howell, Belfast	496 Suzuki							
22	T. Talbot, Dungannon	500 Triton							
23	W. L. Smyth, Newtownards	354 Yamaha							
24	D. Bell, Cookstown	347 Yamaha							
25	J. Lewis, Belfast	495 Suzuki							
26	J. Smyth, Ballymena	348 Allen Yamaha							
27	W. Patterson, Belfast	492 Seeley Suzuki							
28	I. MacIntosh, Cullybackey	352 Yamaha							
29	R. Britton, Enniskillen	500 Triumph							
30	J. Morrison, Cookstown	347 Ducati							
31	W. Kennedy, B/money (1st Res.)	347 Yamaha							
32	G. Miller, Omagh (2nd Res.)	344 Aermacchi							
33	W. Johnston, C/town (3rd Res.)	344 Aermacchi							
34	J. Cooke, Ligoniel (4th Res.)	496 B.S.A							
35	S. Kernohan, Belfast (5th Res.)	352 Yamaha							
36	V. Jones, Raheny (6th Res.)	344 Aermacchi							

Group I—No. 1 to 15.   Group III—No. 16 to 36.

Extract from Cookstown 100 program – note the sponsorship which could only have been for the love of the sport!

Circuit he took a race winning lead 35secs ahead of Dunlop, who had to contend with a fractured Yamaha frame.

McCullough dominated the 250 and 500cc races in which his close friend Ian McGregor was second in the smaller class and Dunlop again second in the 500cc race.

Scottish visitor Jimmy Aird (580 CCM) raced to an impressive double at the Cambridge Motocross organised by the Lightweight Club at Dunmore Mountain.

The tricky 1½mile course saw a number of spills with Irish title pace setter Davy Crockard, Leslie Wright, Dennis McBride and first time Ulster visitor Neil Hudson all disappearing early in the Grade A race, also won by Aird.

TT time and the headline in Motor Cycle News read:–

Herron on top of the world.

Ulsterman Tom Herron leads the world having completed an Island double when he triumphed in the 250cc TT, the last Isle of Man event to officially count for the then world championship, hoisting himself to the top of the current standings to lead Harley Davidson factory rider Walter Villa by one point.

Re-scheduled from Friday to Saturday morning the 250cc TT also gave the Temple team of Herron, Gerry Mateer (17th) and Norman Dunn (29th) the much coveted club team award.

Earlier in the week Herron had won the Senior TT, his first victory since the Killinchy 150 in 1973, despite a stop to refit the chain of his 350cc Rea Yamaha, which had jumped off the sprocket.

After the Senior a tearful Herron commented, "That's my lifetime ambition, because despite all the criticism (many pundits complained it was just a glorified junior race as most of the field were riding 351cc and above Yamaha's) the Senior TT still means something special".

Herron's Senior joy was John Williams despair, as he ran out of fuel coming through Governors Dip surrendering a four and a half minute lead as he pushed his 500cc Texaco Heron Suzuki across the finish line an exhausted seventh having set a new all-time lap record for the Mountain Circuit of 112.27mph.

Herron lost out on a 350cc TT podium when a slipped chain on the last lap relegated him from third to 26th position on the final lap. Thinking his chain had broken Herron free-wheeled and pushed his machine, before realising it had just jumped off the sprocket and he was able to put it back on and finish.

In this race Billy Guthrie, Joey Dunlop and Courtney Junk riding for the Cookstown Club won the team award.

Footnotes from the TT were that Percy Tait was to quit thirty years after making his road race debut after his 'freak' TT accident. Tait, now 47-years old, clouted the wall at Ballig Bridge, but did not fall off despite a left knee injury, cracked bone in his leg, broken left shoulder, several fractured ribs and broken fingers. He simply slowed the machine and laid it against the closest bank.

John Williams on moving from 250 / 350 and 385cc machines to full blown 500cc and 750cc Texaco Heron Suzukis commented, *"The way the Suzuki accelerates I could be hitting the bottom of Bray Hill at least 20mph faster than I have ever done – and on heavier bikes. I don't know if the tyres, suspension or frame can stand it"*

John Williams

In what was described as his most electrifying display of the season Ray McCullough re-wrote the 250cc Killinchy 150 record book setting new race and lap records, his best lap faster than the overall 250cc lap record for Dundrod, set at the Ulster Grand Prix.

For six of the nine laps McCullough and Ian McGregor were wheel to wheel, firstly McCullough in the lead then McGregor in a slip streaming battle.

Near the end McGregor's Yamaha started to slow while McCullough produced his breathtaking 106.33mph lap, streaking to a comfortable win in the end from McGregor, Neil Tuxworth and Billy Redmond.

McCullough doubled up by scoring an easy 350cc victory while Joey Dunlop

Davy Gordon getting clad for battle – no motorhomes then!

won the 500cc race with the fastest lap of the day at 107.40mph, also a Killinchy record.

Davy Gordon on his Rickman Metisse clinched a win in the 750cc race from the Suzuki of George McQuitty while Tuxworth rode the wheels off his little 125cc Yamaha to win the 200cc class from the Rotax of 'RD' McQuillan with Bill Regan continuing his fine form with a sidecar race victory.

Tom Herron scored a brace of seventh places at the Dutch Grand Prix in the 250 and 350cc races. It was recorded at the time that the Ulster rider was the only competitor to figure on three world championship leader boards, namely third in the 250, sixth in the 350 and 500cc classes.

For the first time in nine years Irish scrambling was almost certain to have a new champion after Davy Crockard (Maico) won both legs during the fifth championship round held at Murder Hole Road, Limavady and for good measure won the Foyle Club premier award – The Campbell Donaghy Memorial Trophy.

Despite his rear wheel buckling due to a puncture three laps from home in the first championship race Crockard nursed his machine over the finish line just ahead of the fast closing Winston Norwood (Maico).

Norwood, the defending champion, led the second race, but was soon overhauled by Crockard who went on to take a comfortable victory before dominating the feature race.

Records fell at every turn during an Ulster dominated Southern 100 races in the Isle of Man.

Having taken 2.2secs off the outright lap record in the 750cc race 24-year old Joey Dunlop took another 2.8secs off his day-old record on his way to a brilliant win in the solo championship race.

Fellow Ulsterman Ray McCullough clipped 1.2secs off his own 1973 250cc lap record on his way to victory over Ian McGregor and Dunlop following that up with a win in the 350cc race from Dunlop and 19-year old Trevor Steele, a close neighbour of McCullough's.

Following the Southern 100 a strong Ulster contingent headed to the north of the island for the Andreas Racing Association meeting at Jurby Airfield and continued their winning streak with Dunlop scoring a treble in both solo unlimited and 350cc races where Armoy compatriot Frank Kennedy was second in each race before getting a well-deserved victory racing his 500cc Sparton to victory in the unlimited non-Japanese event.

A broken throttle cable robbed Dunlop of a 250cc victory in which Ivor Greenwood and Con Law finished first and second with Dunlop dropping to third.

Over both the Southern 100 and Jurby meetings Dunlop collected 22 trophies during his barnstorming trip.

The Grand Prix trail took Tom Herron to Sweden and Finland the Ulster rider finishing sixth in the 250 and ninth in the 500cc Swedish event at Anderstorp, where riders were forced to obey the FIM no slick rule for 250s.

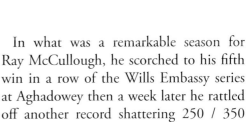

A week later and a major break for Herron when he was drafted into the 'works' Suzuki 500cc team replacing the injured John Williams at Imatra unfortunately retiring early in his first works ride with machine problems.

Herron finished third in the 350cc race and fifth in the 250cc race to make up for his 500cc disappointment.

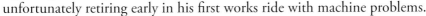

Gordon Bell makes an ackward landing at the Temple (above) while Sam McClements adopts a more traditional pose (below)

In what was a remarkable season for Ray McCullough, he scorched to his fifth win in a row of the Wills Embassy series at Aghadowey then a week later he rattled off another record shattering 250 / 350 double at Ireland's oldest road race; the Temple 100.

The huge crowd lining the roller-coaster 5½mile Saintfield circuit saw Joey Dunlop lead for three-laps of the 350cc race before McCullough moved ahead on lap four with an absolute lap record of 96.59mph to win comfortably from the Armoy man, Trevor Steele and Sam McClements.

Portadown motorcycle dealer Billy Redmond, the 200cc race winner, kept 'Supermac' in his slip stream for four-laps of the 250cc event, but had to give way as McCullough raced past and on to a 15sec victory.

Billy Guthrie was untouchable in the

500cc race, flying the Temple 'jumps' in his own immaculate style to beat Frank Kennedy in what was a drab procession with Adrian Craig the winner of the concurrently run unlimited race.

The McCullough 'road show' turned in a record shattering performance in the Gallaher Mid Antrim 150 250cc race lapping the 6-mile Rathkenny Circuit at 88.50mph to clinch the Ulster championship with five wins from five starts.

Melting tar and flying stones was a problem for competitors in sun-drenched conditions, but no problem for McCullough who went on to win the 350cc race with ease after Joey Dunlop seized an engine during the pre-race two lap practice session.

Mervyn Robinson scored a 500cc victory returning to action after a long lay-off due to injury.

Jack Agnew, a Mid Antrim Club Member, became the first winner of the Enkalon Shield and £10 with the fastest lap by a 350cc Group 'B' competitor – the inaugural donation by the newly formed Enkalon Club that has gone on to pour well over £500,000 into motorcycle sport throughout Ireland.

A little snippet in MCN (now 15p) stated that:–

> Tom Herron was named 'Dish of the Day' during the John Player British Grand Prix at Silverstone by the Lady Marshals Association, which went to the friendliest, most approachable rider at the meeting.

Davy Crockard tamed his Ulster rivals to win the 30-minute Brian Bell Memorial Trophy plus the Experts race at Saintfield. Crockard lead the main race from start to finish, but he had to fight through the field from 20th position in the Experts race having to rely on Winston Norwood suffering a broken chain with the race virtually in his pocket.

Rolls Royce job analyst Geoff Barry (Sid Griffiths 750cc Yamaha) set a new lap record of 114.55mph to win the Ulster Grand Prix 1000cc race in front of an estimated 40,000 fans at a sun-backed Dundrod.

Two-thirds of the circuit had been resurfaced with Tony Rutter the first man to break the four minute barrier with a lap of 3m 58secs during Thursday practice riding Bob Priest's 750cc Yamaha.

Practice had been marred by a frightening four-bike pile up on the fast section approaching Leathemstown in which Charlie Williams received a broken left leg and collar bone, Sam McClements had a plate put in a broken arm, Paul Cott escaped with a minor foot injury and Richard Dowland a broken pelvis.

Race day also brought several crashes in which Dave Hughes suffered arm and leg injuries when he crashed at Quarries, Lee Heeson knocked a knee cap off when he fell heavily at Deers Leap (I was actually a race marshal on the scene that day) and flag marshal Norman Kennedy suffered a broken leg when Surrey rider Jim Gilles crashed.

Ray McCullough picked up a 250/350cc double breaking the class lap records on the way while Stan Woods and Neil Tuxworth set class lap records romping to victory in the 500 and 200cc races respectively.

Paul Cott

Belfast docker Joe Lindsay (Sheilds and McMurray Yamaha) won the Junior Manx Grand Prix at a race record speed of 101.30mph despite riding the last three miles on a deflating rear tyre. In a dramatic race Lindsay was close behind race leader Dave Williams, who crashed out at the 11th Milestone, Lindsay narrowly missing the sliding machine as he sped past the incident on his way to victory.

Lindsay was out of luck in the Senior Manx retiring at Grebba Bridge on the first lap, while fellow Belfast rider Jimmy Heath, who had been fastest in practice with an unofficial lap record of 104.49mph retired at Glen Vine.

Newcomer to the Mountain Circuit Ivor Greenwood, a former stock car champion, from Belfast finished the Lightweight 250cc Manx Grand Prix in fifth position having led at Ballacraine on the opening lap.

Joe Lindsay with his Junior Manx GP winner's trophy at Kirkistown

In a cliff-hanging 350cc road race championship decider at the Carrowdore 100 Ray McCullough pipped Joey Dunlop by half a machine length having shadowed the Armoy man for seven of the eight laps before pouncing on the final run to the chequered flag to snatch victory and the championship with a new track record of 104.82mph.

McCullough made it a double again beating Dunlop across the line in the 250cc race while Robert Hanna (200cc), Billy Guthrie (500cc) and Adrian Craig (750cc) were the other race winners.

Roger Harvey at John Donnelly

Lancashire farmer Bob Wright (Maico) scored two firsts and a second to collect the Carling Black Label Trophy at the John Donnelly scramble.

27-year old Wright was the only rider to have a trouble free run during the three 30minute races. Punctures ruined the chances of many competitors including Pete Mathia, Roger Harvey, Stuart Nunn, Irish champion Davy Crockard, Lars Axelsson and Neil Hudson.

A regular visitor to Ulster events Bill Henderson, originally from Donegal but residing in Coventry, died on his way to hospital following a crash at Gerrards Bend during the 350cc race at Mallory Park Race of the Year meeting.

Making his first appearance in the Motor Cycle News Superbike series Tom

Herron (750cc Yamaha) finished fifth behind Mick Grant, Geoff Barry, Steve Manship and Barry Sheene at Olivers Mount, Scarborough in front of an estimated 65,000 spectators.

In a dramatic last lap at Kirkistown Ray McCullough retained the Wills Embassy championship. From the off Joey Dunlop led, but ran wide at the hairpin with Ian McGregor grabbing the lead with McCullough in hot pursuit. Four laps from the end McCullough moved ahead just before McGregor slipped off at the hairpin.

Going onto the final lap McCullough looked comfortable, but uncharacteristically the Dromara man slipped off allowing Mervyn Robinson into the lead. Picking up his machine, which had a broken footrest and jammed gear lever McCullough got going again. Within sight of the chequered flag Robinson's machine shed its chain and as he toured towards the finish line McCullough sped past for a remarkable win to cap what was a sensational season for McCullough on Mick Mooney's Irish Racing Motorcycle 250 and 350cc Yamaha's meticulously prepared at Queen's University.

Belfast architect student Colin Bell (Bultaco) won both the Turner Trophy Trial at Clandyboye and the Temple Club Terry Hill Trophy Trial at Saintfield to strengthen his lead in the Irish Trials championship. Bell bidding for his first championship winning medal beat Trevor Callaghan by two marks at Clandyboye with a similar margin over defending Irish champion Benny Crawford at Saintfield.

Recounted in MCN that a staggering £100,000 would be made available to riders, mostly in prizes and appearance money for 1977 TT coming from a Manx authorities grant, a raise of over 40%.

With Formula 1, 2 and 3 being the new world championship status events for the TT the result would be three new world champions after a solitary race!

Entitled – Odd TT Ode – the following appeared in MCN written by a Manxman and life member of the TT Marshals Association Iain Marshall;

The FIM have done the deed,
Which doesn't seem to suit Phil Read;
The greatest motorcycle races,
Can now be won by better aces;
While saucer circuit racing scene,
Is left to Ago, Read and Sheene;
Which new riders will become great?
To join Hailwood, Duke (Percy Tait!),
And Frith & Woods from out of the past,
Who won their races, though not so fast.

In boarding houses, hotel or tent,
The air will fill with argument;
Is road race champ a better man,
Than one who circuits round a pan?
We, of the Islands green hills and glens,
Say throttle shuts as well as opens;
As TT marshal and resident,
My love of TT is evident;
Those who don't agree with my views,
Can publish theirs in MC News.

Despite ceaseless torrential rain Robbie Jennings, a diesel fitter from Dundonald, gained his first premier award with a two point winning margin over Derek Russell in the Autumn Trophy Trial at Ligoneil.

The cruel weather conditions meant the organising Lightweight Club reduced the number of laps from four to three – a decision that all 92 starters unanimously agreed with.

Jennings was on a roll and scored his second success of the season comfortably winning the Iveagh Cup Trial at Pond Park quarry by sixteen marks from Ray Pyper with Benny Crawford third.

Pyper hit back a week later at the annual winter trial at Claudy beating Jennings by seven marks while another Pyper, 15-year old Stephen was the clear cut winner of the schoolboy section.

Thick fog reduced visibility to less than 50 yards at the North Armagh trial over a compact quarry course, however it was piano tuner Benny Crawford who called the tune scoring his first Ulster trials championship win of the season taking only two dabs.

200cc Carrowdore start: 3 Richard Hewitt: 2. Robert
Hanna:12. Jimmy Rodgers:15 Norvel Gregory: 8 Ken
Crossett: 19. George Purvis: 23 Stanley Hillis
Starter Joe Boyle, B&D President in the club's 70th year

Graham Young,
at Kirkistown

Mervyn Robinson, entering the 'cement hairpin' at Aghadowey

Steven Cull, Aghadowey

William Johnston explores the limit at Aghadowey

John Smyth Aghadowey

*Joey
Dunlop,
Temple*

*Billy
Guthrie,
Temple*

*Ivor Greenwood,
Deers Leap*

*Ian McGregor,
Mid Antrim
150*

Roy Harris

remembers...The Enkalon Club

By the time I went to work at British Enkalon in the early seventies I already had a keen interest in motor cycle racing having trekked to spectate at events all over the province, initially taken by my father after much pestering and, once I could drive, under my own steam.

As such it was natural for me to get involved with the setting up of a motorcycle club at the Enkalon factory which in turn led to a unforeseen and unplanned part-time career in journalism creating a direct link between the Enkalon Club and this book!

Opened by Queen Beatrix of Holland in 1963 the Dutch owned nylon and polyester producing plant brought an influx of people from all over Northern Ireland into the Antrim area including many who were fans, sponsors, competitors or spectators of motorcycle sport.

Naturally it did not escape these folks' notice that the factory had a huge engineering department which became, unbeknown to the management (or did they turn a blind eye?), an undercover facility for repairs and parts manufacture for many a racer, some of whom worked on site including Mickey Laverty, Rod Coleman, Chris Milner, Ronald and Sam Tweedy and Donny Robinson.

Indeed the story goes that Tom Herron's continental campaigns of the seventies had a hub in the Enkalon workshop where many a mechanical issue was resolved!

Of course, given the clandestine nature of the venture, there were

obstacles to overcome such as how to get parts in and out of the factory gates but "where there's a will there's a way" and I understand that on more than one occasion the late Charlie McClean, who had lost his leg in a road traffic accident, acted as a mule, transporting the parts into and out of the factory inside his false leg – ingenious or what!

Charlie was a real character and racing daft even sponsoring successful seventies short circuit and road racer, Michael (Mickey) Laverty, father of current MotoGP, British Superbike and World Superbike competitors Michael, John and Eugene.

Following the opening of the British Enkalon Sports and Social clubhouse on 1st May 1975 it was natural, given the high level of interest in motorcycling throughout the factory, to look to the formation of a specific motorcycle section within the club. Thus, in July 1976, 25 of these 'racing enthusiasts' met in the clubhouse and formed themselves into a club section under the chairmanship of Joe Hamill, the driving force behind the formation, aided and abetted by Secretary Dougie Morgan, Treasurer Ernie Shaw and a committee of which I was a member – the rest, as the well used phrase goes, is history.

Club meetings were mainly on a Thursday night and those of us working on the factory twelve-hour shift pattern were normally allowed out of work to attend the meetings some of which stretched to maybe beyond midnight for one reason or another before we were back in work.

The membership quickly swelled to over 100 with the early meetings which were to lay the foundations for the club, often resulting in heated debates (and I mean really heated to the extent that chairs were stood on and voices raised in argument) as how the club would spend any monies it raised through functions and what those functions would be.

Eventually a consensus was reached and it was agreed that the main focus of the club would be to support local motorcycle sport and through the small membership fee for the club (I think it was either 50p or £1, I'm not quite sure which) the very first donation was made to the Mid Antrim Club for the 1975 Mid Antrim 150 road race in August.

This consisted of a shield and £25 to go to the competitor with the fastest lap in the 'B' group of the 350cc race to be named the British Enkalon Sports and Social Club (Motorcycle Section) Shield which was first won by Jack Agnew, now Chairman of the Ulster Centre of the Motorcycle Union of Ireland and a Mid Antrim Club (Tarmac Section) member.

To raise more funds the club embarked on a range of events including in September of the inaugural year, a film show when 500 people crowded into the Clubhouse to enjoy two full-length films followed by a 'Talk-in' chaired by UTV sports presenter Jackie Fullerton with a panel of motorcycle racing personalities past and present including Malcolm Templeton, Billy McCosh, Joey Dunlop, Mervyn Robinson, Joe Lindsay, Ivor Greenwood and Harold Crooks alias 'Hi-

Cam' correspondent for the Ballymena Guardian and Downtown Radio reporter.

The film shows became legendary but, for me, one in particular will be forever etched on my memory when, after the Enkalon evening, the films were loaned to Derek Mason (the late 'Big D') who was to show them at a function in Davy

Inaugural function of the Enkalon motorcycle club reported in Enkalon News.
L-R: Dougie Morgan, Jackie Fullerton, Billy McCosh, A. N. Other
Joe Lindsay, Ivor Greenwood and Harold Crooks.

Gordon's Hawthorn premises outside Portglenone the next night.

Now these films were obtained from Danny Keaney in Dublin and had to be guarded with your life or you would never have got the loan of another so you can imagine the panic when Dougie Morgan, Sean McClarnon and myself arrived at the Hawthorn to find 'Big D' standing in front of his projector with one of the films completely unravelled from the spool and Derek standing up to his ankles in celluloid trying to get it rewound!

I can assure you that, after a long night and a marathon journey to Dublin the next day, it was with much relief that the film was returned as received along with a grovelling apology to Danny for being late.

Alongside the film shows, a full calendar of sponsored walks, cabaret shows, raffles and chat shows (including on one occasion the full Honda GB Endurance squad of Charlie Williams, Tony Rutter, Stan Woods and Geoff Barry, while another had Jackie Fullerton interviewing the great Stanley Woods on stage in the Clubhouse), all ensured the purse was always replenished and ready to be emptied for the good of motorcycle sport.

Not long after the formation of the club it was decided we should put on a motorcycle show which, in time, would become the major fund-raiser for the club. The brainchild of Joe Hamill, the show first ran in 1977 and saw a dozen exhibitors take space in the clubhouse dance hall with Cyril Smith of Ulster Television opening the venture and a steady stream of punters paying into the exhibition.

This show became the key social gathering of the winter months and grew to such an extent that after 2,000 people attended the 1979 show a new larger venue had to be sought, hence the move to nearby Antrim Forum from 1980.

Organised in those early days by every day workers, who did all the organisation in their spare time for absolutely no personal gain, the profits always going straight into club coffers, the event quickly gained the motto 'Support the show that supports the sport.

Off and running with money to spend, the next venture was to become one of the longest running sponsorship involvements in Ulster Motorcycle racing when in the 1977 season a tie-up with the Motor Cycle Road Racing Club of Ireland was forged which continues until the present day.

6th Round. Wills. Embass. C/ship
1 Joe Dunlop 750. Yamaha
2 Adrain. Craig " "
3 Joe Lindsay 347 "
4 Trevor Steele " "
5 Ray McCullough " "
6 Graham Young " "
7 Courtney Junk " "
8 Jim. Dunlop " "
9 Brian. Hewitt 247. "
10 Ernie. Coates. " "
11 Jackie. Hughes 347 "
12 Billy Redman. 351 "
13 George McQuitty 750. "
14 David Gordon 525 Sparton.
15 William B. Johnston 347 Yamaha
16 Bill Simpson. 247. "
17 Donny Robinson. " "
18 Connor McGinn 347. "
19 Sam. McClements " "
20 Raymond McKee 351. "
21 Ian Macintosh. " "
22 William J. McKillop " "
23 Alex Ritchie 110. Kawasaki.

1st British. Enkalon. Trophy
RACE
1 Raymond. McCullough 347 Yamaha
2 Joe. Dunlop " "
3 Steven. Cull 750 Suzuki
4 Stanley. Junk 373. Yamaha
5 Courtney. Junk 347. "
6 Connor. McGinn " "
7 Jackie. Hughes. " "
8 Jim. Dunlop " "
9 Trevor Steele " "
10 John. Smyth 351. "
11 Adrain. Craig 750 "
12 David. Gordon 525 Sparton

Initial contacts were made between the two clubs and Dougie Morgan and myself went along to a MCRRCI club meeting to put forward a proposed sponsorship deal whereby we would contribute half the prize money for the meeting as well as sponsoring an invitation race on the day. In return we would receive back half the profit on the meeting after all the bills were paid.

Now that could have worked either way as we could have had half of nothing if it was a poorly supported meeting or half of a good profit at a well supported meeting – but after some discussion the deal was agreed and the foundation for the Enkalon Trophy meeting was laid.

Displaying the support that motorcycling had throughout the Enkalon operation, Mr R. L. Schierbeek Chief Executive of the

PERMIT No. 77/22

Motorcycle Road Racing Club of Ireland

AGHADOWEY SHORT CIRCUIT ROAD RACES

SATURDAY, 23rd JULY, 1977
First Race 1.00 p.m.

FEATURING

BRITISH ENKALON

TROPHY INVITATION RACE
and Sixth Round Embassy Championship

THIS MEETING IS SPONSORED BY BRITISH ENKALON SPORTS & SOCIAL CLUB (Motorcycle Section)

Presentation of cheque for first sponsorship of Enkalon Trophy Meeting

factory donated a Trophy and on Saturday 23rd July 1977 thirty invited riders vied for the trophy over fifteen laps of the Aghadowey Circuit with Ray McCullough emerging victorious to become the first recipient of the Enkalon Trophy.

Another unique and significant feature of the clubs activities was the introduction of the Irish Motorcyclist of the Year Award evening, the winner decided by a vote by the general public for who they

Joey Dunlop, regularly voted Enkalon Irish Motorcyclist of the year, pictured here with Barry S,ymmons (Honda Team Manager) and Roy Harris (Enkalon Club)

thought should be crowned champion. The idea caught on and thousands voted for the first winner, Tom Herron, in 1978 and a year later Joey Dunlop. Such was the popularity of this award that huge crowds attended the presentation evening in the Sports and Social Club, one of the nights of the year on the social calendar which still plays a significant role in the Adelaide Awards Gala evening in Belfast.

Competitors soon became aware of the input this new club, not affiliated to the MCUI, was having with increased prize money and new ideas and they always bent over backwards to a man to support any of the functions organised by the club.

The alcohol in the clubhouse was cheap and although, according to the rules, one member could only sign in one non-member, for a club whose members could smuggle motorcycle parts inside an artificial leg this was a fairly minor hurdle and many a ruse was pulled at getting non-members (virtually everybody who attended the motorcycle functions) signed into the clubhouse. Of course, despite the odd complaint from management and executive committee, the clubhouse benefited greatly through the sale of many pints and half 'uns to the thirsty motorcycle crowd and many a blind eye was turned, as the motorcycle section was renowned for pulling in the biggest crowds and contributing most to the day to day running of the venue.

The activities and contribution made to the sport in the first three years when over £4,000 was contributed to motorcycling is concrete evidence of the graft of the committee who worked hard and played hard in their efforts to further motorcycle sport in Ireland.

Richard Agnew

remembers... Timekeeping

Attending events with his father Joe since he was eight, he joined the timekeeping team when he was thirteen and after nearly 40 years timekeeping Richard has overseen the progression from a manual system to today's 'almost' automatic transponder system.

By day he is a chemical engineer and whilst working in England was a timekeeper at the Transatlantic Trophy and Powerbike meetings at Brands Hatch. A keen historian of our sport he's a Banbridge man, now living outside Randalstown, and was part of the 'Banbridge Mafia' scene of the 80s/90s when it seemed like every other road racer came from that locality.

As a boy growing up in the 1970s I remember long warm summer days and discovering the magical world of motorcycle sport for the first time. I was just too young to remember Ray McCullough's famous World Championship 250cc win at the Ulster in 1971 or indeed the season that didn't start until July in 1972 on account of the troubles. So my first definite memory was the 1973 Ulster Grand Prix.

I was eight years old, was given a job and have been working at motorcycle races ever since. Sydney Steel ran Race Control which was manned by people using wind-up field telephones to receive messages from points around the Dundrod circuit. I was one of the runners for the timekeepers. At the end of each lap they wrote down the leading six riders with times and speeds on little strips of paper. There were two runners and we swapped the two runs between us – one lap you ran up the stairs, rolled the piece of paper up and pushed it through a hole in the trap door to the "crow's nest" for the commentator; the next lap you ran down the stairs to take the note to the press in their caravan just outside Grand Prix House. Each time you had your own personal race to be first back to the timekeepers' office in time to see John Williams complete another lap. For 1973 was the year that Williams became the first man ever to win three races in one day at the Grand Prix – my first motorcycling hero.

The following year 1974 I met another hero at Dundrod – Peter Williams, who would suffer career ending injuries just days later at Oulton Park. I also met Tommy Robb that year too as he autographed his new biography for my dad, but I must confess that at the time I didn't know who Tommy was!

As I was getting older I was going to more and more events. There was a first trip to Clandeboye in 1975 for the Hurst Cup, a round of the new world trials championship. Dave Thorpe won the trial, but my memory is of seeing Sammy Miller in competitive action for the first time, riding the new Honda that he was developing, although by that time Sammy was a long way from the dominant force that he had once been.

In future years I saw all the greats of that period at Clandeboye, Martin Lampkin, Malcolm Rathmell, Yrjo Vesterinen, Bernie Schreiber and Rob Shepherd who won the trial in 1979 on the latest version of the Honda. By then Miller had left the Japanese giant and joined Italian minnow SMW, bringing his new team of John Reynolds and local rider Colin Bell to the 1978 event. Although Colin had been achieving excellent results at British Championship level the new machine and the step up to the World Championship wasn't successful and he left the team after only a few months.

Unlike top level trials of the last ten years that can only attract a handful of competitors, the Hurst in the 70s had an entry list of close on one hundred with many local riders taking the chance to compete against the best in the world. In particular I can remember the extremely versatile Davy McBride and also Bryson Perry. On his day Davy was one of the top Irish riders whilst I would describe Bryson as more a clubman rider and whilst they would exclaim how difficult the trial was each time that you met them, they were enjoying themselves to the full.

Back to 1975 and another memory was the 250cc Harley Davidson that Ray McCullough rode that season. The Italian rider Walter Villa had won the first of three successive world title the year before, but Ray had very little success with this machine retiring from nearly every race that he started.

Bryson Perry

While I thoroughly enjoyed my first trip to Skerries, my favourite race of the year was the Temple 100, where Ray finally won a 250cc race on the Harley.

The Temple on the last Saturday in July formed a unique double-header with the Mid-Antrim 150 on the Rathkenny circuit the following weekend, the first Saturday in August. These events held at the height of the summer had an atmosphere that made the hairs on my neck stand up. Music playing over the tannoy – every time I hear *The Rhinestone Cowboy* or *The Crystal Chandelier* I am taken back to those days – crowds milling about, a walk through the field that was the paddock, a visit to scrutineering, watching the bikes being prepared on the grass in an open air workshop at the rear of a Transit van, the start of the race as the riders pushed their machines before bumping them into life, the crackle of exhausts and the smoke that enveloped the whole scene and when it cleared one or two riders still pushing, trying to coax their machines to start.

Back in 1975 I remember my first John Donnelly Scramble in September – Ireland hadn't adopted the continental name of motocross at this stage. Anyway at Killinchy I don't remember getting out of the car all day as it rained and rained the whole time, but I still recall the dominance of the Swedish visitors that day with Arne Kring winning from Bengt Aberg. Again I was unaware of the quality of the riders that I was seeing – Aberg had been double 500cc world champion

Lasse Axelsson in 1977, one of the many Swedish visitors to the John Donnelly

in 1969 and 1970 whilst Kring was also a Grand Prix winner and runner-up in the championship in 1970.

My father was a member of the Ards Motorcycle Club and whilst better known for their trials events they also organised short circuit races, a big holiday grass track meeting on the 13th July and also the McClay scramble.

In those days visiting riders wheeled their machines onto the ferry and the organising club sent

Lief Gustaffson, one of the many GP riders encouraged by Tom Herron to come to the Grand Prix

a van or lorry to meet them and though I can't remember which year, it must have been in connection with the McClay scramble that I remember tagging along with my father to collect four burly Scottish scramblers from Larne docks – among them notable competitors Norrie Lymburn and Peter Reid – and the only room left for me in the car was to sit on one of their laps in the front seat. I was asked who my favourite rider was and straight away I answered Ray McCullough, but off course they had meant a scrambler and again I quickly replied Winston Norwood, which made them all laugh. I don't recall who won that day but Winston was a serial winner of Irish scrambles and grass tracks and a multiple Ulster and Irish Champion in the 1970s.

Other memories that stand out are the 182cc Hondas ridden by the like of Courtney Junk, David Gordon and Liverpudlian Roy Garnett in the 200cc class, some of the last four-stroke machines still being raced in the two-stroke era, although there was still the odd Aermacchi and of course Sam McClements on the Ryan Norton.

I can still picture The Green Meanies (Kawasakis) ridden by Mick Grant and Barry Ditchburn at the North West 200 in 1975 and when Grant raised the lap record to over 120mph for the first time, I got a taste of the future when I timed that lap using my wrist watch and knew that the lap record had been broken before the official timekeepers could confirm the time for the commentator to announce to the expectant crowd. In just three more years I became a timekeeper for the first time when Bobby Hewitt invited me to be a lap scorer at the Killinchy 150 and I haven't stopped since.

Another fond memory was the Ulster Grand Prix in 1977 which must have been a throw-back to the world championship days as Tom Herron encouraged leading GP privateers, Jon Ekerold and Alan North from South Africa, Finland's Pekka Nurmi and French-Australian Vic Soussan to Dundrod. Herron just pipped North in a 250cc photo-finish. I remember going out round the circuit with Gordon Flinn and Marcus Blain and we made our way across fields to watch these riders through Budore – now that's one experience that I will never forget. What a spot although I'm sure that you are no longer allowed to lie in the hedge like we did that year.

Dundrod will always be a special place for me. My father was Chief Marshal from the mid-60s to the mid-70s which meant that not only was he responsible for the marshals but also the setting up of the course, erecting the corner boards, putting up the straw bales and the million and one other jobs that need to be done before any race can run.

Richard in his 'office' at Dundrod

My fondest motorcycling memories are the many non-race day summer evenings that I spent at Dundrod with the group of men that helped prepare the course, men like Marcus Blain, Phillip Campbell, Fred and Gordon Flinn, Jimmy Henry, Leslie Kirk, George McCann, WR Neill and Rab Nightingale. Apologies if I've forgotten anyone. For a young boy it was a magical time, the camaraderie, the joking, the common purpose for no reward other than making the race happen.

For me the 1970s will always be the best period in motorcycle sport and there is no better sound than listening to the hum of a two-stroke engine all the way down the Flying Kilo at Dundrod. Then again it's probably true that every young boy remembers the first time that they are introduced to this sport as being the best period as nothing can quite match that same sense of wonder again.

1977

Budget cuts income tax from 35p to 33p in the pound as inflation hits 15.8% – Freddie Laker launched Skytrain, single fare Gatwick to New York £59 compared to normal price of £186 – Star Wars screened in Britain for first time – Barry Sheene retained 500cc world championship.

John and Charlie Williams (unrelated) were guests of Tom and Andrea Herron to herald in the New Year. John and Tom competed in the Temple Club 130mile Marathon Trial centred on Saintfield and both finished – Tom 17th with John 31st and last.

Tom then switched to four wheels competing in a stock car meeting at Portadown finishing third in his heat and second in the final.

The mini ISDT held in icy cold conditions was won by Raymond Davidson from Wallace Seawright, Winston Norwood, George McCann, Bryson Perry and Hugh Simpson.

Drama at the Knock Club Kelly Cup trial at Crossgar where 16-year old Billy Wightman was awarded the trophy as top Grade 'C' rider after a tight tussle with Mark Neill only to be disqualified for allegedly switching machines handing victory to Neill.

Following a decision by the North West 200 organisers to drop the 350cc race from the programme and run a 300cc to 500cc that would have seen 350cc Yamaha's pitted against 500cc Suzuki's brought this response from Mick Mooney, sponsor of Ray McCullough, who thought that the Ulster riders would lose out, "Include a 350cc race or we won't be there." Almost four weeks

Billy Wightman

195

Tom McBride 'smokes' a section watched by John Heenan

later after a meeting between competitors and Coleraine Club officials the separate 350cc race was re-instated.

The McBride Brothers made it a family double in the two holiday trials with Tom taking the Rusk Trophy Trial and Davy winning the Jack Hunter Trophy Trial, both held at the Lead Mines and coincidentally both Tom and Davy lost 18 marks on their way to victory.

Colin Bell, a Belfast University student took another step towards his first ever Irish Trial Championship when he won the eighth round of the current series, The Larkin Cup, at Ballynahinch.

Robbie Jennings scored his fourth victory of the season when he beat Raymond Davidson by five marks to win the Road Racing Club trial at the Lead Mines.

Tom Herron was crowned Ulster Sportsman of the Year for 1976 in a poll carried out by the Sunday News narrowly beating motor racing ace John Watson and Fulham football star George Best.

Wetherby teenager John Reynolds, a technical college student, riding a cantilever Ossa came within a whisker of pulling off the most sensational result in the Hurst Cup, first round of the world trials championship, when he finished two tenths of a mark behind winner Malcolm Rathmell (Montesa) with Rob Edwards making it a mainland 1-2-3 by finishing third having lost 94.1 marks.

With marks being docked at the rate of a tenth for each minute over the allotted 4½ hour time to complete the trial at Clandyboye Estate, where over 3,000 spectators turned out, Rathmell was 28mins late incurring 2.8 time penalties squeezing out Reynolds by a margin of 78.8 marks lost to 79.

The course was made treacherous by six days of continual rain with the best local competitor Colin Bell in fifteenth position.

The organising club raised a few eyebrows by charging 20p for a programme and motorists 50p for admission in an effort to make the event financially viable – charging was unheard of at trials and frowned upon by many visitors from the mainland as against the trials tradition.

John Reynolds

Colin Bell was on a brilliant run of form and won the Presidents Cup Trial his eighth Irish championship success of the season and his seventh in a row, a week later he added the McMaster Cup Trial to his success run to make it eight in a row at Crossgar, eventually clinching the Irish championship by winning the Allen Cup event at Glen of Imaal, Co. Wicklow.

Northern Ireland schoolboy motocross champion 16-year old Dave Watson, now riding a Maico under the Bryan Goss – Winston Norwood banner took five wins from six starts in his debut season in the senior ranks with a treble at Richhill, Co Armagh and the following week added a treble at a Northern Ireland Motorcycle Club March Hare event, where a four-timer was on until a faulty chain cost him certain victory.

Motor Cycle reported that a storm of protest had broken out among Ulster 200cc competitors following a decision by promoters of the Ulster Grand Prix to

No.	Name and Address	Machine	Grade
	BELL BROTHERS 200 c.c. CLASS — 6 LAPS		**START 1.00 p.m.**
1	R. D. McQuillan, Muckamore	191 Rotax	A
2	J. R. Hanna, Belfast	123 Honda	A
3	R. L. Nesbitt, Belfast	196 Yamaha	A
4	D. Lowry, Belfast	195 Yamaha	A
5	R. J. Hewitt, Carrickfergus	196 Suzuki	A
6	B. Redmond, Portadown	196 Suzuki	A
7	B. Simpson, Belfast	196 Suzuki	A
8	D. G. Wood, Belfast	182 Glover Honda	A
9	J. Lennon, Downpatrick	196 Pilot Bultaco	A
10	D. Gordon, Portglenone	185 Spartop	A
11	S. McKee, Newtownards	195 Yamaha	A
12	J. Ogle, Belfast	195 Yamaha	A
14	W. L. Smyth, Newtownards	195 Yamaha	A
15	S. Murray, Chester	182 Honda	A
16	S. Dempster, Bangor	174 Fahron	A
17	J. Rodgers, Killinchy	125 Maico	A
18	G. Bell, Moira	125 Maico	A
19	L. W. Walker, Belfast	196 Suzuki	A
20	J. Melvor, Belfast	200 Suzuki	A
21	J. Donnan, Belfast	198 Suzuki	A
22	T. Kelly, Kircubbin	196 Suzuki	A
23	S. Stewart, Monkstown	196 D.F.R.	A
24	N. Gregory, Belfast	196 Yamaha	B
25	J. Dunlop, Ballymoney	195 Yamaha	B
26	R. Niblock, Crossgar	174 Rotax	B
27	G. Farlow, Belfast	200 Yamaha	B
28	R. Thompson, Bangor	196 Suzuki	B
29	S. McNaul, Ballyclare	184 Suzuki	B
30	S. Smyth, Holywood	196 Suzuki	B
31	H. Boal, Lisburn	125 Yamaha	B
32	N. Lindsay, Lisburn	196 Suzuki	B
33	C. Spence, Crumlin	124 Yamaha	B
34	I. Boyd, Ballymoney	182 Honda	B
35	R. Hanna, Tandragee	195 Yamaha	B
36	L. Allen, Crumlin	165 Honda	B
37	H. Howell, Belfast	196 Suzuki	B
38	I. Porter, Castlewellan	196 Bultaco	B
39	N. Boyd, Ballymoney	182 Honda	B
40	J. Lewis, Belfast	198 Yamaha	B
41	E. McHenry, Dublin	125 Yamaha	B
42	D. Beattie, Banbridge	195 Yamaha	B
44	R. Peile, Richhill	124 Thor Yamaha	B
45	T. Gray, Banbridge	196 Suzuki	B
46	K. Crozier, Belfast	195 Yamaha	B
47	K. Ferguson, Newtownards	124 Suzuki	B
48	D. Carlisle, Ballyclare	125 Manx	B
49	A. McVicker, Ballymoney	123 Minarelli	B
50	R. Howell, Belfast	195 Yamsel	C
51	D. McKinnie, Comber	196 Yamaha	C
52	F. Shaw, Belfast	195 Yamaha	C
53	J. Patterson, Belfast	200 Suzuki	C
54	T. Smyth, Lisburn	196 Suzuki	C
55	M. Robinson, Belfast	196 Suzuki	C
56	J. Gordon, Belfast	165 Honda	C
57	J. McQ. Patterson, Lisburn	196 Suzuki	C
58	B. Laverty, Carrickfergus	196 Bultaco	C
59	F. McConnell, Holywood	195 Yamaha	C
60	H. Patterson, Crossgar	196 Bultaco	C
61	D. Ross, Belfast	177 Bridgestone	C
63	A. Irwin, Monkstown	195 Yamaha	C
64	M. Brown, Belfast	198 Yamaha	C
64	G. Murphy, Killyleagh	196 Bultaco	C
65	D. McClements, Belfast	125 Maico	C
66	V. Kelly, Richhill	196 Suzuki	C
67	E. McKinley, Lurgan	196 Suzuki	C
68	D. Hughes, Cookstown	200 Suzuki	C
69	N. Nixon, Lisnaskea	200 Suzuki	C
70	D. Wallace, Bangor	196 Suzuki	C
71	A. Gibson, Dundrum	196 Bultaco	C
72	J. McFarland, Carnmoney	195 Yamaha	C
73	G. Kelly, Dublin	196 Bultaco	C
74	B. McDowell, Dundrod	124 Yamaha	C
75	R. Simpson, Dungannon	124 Yamaha	C
		199 Triumph	C

18

Despite being axed from the UGP the 200cc class was still immensely popular as the entry list from the 77 Killinchy 150 testifies

exclude the class from their race this year, as it was an all-international meeting with sidecars replacing the 200cc race in operation since 1973.

Spokesperson Richard Nesbitt was quoted as saying, "This decision is scandalous and we aim to fight it all the way."

The Prix benefited from a £10,000 donation from the supporters club in a bid to improve the entry.

Tom Herron was the best British finisher in the 250cc race at Daytona working his way through from fortieth to finish seventh by the chequered flag in the two wave start.

The waves were separated by 10secs, but Herron on the front row of the second group forgot and when the flag dropped for the first group he started, then realised his error, pulling to the side of the track and waited for the second wave to go before he started towards the rear of the field.

Herron only lasted a couple of laps in the Daytona 200 race, reduced to a '100 miler' because of rain, when his new 750cc Yamaha went onto two-cylinders.

Ulster's first championship motocross of the season sank in a sea of mud when the Wills Trophy meeting at Dromore had to be abandoned before half the programme had been completed.

Before the abandonment young newcomer Dave Watson won the Grade 'A' race from another former schoolboy star Laurence Spence.

The first ever international sidecar motocross in Ireland was held at Whitehead in March.

Former British champion Nick Thompson and passenger Gary Withers (750cc Heanes Wasp) scored three of the easiest victories of his career racing through a quagmire due to heavy rain. Thompson was the only rider to get to grips with the diabolical conditions.

Experience defeated youth in a dramatic finish to the Ulster championship scramble in Newry when Irish

Dave Watson

champion Davy Crockard just got the better of exciting newcomer Dave Watson in the Tom Henning Scramble.

The 30-minute race saw Watson overtake Crockard, but Watson tired and Crockard, twice Watson's age closed the gap coming to the final bend side-by-side with Watson reported as sailing through an adjoining hedge recovering to finish second.

The tarmac season in Ulster looked like developing into a two-man show after Ray McCullough and Joey Dunlop dominated the Easter Monday meeting at Kirkistown, Dunlop taking a treble and McCullough the opening round of the Wills Embassy series.

Both ran out of fuel at vital stages of races when leading – McCullough the 350cc with a lap to go and Dunlop the feature race with two laps remaining.

Dunlop's Embassy jinx continued five-days later at St Angelo when he clipped a course marker while dicing with McCullough ending up in hospital with an arm injury, where he joined brother-in-law Mervyn Robinson, who had crashed earlier during practice.

Dunlop was back on form at Aghadowey a fortnight later scoring a four-timer during an action packed meeting with victories in the 250, 350, Ace of Aghadowey and Embassy races.

Tandragee Road Races were marred by the tragic death of Dubliner Michael Shanahan during the two lap sidecar practice with the race cancelled.

Prior to this incident Joey Dunlop (Rea Yamaha) scored a double in the 350 and 750cc races.

Ray McCullough, who won the 250cc event, made a poor start in the 350cc race made it through to second by lap three and was only ten seconds behind Dunlop at the start of the final lap, reduced to four half way around the five-mile circuit failing by two-seconds to reel in the winner.

Abe Alexander clinched the 500cc victory while Billy Redmond beat Richard Hewitt and Davy Lowry in the 200cc contest.

Dave Watson, Ulster's teenage sensation, taught local scramblers a lesson when he won the Brian Bell Memorial event at Saintfield winning by more than 40secs from Davy Crockard.

However having taken out an ACU licence Watson had effectively ruled himself out of the Irish title chase, as he did not have, as required, a MCUI licence.

Mick Grant winning Superbike race at NW200

The Morans Limited North West 200 saw an epic 60-mile 350cc dice with Ray McCullough and Tony Rutter crossing the finish line side-by-side a dead heat the verdict.

Rutter got his revenge by winning the 250cc race while John Williams riding Appleby Glade 500cc Suzuki and 750cc Yamaha machines produced a majestic double in the 500cc race and the feature North West 200 event pushing the outright lap record 124.06mph – the fastest in the British Isles on a day of intense heat.

Mick Grant (Kawasaki) won the 750cc race, the last time a Kawasaki won a superbike race around the Triangle.

Tom Herron reported in MCN as

"having a DIY splint done on his injured thumb after a prang at the Spanish Grand Prix – a piece of old plywood backed by two lollipop sticks, the whole lot held together by waterproof tape normally used for visors and machine parts.

Dr Costa from the travelling Clinic Mobile that attends each Grand Prix replaced the splint with a more professional job at Paul Ricard during the French Grand Prix."

Ulster's 'big two' Ray McCullough and Joey Dunlop brought the 100mph lap to the Cookstown 100, as they re-wrote the record books around the Sherrygroom Circuit.

McCullough was first to break the 'magic ton' barrier with a lap of 100.17mph on his way to a 350cc victory, but in the last race of the day Dunlop lapped at 101.05mph taking his 350cc Rea Yamaha to an easy 500cc race win.

Dunlop a week later gave his host of supporters a timely TT boost by scorching to five sensational victories at Kirkistown.

Just a few hours before heading across the Irish Sea Dunlop triumphed in the 250, 350, Unlimited, Embassy and King of Kirkistown races.

The Schweppes Jubilee race on the Friday of TT week was a historic day with Joey Dunlop, not all that well known outside Ireland at the time, in only his second visit to the 37¾ mile Mountain Circuit racing to the first of his eventual twenty-six victories by winning the 4-lap 1000cc race on his Rea Yamaha – taking time on the last lap to stop in Ramsey to check his rear tyre (which tended to wear out after two-laps) had enough tread for the fast sweeps on the final mountain climb.

In a Motor Cycle article Jimmy Walker, the doyen of Ulster sports writers claimed that:–

'the tiny Co. Antrim rider with the long-haired look of a wild Irish leprechaun had a wall of death style which would have made Evil Knievel turn white, yet rarely fell off. Tucked down behind the fairing he resembles a high-speed Pony Express rider escaping from redskins – and he rarely failed to finish the trip.'

Joey started with a lap of 110.80mph increasing that to 110.93mph on the second lap, the third fastest in TT history at the time, including slowing for his pit stop going on to win by 51.4secs from George Fogarty and Steve Tonkin.

This was the day that Joey announced himself to the world just how good he was – although of course here in Ireland everybody knew that anyway.

This was also the TT that 7-times world champion Phil Read, who had turned his back on the event five years previous, made a dramatic return and promptly won the first rain-lashed F1 TT and instantly became the first ever Formula One World Champion – the TT the only race to count towards the new championship.

Read made it a double by winning the Senior TT held in atrocious conditions in which Tom Herron was second, Dunlop fourth, Joe Lindsay sixth, Billy Guthrie ninth and Jim Scott tenth.

Herron described the conditions as, "The worst I've seen. The last lap was really bad and you could go no more than 20 or 30 mph in places, I could not even see the white line on the road on parts of the mountain."

Geoff Barry and Ron Haslam at Dundrod

The Killinchy 150 at Dundrod proved a dark day with the death in hospital of Geoff Barry, a favourite with fans in Ulster.

Barry died from serious head injuries following a crash at Tornagrough on lap six during an epic dice

with Ron Haslam having just set a new lap record of 111.68mph on the previous circuit.

Haslam making his Dundrod debut went on to win the race from Ray McCullough on only his second outing on an OW31 Yamaha with Joey Dunlop third.

McCullough scored a 250 / 350 winning double while Dunlop won the 500cc race and Ronnie McQuillan the 200cc on his Rotax.

The Co. Antrim Junk brothers wrapped up an Enniskillen treble with Courtney winning the fifth

Joe McArdle (with bandaged hands) watches the Yamaha which he had crashed in the Killinchy 150 being pushed from the field at wheelers by Frankie Corrigan.

round of the Embassy championship and a cracking 350cc race while Stanley clinched victory in the 500cc event.

Joey Dunlop took time out from his local appearances finishing eleventh in the first leg of the new Formula 750cc world championship at Brands Hatch.

After six-weeks on the sidelines Davy Crockard bounced back with a grand slam treble in the Campbell Donaghy Memorial motocross organised by the Foyle Club.

Meanwhile Blackburn rider Bob Wright returned for the fourth time to Ulster and so far has won every race he has contested, the latest a four-timer at the Ards Club Wednesday evening holiday festival event.

Joey Dunlop proved he was 'King of the Roads' walking away with three wins including retaining the Southern 100 Solo Championship title having already won the 250cc and unlimited events smashing records in every race on his Rea Racing motorcycles.

The Armoy man travelled back to his home track at Aghadowey to reel off another treble taking the sixth round of the Embassy, the 750 and 250cc races.

However biggest rival Ray McCullough won the richest race of the day – the first running of the Enkalon Trophy Race that had a £110 cheque for the winner, the Antrim based club providing the entire prize fund on the day.

Ray McCullough won the 1st Enkalon Trophy Race

Stanley Junk had led the 15-lap Enkalon race, but tired three laps from the end handing victory to McCullough from Dunlop, Steven Cull and Junk.

Dunlop blotted his copybook in the 350cc race when he clipped the back of race leader Courtney Junk and crashed out at the hairpin with Junk staying onboard and winning.

Ballymoney competitor George McQuitty was killed during practice for Fore Road Races in Co Westmeath.

Hi Fliers McCullough and Dunlop at the Temple

The high-speed – low-flying double act by Ulster's top two road racers McCullough and Dunlop had the Temple 100 crowd in frenzy with strong men reaching for their tranquilisers, as the pair diced around the narrow, twisty, bumpy 5½ mile road course – races that will be talked about for a long time.

Reported at the time by Motor Cycle, as *"short circuit racing over an open road race course only five yards wide in places"*, the pair raced side-by-side for most of the 350cc race well clear from the rest of the field.

McCullough equalled the course record but was 100 yards adrift as they approached Rectory Corner for the final time only to see Dunlop run wide handing victory to the Dromara man.

Drew Alexander

The 250cc race was an action replay with McCullough again breaking the class lap record holding off Dunlop after a thriller.

Surprise winner of the 500cc race was Drew Alexander, who took over injured brother Abe's machine in a race that saw Stanley Junk loop his Yamaha at the roller-coaster section escaping with hefty arm and leg injuries.

Final corner problems followed Dunlop to East Fortune in Scotland the next day when he slid off leading the invitation race on the last lap at the final bend having earlier won the 250cc race.

Dunlop was second in the 1000cc race and set a new absolute lap record for the Scottish venue in the invitation event. Travelling companion Ernie Coates was second in both the 250 and 350cc events.

Returning to Kirkistown Dunlop scored another treble in the 350, 750 and final qualifying round of the Embassy.

Tom Herron rode a magnificent race to finish second to Johnny Cecotto in the 350cc Czech Grand Prix to move into second place in the world championship. Herron also lies in fifth position in the 250cc series having finished fifth in the Czech race.

In the British Grand Prix a week later a battered and bruised Herron lay back in his caravan as he clinched the runner-up spot in the 350cc world championship. He had retired from the race at Silverstone with an ill-handling Yamaha that had threatened to throw him off, for what would have been the third time that weekend.

With closest rival Jon Ekerold also retiring Herron was assured of second place in the championship behind Japanese ace Takazumi Katayama.

Despite crashing out of the 250cc race when his front wheel hit oil, Herron maintained his fifth position in the final 250cc world championship standings in what had been a tremendous season for the Ulsterman.

250cc Podium UGP L-R Alan North, Tom Herron, Pekka Nurmi

Tom Herron had assisted the Ulster Grand Prix organisers by approaching a few of his world championship rivals to see if they would consider riding at Dundrod and thanks to a considerable cash injection from the UGP Supporters Club Finn Peka Nurmi, South Africans Jon Ekerold and Alan North plus Vic Soussan all took up the challenge of Dundrod – and boy did they do well.

An epic 250cc race went to the judges after Tom Herron, giving Terry Shepherd's new machine its debut and Alan North flashed across the finish line side-by-side both credited with the same race time and average speed.

The judge's verdict gave the win to Herron, who despite a misfire that dropped him to third at one stage before clearing, had set a new class lap record of 110.65mph in his charge back into contention, bettering the earlier record of North.

Herron, returning to the 'Prix' after a two year absence, completed a double with a more comfortable two second victory over Ray McCullough who had scythed his way through from a diabolical start, 14th at the end of the first lap.

McCullough set a new lap record of 113.86mph on his charge through to

second eclipsing the John Williams, Ekerold, and Nurmi battle that saw Ekerold snatch third spot.

Jon Ekerold at Leathamstown

John Williams was also a double winner taking the 500cc race win with ease from over a minute and a half clear of Bill Smith with New Zealander John Woodley third.

Fellow Kiwi Stuart Avant had the misfortune to 'step off' his 500cc Suzuki at Deers Leap luckily walking away unscathed from his 120mph crash.

Courtney Junk, UGP

Williams, who had set a new 500cc lap record of 115.04mph, upped the absolute lap record for Dundrod to 117.48mph on his way to victory in the 1000cc race to finish four seconds clear of Tony Rutter with Dave Potter in third after the late retirement of Roger Marshall.

Tragedy marred the sidecar race when Manx pair George Oates and John Molyneaux died after crashing at Tornagrough. John was the father of today's Isle of Man 16-time sidecar winner Dave Molyneaux.

The race continued and victory went to Mick Boddice and Chas Birks, who just edged out Swedish pairing of Gote Brodin and Bengt Forsberg by half a second while Scottish legend Jock Taylor with Lewis Ward in the chair set a new lap record of 105.06mph settling for fourth reportedly having been shown a red flag at the fatal incident, before being waved on!

In another tragic moment during the 350cc race Ivor Greenwood crashed at Dawson's Bend and his machine left the track, careering into a nearby garden where spectator Mary Jane 'Jean' Cardwell lost her life.

Jimmy Heath fell foul of pit lane marshals during the Manx Grand Prix on two occasions when quick fuel stops turned into lengthy delays by their insistence that he should re-tighten his chain.

Running second in the 350cc race a minute behind Kevin Reilly at the end of the fourth lap of six the resultant pit lane delay of 3m 28secs dropped him to fourth and 5m 25.2secs behind winner Riley.

An action replay came in the Senior Manx when Heath was leading at the end of the fourth lap this time costing him 2m 15secs, although he was forced to pull out of the race on the last lap, reported walking near Ballaugh Bridge!

Con Law a future Manx winner finished tenth in the 250cc race.

Broughshane rider Ivan Houston (27) died in Nobles Hospital from multiple injuries after crashing his 250cc Yamaha in practice on the approach to Cronk-ne-Voddey and being hit by a following competitor.

Out of the saddle for four months due to injury Mervyn Robinson made a welcome return to action over his home course where he finished seventh in the 350cc Mid Antrim 150 race.

Joey Dunlop's brother Jim fractured a leg after crashing in the same race and Conor McGinn also had a trip to hospital following a crash.

The injury list mounted, as Frank Kennedy was already sidelined with both wrists in plaster, Abe Alexander had an ankle injury, Stanley Junk was still in hospital with arm and leg injuries following his Temple spill and John Smyth also had a hand in plaster.

At the Mid Antrim there were five different winners of the five races – Billy Redmond (200), Ray McCullough (250), Courtney Junk (350), Noel Hudson (500) and Adrian Craig (750).

37 year old Mike Hailwood on his planned return to the TT in 1978 after

11-years away was quoted in August MCN as saying, *"Am I crazy? I think I am and a lot of other people will probably agree with me. However racing and especially the TT gets in your blood, remember it has been my life for the past twenty years and it's not easy to give up."*

Ray McCullough ruled the roost at Carrowdore 100 the final road race of the Ulster season collecting two memorable wins.

In the 350cc race McCullough and Courtney Junk were inseparable for the entire nine laps. Apart for two laps McCullough led the way in a thriller as Junk tried all he knew to oust the master, losing out by two seconds at the chequered flag.

The flying trio of Steven Cull, Graham Young and McCullough all took turns to head the 250cc race, but again McCullough with a new lap record of 100.21mph used all his experience to fend off his rivals in the end.

Punctures were numerous at a gruelling Tennents Lager John Donnelly motocross at Killinchy where after three stamina-sapping legs held in continuous rain it was Bob Wright who emerged successful for the second year in a row.

ACU stressed that while MCUI licence holders may ride in national motocross events they may not compete in the British Motocross Championship – the reason being that they had their own MCUI championship!

Joey Dunlop turned the Embassy Championship final into a one-man show taking his 750 Rea Yamaha to the prestigious title for the first time, pocketing his best ever short circuit cheque of £190 in front of an estimated 8,000 spectators and BBC Television cameras.

Alan Morrison in later years

He led the 15-lap final from start to finish easing to a seven second victory over Adrian Craig, who cracked the Kirkistown lap record with a speed of 89.40mph to pass third place finisher Courtney Junk, with Graham Young fourth, Joe Lindsay fifth and Mervyn Robinson sixth.

Ten year old Alan Morrison from Shrigley brought home the British Junior schoolboy motocross championship going on to become a motocross Grand Prix winner, a top short circuit competitor and a leading contender in the British Touring Car championship.

Sixteen-year old Belfast rider Laurence Spence became

the youngest ever Irish Scrambles champion in his first year among the seniors.

Spence took advantage of the mercurial Dave Watson's many English excursions to take a grip on the series from halfway through the season to clinch the championship with a double success in the final round near Dublin.

Ulster clubs showed a lack of interest running only two of the six counting rounds.

Joey Dunlop ended the season with a double at Aghadowey in the 250 and 750cc races emphasising that he was Ireland's leading short circuit rider according

Laurence Spence

to the report on the meeting in Motor Cycle. He also led the 350cc race before retiring and in a rare outing, if not his only outing, on a Sparton he led the 500cc before the chain broke.

In October the rumour mill was in overdrive with reports that the Ulster Grand Prix, without a world championship meeting since 1971, hoped to get back through the medium of the Formula TT races.

Glue-pot conditions following a mid-meeting thunderstorm did not deter Belfast teenager Stephen Russell from winning the Jimmy Geddis Trophy at the final high profile meeting of the season.

Joey Dunlop clinched three Ulster short circuit championships, but failed to win an Ulster Road race championship.

Stephen Russell

Noel and Geoffrey Ingram, leading contenders in sidecar-X

On the short circuit scene Dunlop won the 250, 350 and 750cc titles whole Stanley Junk won the 500, Richard Nesbitt the 200 and Norman Taylor the sidecars.

The Ulster road race champions for 1977 were 200cc Billy Redmond, 250 and 350cc Ray McCullough, 500cc Jim Scott and 750cc Adrian Craig.

The Ulster sidecar championship was not awarded owing to the cancellation of the race at Tandragee following a fatal accident.

An Ulster sidecar scrambles champion-ship, re-introduced af-ter a lapse of a number of years, was won by the sixth round by Wilson McKibbin and passen-ger Cyril Gardner.

As a row over track safety at Grand Prix level raged on Ulster ace Tom Herron waded in reportedly saying,

"If what Barry Sheene and his friends want from the FIM means the end of road racing then I'll not go along with

them. What is the dividing line between a safe circuit and a dangerous one and who actually draws that line? If riders don't want to be forced to ride at circuits that they do not feel comfortable with then make just nine from twelve rounds count for the series giving riders a choice to ride or not at some venues."

It was announced in Motor Cycle that Ireland's champion road racer Ray McCullough had stepped down as No.1 rider for Irish Racing Motorcycles to be replaced by 21-year old Graham Young, who is stating his fourth year of racing.

Meanwhile McCullough is to test a three-cylinder Yamaha and will have some outings on that plus the 750cc Yamaha he rode three times in 1977.

Best of three Irish riders who took part in arduous conditions of rain, sleet and hailstones during the British Experts Trial was Colin Bell, who proved the value of his move to Yorkshire by finishing a fighting sixth amongst the best trials exponents in the country. Davy McBride was 23rd and Norman Colin retired.

Bell maintained his good form across the water by recording seventh position in the Peak Trial.

A tight time schedule of three-hours for completing three-laps of an ice-bound 16-section course caused controversy at the Terry Hill Trial at Saintfield, the sixth round of the Irish championship.

Tom McBride lost 41 marks on observation and a further 17 on time to win by a solitary mark from 20-year old Ian Davidson who lost 59 in total 12 of those on time.

No rider escaped without a time penalty with competitors complaining that it was impossible to complete the trial inside the allotted time; in fact it took some over two-hours to finish their first lap.

After what was a record year for the UGP Supporters Club when they handed £10,000 to the organisers and 1977 membership standing at 4,300, Chairman for the past ten years Dan Jordan did not seek re-election at the recent AGM becoming a vice-president with Harry Ingram and Esdale Dowling.

The new Chairman elected was Randall Stewart while Des Jardin and Tommy Robb retained their posts as Secretary and President respectively.

Joey Dunlop at Kirkistown

Donny Robinson, Mondello

*Jackie Hughes
at Castle Corner,
Tandragee*

Jim Dunlop, Temple

Dave Potter

Neil Tuxworth

Tony Rutter

Charlie Williams

Roger Marshall

In a break between races stunt rider Dave Taylor rode an entire lap of the NW200 course on one wheel

Davy McBride and Jim McCrea, Sidecar Trials

Davy McBride, solo trials rider

Davy McBride, Classic road racer

Denis Quinn

remembers... The 200 Class

Introduced to the thrills and spectacle of motorcycle racing in the mid 70's by Shorts workmate Jim Esler, I was immediately hooked and spent the next couple of years following my leather clad heroes around the racetracks and road circuits of Ulster. However by 1977 I was itching for something more .... I wanted to be on the other side of the hedge!

But how to get there? A quick review of the options for a young aircraft fitter strapped for cash showed there was only one way to go and that was the entry class to racing in the seventies, the 200 class.

Starting out with a stock showroom bike, there were virtually no restrictions on how the engine could be modified provided it did not exceed the 201cc limitation. The frame and suspension set-up could be almost anything as long as it stayed together. Bits welded here and there, holes drilled everywhere to reduce weight (though weighing only around 9st at the time I had a natural advantage in that department!) and parts used from other machines to help turn an 80mph road-going bike into a 120mph racer. Everyone had their own thoughts on how to make a winner and, armed with a loan of £1000 from the bank, I was no different.

Abe Alexander's on the Castlereagh Road and Ernie Coates on Grand Parade were two of the main suppliers

Denis began racing in 1977 while working as an aircraft fitter in Short Brothers., building his own bike to race in the 200 class. He won the Irish championship in 1982 before moving up to the 250 class where he competed until a serious crash at the 1985 Killinchy 150 ended his career.

Married to Lynn in 1986, they settled outside Hillsborough with their daughters Alison and Sarah.

Now working for Jeppesen Uk as a Snr Aviation Emissions Consultant, Denis is still in aviation after 45 years, but now-a-days when he gets free time, rather than slaving over a stripped down bike in a cold garage, he indulges in his other hobbies of fly-fishing and golf.

to the racing fraternity and before long I was standing in Abe's workshop fleshing out a plan to buy a brand new 200 Yamaha and strip it down to race. The mechanic working there, Davy Lowry, was a racer himself and seemed to know just about everything there was to know about bikes in general and 200 racing in particular. Tuning, building wheels and cranks and fixing just about anything that broke – there would be lots of broken things to take to Davy over the coming years!

Though there was rivalry on the track, there was always great comradeship among the 200 class racers. The older hands were always willing to help out the newcomers with advice and tips and I'd regularly meet with other racers in sheds and garages around the city, all displaying a remarkable level of inventiveness and problem solving which would have made them stand out in any walk of life. Typical of the breed was John Menagh who raced a 200 and lived in a terrace house off the Woodstock road with no shed or garage. Undaunted by this lack of facilities he'd converted his downstairs front room into a neat and tidy workshop, complete with lathe and tool cabinet and work bench – bike in the middle of the room!

In today's parlance, Davy Lowry's shed was a centre of excellence for 200 racers from all arts'n parts. Just being there with a few guys needing something fixed or repaired and to watch the skills of a gifted motorcycle mechanic in action was a lesson in how-to-do. We got to know specialists in every area: welding, turning, spraying, tank repairing, fiberglass repairs etc… all were needed at some stage when something broke or needed repaired after a fall. Up and down the country there were garages being worked in until the wee hours to build unique versions of a 200 racing bike.

Of course while basic information was freely swapped, there were some detailed tuning tricks to extract the last few miles an hour from these highly strung machines which were closely guarded secrets. Through trial and error and just plain "chance", something would be found that made a difference and once found such hard won knowledge might be worth keeping quiet about for as long as possible. For example when silencers were introduced, the whole engine performance of 2 strokes was affected and I remember taking this problem to a guy who worked at Shorts and who was renowned for his calculating skills. Given the porting layout of my barrels, he was able to calculate the best possible size of expansion box with silencer to get the optimum performance from the engine. With his long-hand figures on a graph sheet I was then able to develop a set of templates that formed the components of the expansion box and have them cut, rolled and welded together. It worked!! That year both the speed and 'rideability' of my bike were transformed. This was valuable information shared exceedingly sparingly for a long time!

Other mods were less successful. At one time someone suggesting drilling a

No.8 bike pic - my 2nd year at Agahadowey

13mm hole in the back of pistons to allow a pre-induction before the piston reached its stroke limit. It appeared to improve performance but no matter how carefully the drilled hole was smoothed, cracks started and seizures were inevitable.

Of course sometimes the level of secrecy was taken to extremes such as when one particular rider made cardboard blanks to insert into the barrels to prevent a particular scrutineer from seeing the porting arrangement in his engine, should it be selected for a spot inspection to check its legality.

Winters were long and just the anticipation of the forthcoming season to 'unveil' the latest changes to 'the bike' was a great feeling. The engineering firms around the country that unwittingly contributed to the success of 200 racing were many. Frames sand blasted and stove enamelled, engines modified in machine shops, barrels re-bored on vertical mills and parts turned on lathes, all done as 'homers'. A small industry revolved around the 200 class, mostly unpaid!! Access to aircraft alloy and parts we could use on a racing bike gave an 'edge' to those of us who worked at Shorts and would be the envy of other riders when displayed at a race meeting. It was all a bit of one-upmanship at times to produce something nobody else had on their bike, especially if it looked good. At each race event it was normal to have a walk around the paddock and see what was new on various bikes. Occasionally someone would have a cover draped over a bike just for badness to make believe there was something secret to hide. It was always good for gossip even if there was nothing new.

The racing season took us all over the country and the craic was always mighty and the banter and "wind-ups" hilarious at times Starting with Aghadowey and Kirkistown to Mondello Park and back to St Angelo. Then the Cookstown100, Tandragee 100, Temple 100 (probably my favourite because of the high speed jumps), Killinchy 150, Mid Antrim 150, Carrowdore 100, interspersed with Carrik-on-Suir, Fore, Skerries, and Bandon.

Davey Ross and I shared a lot of the transport to the races. We'd progressed from a trailer hitched on to a Mini to a series of transit type vans and acquired a small caravan that was hand painted to match the race van. On one return journey from a Southern race we were passing a line of travellers on the road out of Dublin and got great waves from them as we passed. They must have thought we were fellow travellers which raised a lot of laughs with the boys.

Carrick-on-Suir was a really fun event. It normally fell during the 12th fortnight and attracted a big turn-out of us Northern racers during the holiday. Most made a small holiday out of it and pitched tents and caravans in the paddock. There was always a bit of craic going on somewhere and we'd move from camp to camp as the evenings went on. Guys slept in their vans, tents and awnings and were up at the crack-of-dawn with paraffin stoves making fried breakfasts, tinkering

Carrick-on-Suir RR with 200 riders L-R Grant Anderson, Davy Ross and myself sitting on the bikes and John Borne inspecting the front tyre

at bikes, mixing petroil for the 2 strokes and generally getting prepared for the race. I recall one year when John (Loopy) Lewis and his family were getting their tent set up and had a pile of burgers and meat set aside for a barbecue. Davey Lowry and his wife Sandra had brought along their Springer Spaniel and it bounded over and ate the lot. John berated everyone for hiding the meat and nobody could convince him the dog had eaten it.

Of course while everyone was willing to help each other out to go racing, once the flag dropped it was a different story as we fought the bit out for race honours, though even in the heat of action there was plenty of fun and humour.

On one particularly memorable occasion I was leading the 200 class at Mondello Park and another competitor kept coming up alongside me as we braked for the hairpin. After about the third time, instead of sitting up, I braked hard but stayed on the tank. Waiting for me to sit up before he braked, he totally missed his braking point and next thing, he came past sliding on his back but with the admirable presence of mind to look up at me and give me the two fingers!

From my earliest days in the sport there were highs and lows, machine failures where success was almost in sight, crashes that left me with wounds and broken bones to heal and the constant urge to be back out there on the track and road. Everything revolved around racing. 5 or 6 nights a week in the garage or someone else's garage making parts, modifying parts, fixing broken engines, watching and learning.

Small successes came slowly – actually, just finishing a race was success in itself in the early days as I learnt how to make the bike 'go' and keep it reliable. But there were finishes in the top ten and occasional better placings.

It wasn't until my 3rd season that things started to move forward. Road Racing was a great thrill! It wasn't like Short Circuit racing where there were a dozen lines into a corner, it was all about learning the road and knowing lines and braking points, bumps and jumps, cambers and surface changes. The great Ray McCullough and names of the seventies were experts on the roads and I wanted a bit of that.

By the late seventies/early eighties the 200 class probably was at its peak. A Kirkistown or Aghadowey race may have

First Road race win at he Mid Antrim 150.

RACE 1	200cc CLASS HEAT 1	6 LAPS	
No.	Name	Machine	Place Finished
1	Fred Boyd	124 Honda	- - - -
2	Sam Stewart	195 Yamaha	- - - -
3	Robt. Hanna	196 Purvis	- - - -
4	Norvel Gregory	196 Yamaha	- - - -
5	G. Anderson	198 Yamaha	- - - -
6	Terence Smyth	195 Yamaha	- - - -
7	David Wood	124 Honda	- - - -
8	David A. Lynn	196 Suzuki	- - - -
9	Steven Martin	195 Yamaha	- - - -
10	Noel Dorman	196 Yamaha	- - - -
11	Gary Johnston	196 Suzuki	- - - -
12	Richard Piele	196 Yamaha	- - - -
14	Desmond Lynas	196 Yamaha	- - - -
15	Steve Murphy	124 Honda	- - - -
16	Frank McConnell	196 Suzuki	- - - -
17	Ciaran Collins	195 Yamaha	- - - -
18	Robert Scott	196 Yamaha	- - - -
19	James Knox	196 Yamaha	- - - -
20	Alan Crozier	196 Yamaha	- - - -
21	David Ross	196 Yamaha	- - - -
22	Dennis Quinn	196 Yamaha	- - - -
23	Richard Bingham	195 Fahron Yam.	- - - -
24	Stephen McClements	196 Suzuki	- - - -
25	Gary Ferguson	195 Yamaha	- - - -
26	R. Walkingshaw	195 Yamaha	- - - -
27	Mervyn Salmon	195 Yamaha	- - - -
28	Maurice Laverty	195 Yamaha	- - - -
29	Bertie McDowell	125 Yamaha	- - - -
30	Mark Carter	192 Yamaha	- - - -
31	Gerry Mullen	156 Bultaco	- - - -
87	Michael Robinson	196 Yamaha	- - - -

First 10 qualify for final

Winner's Time   Speed   m.p.h.

Fastest Lap No.   Time   Speed   m.p.h.

RACE 2	200cc CLASS HEAT 2	6 LAPS	
2nd Round George Purvis Prize			
No.	Name	Machine	Place Finished
32	Michael Moore	196 Suzuki	- - - -
33	Leslie Junk	195 Yamaha	- - - -
34	John Borne	"	- - - -
35	Ronnie Anderton	"	- - - -
36	Willie Kennedy	"	- - - -
37	Mark Russell	125 Suzuki	- - - -
38	Stanley Rea	200 "	- - - -
39	Paul Allen	195 Yamaha	- - - -
40	Joe O'Kane	196 Suzuki	- - - -
41	Ken Ferguson	195 Yamaha	- - - -
42	Brian Turkington	198 Yamaha	- - - -
43	Ronnie Nicholl	"	- - - -
44	Stan Arbuthnot	196 Suzuki	- - - -
45	R. Patton	195 Yamaha	- - - -
46	Steven Smyth	200 Suzuki	- - - -
47	Wm. Smyth	175 Yamaha	- - - -
48	Kenny Craig	196 Suzuki	- - - -
49	Sam Stewart	196 "	- - - -
50	Robert Howell	196 Yamaha	- - - -
51	Carl Wilson	"	- - - -
52	Chris Wheeler	"	- - - -
53	Raymond Hanna	"	- - - -
54	John McFarland	"	- - - -
55	Marcus Brown	175 Rotax	- - - -
56	Robert Niblock	"	- - - -
57	John Menagh	196 Yamaha	- - - -
58	D. Morrison	"	- - - -
59	William McMinn	"	- - - -
60	Noel Lindsay	"	- - - -
61	David Hallowell	195 Yamaha	- - - -
95	Gerry Hyland	200 Yamaha	- - - -

1st £5   2nd £3   3rd £2

200cc & 250cc heats start 11 a.m.

First 10 qualify for final

Winner's Time   Speed   m.p.h.

RACE 3	200cc CLASS HEAT 3	6 LAPS	
No.	Name	Machine	Place Finished
62	Alan Gibson	196 Yamaha	- - - -
63	Jim McCullagh	196 Suzuki	- - - 2
64	Richard Nesbitt	196 Yamaha	- - - -
65	John Ogle	196 Yamaha	- - - -
66	Martin Elliott	"	- - - -
67	Dennis Todd	124 Honda	- - - -
68	Norman Boyd	196 Yamaha	- - - -
69	Jim Patterson	196 Bultaco	- - - -
70	Martin Storey	125 Yamaha	- - - -
71	Richard Hewitt	196 Suzuki	- - - 1
72	Sammy Bentley	125 Maico	- - - -
73	Jimmy Rogers	"	- - - -
74	Ivor Holland	196 Bultaco	- - - -
75	John Donnan	196 Yamaha	- - - -
76	Sam Dempster	200 Fahron	- - - -
77	Michael McGarrity	124 Honda	- - - -
78	Jackie Patterson	200 Suzuki	- - - -
79	Ken Crossett	125 Morbidelli	- - - -
80	Victor Kelly	196 Yamaha	- - - -
81	D. Donnelly	196 Suzuki	- - - -
82	Norman Nixon	196 Suzuki	- - - -
83	A. Nettleship	"	- - - -
89	Jerry Webb	195 Yamaha	- - - -
101	Joe Seeley	200 Yamaha	- - - -
86	Alan Irwin	198 Yamaha	- - - -
100	Brian Thompson	200 Suzuki	- - - -
99	Gordon Murphy	198 Yamaha	- - - -
96	Ron Shaw	198 Suzuki	- - - -
90	Jack Patterson	196 Suzuki	- - - -
91	Cyril Simpson	195 Yamaha	- - - -
92	Gerry Bradley	196 Suzuki	- - - -
93	T. C'Neill	124 Yamaha	- - - -
94	Pat Robinson	196 Yamaha	- - - -

1st £5   2nd £3   3rd £2

Winner's Time   Speed   m.p.h.

Fastest Lap No.   Time   Speed   m.p.h.

200cc and 250cc heats start 11 a.m.

Typical packed 200 class at 1979 Ace of Aghadowey meeting

had 3 heats of 30 bikes and racers all vying for a top ten placing to reach the 200 Final. It was tough going just to get there, no matter get a placing in the final.

By '79/80 I'd built up a stock of engines and parts that were constantly being dismantled and modified for the race bike and parts sought by lots of the 200 racers. Cranks, clutches, gearboxes, barrels and crank cases. I'd acquired a Spondon frame with Campag wheels and twin discs, and now had a Barton water cooled engine complete with race gearbox. There were only 4 of these frames in the country and I recall when it arrived, much to my Mother's disdain, I gave it pride of place in our 'front room' such was its beauty! The word got around quickly and there were lots of callers to see the rolling chassis – in my eyes

Lining up at Aghadowey 1981

then the best that money could buy.

In '82 and with a lot of new modifications to the bike I managed to finish in the top 3 at several events with wins at the Mid Antrim and Fore. At the Mid Antrim Ken Ferguson was leading when his bike expired leaving me with my first road race win.

At Fore, Dickie and I shared the lead for 4 or 5 laps and he left me with a comfortable lead when his bike expired crossing the start/finish line with a carb drain nut loose and fuel spilling out. The win in front of a crowded road circuit was memorable.

The season was hotly contested with Gerry Brennan, Ken Ferguson, Alan Crozier and myself all chasing points in the Irish Road Racing Championship and it all came down to the last road race of the season at Carrowdore with only a couple of points separating Gerry, Alan and myself. Gerry had gone to the IOM for the Manx GP with his 350 but flew home after the practice week to contest the Carrowdore. The three of us shared the lead for several laps until Gerry's Yamaha expired leaving Alan and I to sort it out. On the last lap and approaching the finish line almost side by side, Alan's gear lever broke off leaving me with the win and the Championship. This was just another of those things that happened with home made parts and confirmed the fickle reliability of 200's which we were all hostages to – I found out afterwards that I'd had an oil leak from the clutch most of the race and how my bike managed to stay the distance was a mystery. All in all it was the end of a great season for me and the perfect way to finish

Spondon Bike 200cc at Killinchy 150 - Leathemstown corner at Dundrod

my time in the 200 class.

I moved to 250 and 350's for a couple of years before lady luck deserted me and I suffered a crash that ended my racing career. I was leading the B group in the 250 class in the 1985 Killinchy 150 at Dundrod when I came off at the Flow Bog crossroads and was flung through the air, ending up in a Blackthorn tree. Unconscious for seven hours, I broke my right arm badly, damaged the nerves and couldn't use it for about a year. Despite 12 months of rehabilitation, I have never got full extension back in my hand.

That put an end to my racing. I didn't go back for a long time and when I did, it was very difficult to go and just watch. Life gradually changed. I got married in 1986 and a few years later I remember taking my four-year-old daughter Alison to the Carrowdore 100. As we walked through the paddock, I was greeted by so many old friends that she asked in amazement: 'Do you know everybody?' It was still like one big family. They were great times.

1978

The world's first IVF baby born – Summer Nights by John Travolta and Olivia Newton-John made No 1– a gallon of petrol was 76.5p, pint of milk 25p, loaf of bread 31p, pint of beer 96p, packet of ten cigarettes 66p and Kenny Roberts became the first American to win 500cc world championship.

Belfast Shipyard builders Harland and Wolff launched themselves into the manufacture of high-class motorcycle accessories after receiving an order from Heron Suzuki GB.

Colin Bell

Irish Trials champion Colin Bell (Bultaco) scored his best result in a British Championship Trials round finishing fourth in the Vic Brittan event in fourth position just 10 marks behind winner Martin Lampkin.

The Lakes Two-Day trial in Cumbria saw snow and gales on Saturday followed by torrential rain, sleet and bitter cold wind on Sunday where Bell finished in seventh position losing 17marks on Saturday and 63 on the more difficult Sunday.

Shortly afterwards Bell finished eighth in the Colmore Cup having switched to an Italian SWM machine. 11-times British champion Sammy Miller had just joined the Italian manufacturer as British team manager and development rider.

92 starters tackled the Ulster Championship trial at Ballycarry with Benny Crawford coming out on top losing 24 penalties seven better than runner-up Davy McBride with Robbie Jennings third.

Benny Crawford

Dubliner Trevor Callaghan (Montesa) chopped half a point off Benny Crawford's lead in the 1977-78 Irish Trials championship when he won the Larkin Cup in sub-zero temperatures at Drumkeeragh Forest and Dunmore Mountain, Co. Down.

Despite a last lap panic when he stopped with a broken chain Callaghan reduced the deficit by a further two points by repairing the chain and still winning the Presidents Cup organised by the Killinchy Club four weeks later.

Another week and the deficit was down to half a point and the championship in the melting pot as Callaghan finished second in the Knock Club McMaster Cup at Crossgar just two marks behind fellow Dubliner Derek Burton. Championship leader Benny Crawford had a shocker of a day eventually finishing in eleventh position.

Meanwhile Belfast painter Billy Rodgers was splashing out after winning the MCRRCI trial at the Lead Mines – the reason to celebrate, this was Billy's first win in 20-years competing in trials. Riding a Montesa Billy lost 29marks to win by six from Harry Dunwoody.

Billy went on to become a trial aficionado, respected around Europe, Clerk of the Course at local world rounds, Chairman of the Ulster Centre, President of both the Ulster Centre and Motorcycle Union of Ireland.

Finnish rider and world champion Yrjo Vesterinen (Bultaco), with a performance of pure magic on his third and final lap, came from behind to beat Martin Lampkin during a frozen Hurst Cup. Lampkin rode the last four sections with a flat front tyre rather than go back to the paddock to change the tube, Vesterinen winning by 101 penalties to Lampkin's 112.

Best local competitor was Colin Bell (SWM) in twentieth position having accumulated 223.7 penalties!

On his Daytona debut Joey Dunlop finished a creditable eighth in the 250cc race, but his luck was out in the main 200-miler when his new 750cc Rea Racing Yamaha sheared a cylinder head bolt after thirty laps, just over half race distance.

Benny Crawford put a string of mediocre performances behind him to win the Slemish Cup Irish championship trial and extend his lead of the series to 3½ points.

Held in continuous rain Crawford lost 132 penalties to come home six less than schoolteacher Davy McBride.

It was announced through the media that Ulster Grand Prix Supporters Club was to donate £15,000 towards the running of this year's race, an increase of 50% on last year, in a bid to attract an even higher standard of competitor. Membership of the club at the time was 50p minimum.

Mondello Park Co. Kildare was the usual St. Patrick's weekend opener for the Irish short circuit season and Ulster riders dominated with Mervyn Robinson taking three wins, Graham Young two including the Radio Dublin St Patrick invitation feature race, Donny Robinson won the 250cc race and Con Law the unlimited.

At this meeting when asked if an arrow pointing in the wrong direction was supposed to be a guide to fitting a tyre Joey Dunlop in his Armoy brogue said, *"The front tyre's a rear tyre fitted the wrong way round, that why the arrow's pointing the wrong way!"*

Rob Wilkinson and David Watson, both now resident in England and holders of Auto Cycle Union (ACU) licences were among the 35 riders entered for the opening British Motocross Championship round at Tenby in Wales.

Wilkinson (Maico), who had finished second and third before crashing out of the third leg on lap one of the Mendip Club event a week earlier, finished eleventh overall and Watson 16th in the championship opener.

Davy Crockard the 1976 Irish scrambles champion and Laurence Spence the defending champion could not be separated after the first two championship races of 1978 each scoring a win and a second in the two legs over a new course at Strangford, However when it came to the feature Ayton Trophy race Crockard, riding a Maico borrowed from rival Winston Norwood, won with ease while Spence having carved his way through from seventeenth to third by half distance was forced out with a flat rear tyre.

Joey Dunlop travelled to the South of France for the second round of the Formula 750 world championship and finished fifteenth in the 54-lap race, two laps down on winner Johnny Cecotto.

During an FIM meeting in Geneva it was announced that the MCUI had been awarded its first world championship motocross Grand Prix for 125cc machines while a European sidecar cross championship round was also awarded, both events to be held in 1979.

Robert Wilkinson, now based in Bristol, returned to one of his favourite courses to win the Tom Henning Trophy and Grade 'A' race at Tinker Hill, Newry while Laurence Spence beat Stephen Russell in the first round of the Northern Ireland U-21 championship.

It was reported in Motor Cycle that Joey Dunlop won his first race on the mainland when he was victorious in the 15-lap 250cc race supporting the world 750 championship meeting at Brands Hatch. Dunlop took over the lead of the race after Australian Greg Hansford crashed his Kawasaki, the result then never in doubt with the Ballymoney man winning from Clive Padgett, Derek Huxley, Ian Richards, Derek Chatterton and Tony Rutter – all top class short circuit competitors and well known to Ulster fans.

Fellow Ulster riders Graham Young and Steven Cull had a coming together on the first lap with Young brought down, remounting to storm through the field to finish seventh.

Ray McCullough gave the new QUB 3-cylinder Yamaha its first victory, by the width of a wheel from Noel Hudson, in the 350cc race at St Angelo in April, but when it came to the second round of the Embassy championship Noel Hudson riding a 750cc Yamaha out gunned McCullough's 350cc machine.

A race long three-man 250cc dice saw victory going to Jackie Hughes from Hudson with Donny Robinson crashing out in the closing stages.

Jim Dunlop, brother of Joey, won the 500cc race while McCullough won the

Ray McCullough gives the 3 cylinder 350cc QUB Yamaha its debut win at St. Angelo

750cc race on a rare outing on his 750cc Yamaha; Richard Nesbitt took the 200cc win while Ronnie Perry and passenger Fergus Bevan were the sidecar victors.

A week after his Brands Hatch win Joey Dunlop had an up and down day at his home track, Aghadowey,

Richard Nesbitt on 200cc winner at St. Angelo

winning the Ace of Aghadowey the richest race of the day before easing off too soon allowing Noel Hudson through to clinch the 750cc event and then crashing out of third position in the 250cc race suffering a shoulder injury.

Despite being bruised and bandaged, Dunlop turned up at Kirkistown on May Bank Holiday Monday and chalked up four wins in the 250, 350, 750 and the fourth round of the Embassy championship.

Tandragee 100 was the first road race of 1978 and Ray McCullough won the 350cc race at a canter with Joey Dunlop, still stiff and sore from his Aghadowey spill, holding off Graham Young for second.

Con Law at Tandragee

Young recorded his first ever road race win beating Noel Hudson, Jackie Hughes and Dunlop into second, third and fourth in the 250cc race.

Another first time winner on the roads was 24-year old Michelin engineer Con Law who won a thrilling 500cc race that involved Jack Wilkin and Ivor Greenwood before Law gunned his Glen Cowell Yamaha into the lead at half distance going on to win by ten seconds from Wilkin and Greenwood while in the concurrently run 750cc event Dunlop was the winner having started from the back of the grid with a 'pusher' to earn the Man of the Meeting award for the second year running.

Teenager Laurence Spence (Suzuki) continued his fine form by winning the Brian Bell Memorial Trophy at Saintfield, also winning the third round of the U-21 Dealers championship, however his chance of a hat trick disappeared when he fell while challenging for the Grade 'A' lead with victory going to Davy Crockard (Maico).

Ulster's Grand Prix contender Herron returned to the Morans North West 200 for the first time in four years and re-wrote the record book.

Riding his new Finlay – Kangol TZ 750E Yamaha Herron smashed John Williams's absolute lap record around the 10.1mile circuit scorching to a lap speed of 127.63mph in the 5-lap feature NW 200 race, a record for a British circuit – but he did not win the race, as his rear tyre shredded with the sizzling pace and he dropped to sixth despite the race distance being reduced to suit the Dunlop slick tyres.

Tony Rutter capitalised on Herron's woes collecting the £750 cheque for winning the race from young debutant Kevin Stowe while Ray McCullough had a lucky escape when he crashed his 750cc Irish Racing Motorcycles Yamaha at

Tom Herron sets lap record at NW200

high speed on the fast run from York hairpin towards Station Corner suffering two broken bones in a foot and losing a considerable amount of skin.

Herron did manage a double by showing a clean pair of heels to the opposition with a lap record in the 250cc race heading home Ray McCullough in an Ulster 1-2, Herron also winning the opening superbike race.

Rutter also completed a double after a superb 350cc battle with Graham Waring and Steve Tonkin while John Newbold edged home ahead of George Fogarty and John Williams in the 500cc race.

It had been a record breaking meeting in which every lap and race record fell with the top 750cc machines clocking in excess of 175mph on the plunge towards Metropole, remember no chicane at Magherabuoy then.

Three riders were awarded long service awards by the Coleraine Club – Wilfie Herron received a plaque to commemorate the 26-years since his North West debut when he rode a 350cc BSA Gold Star, Steve Murray first rode at the North West in 1953 riding an Excelsior Manxman when he fell at Black Hill and Bill Smith's 21 North West years were highlighted by his 1968 350cc win.

Turned down for the TT because he was considered not good enough Graham Young had a ding-dong battle with third fastest Mountain Circuit rider Joey Dunlop during the 500cc Cookstown 100 race, Young squeezing past the Rea Yamaha in the final run to the chequered flag , both judged to have set a new lap record of 101.42mph.

Young was declared the man of the Meeting after finishing second to Courtney Junk in the 250cc race and third behind Dunlop and Steven Cull in the 350cc event.

TT Special headline June 5th

Storybook TT win for Mike Hailwood

Fans flocked in record numbers to the Isle of Man to witness the return of Mike 'The Bike' Hailwood to race around the 37¾ mile Mountain Circuit after an eleven year absence.

Riding a Ducati in the Formula 1 race Hailwood led our own Tom Herron by nine seconds at the end of lap one with arch rival Phil Read third.

By lap three Herron had retired with a broken frame on his Mocheck Honda and Hailwood had caught Read on the road to lead by over fifty seconds and then on the penultimate lap Read was forced to retire and the fairy tale was complete with Hailwood taking the chequered flag for his 13th TT success and recording his tenth world championship.

Herron made up for his F1 disappointment by winning the 500cc Senior TT at record speed to beat fellow Ulsterman Billy Guthrie into second position.

Mike Hailwood Ducati

Herron was reportedly fined £17 for speeding when caught doing 47mph on Lezayre Road Ramsey where the speed limit was 30mph. Herron joked afterwards, *"Pity they didn't get me on race day. I was doing 167mph then."*

In the Schweppes

Classic won by Mick Grant, who set an absolute lap record of 114.33mph, the three main Ulster hopes all retired – Herron on lap one with a leaking gearbox, Guthrie at the Verandah with gearbox problems and Joey Dunlop out at Greeba Castle on lap two with a broken exhaust when fifth.

Joe Lindsay

Better luck for the locals in the 250cc TT with Herron third, Joe Lindsay fifth, Dunlop eleventh, Ernie Coates fifteenth, Steven Cull twenty-first, Jim Scott twenty-fifth and Courtney Junk twenty seventh and last silver replica finisher.

North West 200 winner Tony Rutter had the misfortune to tumble during practice at the TT suffering a broken right leg.

Tragedy struck the first sidecar TT race when seconds after the start Mac Hobson and passenger Kenny Birch were killed instantly in an accident at

Joey Dunlop on Devimead Honda in F1 TT

the top of Bray Hill and only 300 yards further on Swiss driver Ernst Trachsel was also killed in a separate incident with his passenger taken to hospital with a broken leg.

American Pat Hennen, factory Suzuki rider, was seriously injured on the final lap of the Senior TT after crashing at Bishopscourt near Ballaugh Bridge.

Less than a fortnight after his Senior TT victory Tom Herron came to the Killinchy 150 and was humbled by a stock car champion, Ivor Greenwood riding Hector Neill's RG 500 Suzuki, over eight laps of the Dundrod Circuit.

Greenwood led for five laps before Herron steamed past to take the lead, despite a bent gear lever. Greenwood, the underdog didn't lie down and gave chase the pair passing and re-passing thrilling the crowds lining the world famous circuit.

Ivor Greenwood at the top of the Deer's Leap in 1976 on Hector Neil's 250 Yamaha

Coming around the final bend Greenwood was in front and despite Herron trying all he knew, the stock car driver hung on to win by a hair's breadth, a memorable result for the Greenwood / Neill combination over the TT winning combination of Herron and sponsor Jim Finlay.

South African Dudley Crammond scored a 'lucky' victory in the 1000cc race on his Dundrod debut following the retirement of Joey Dunlop whose Rea Yamaha packed up with oil filter problems having set a new Killinchy lap record of 114.73mph.

20,000 had turned out to see Herron, but he was a non-starter in the 250 and 350cc races with his machines being prepped for the Dutch Grand Prix a week later with these two races dominated by Dunlop and Courtney Junk.

Richard Nesbitt scored his first ever road race win in the 200cc class while English visitor Dave Hallam beat Lowry Burton by a whisker in the side car race while it was noted that a young Brian Reid scored a best road race finish to date with fifth in the 250cc race

Rapidly rising star Graham Young was right out of luck at the Killinchy where he crashed out of the 350cc race at Leathemstown trying to make up for a poor start reported as having, 'landed at his mother's feet,' then his 250cc Yamaha that had seized in practice the

Graham Young, turned down for the TT in a questionable decision by the organisers

previous evening suffered the same problem in the race.

Gamble on tyre choice for the 350cc Dutch Grand Prix cost Tom Herron when he could only finish in sixth position on slicks after dicing for the lead before the rain came down and he was forced to ease his pace on the dampening track.

Herron followed this result with two fifth places in the 250/350cc Swedish Grand Prix.

Noel Hudson was a treble winner at Aghadowey winning the second running of the Enkalon Trophy, the 750 and Embassy Championship races picking up a best ever £200 cheque..

Graham Young was a double winner at the MCRRCI meeting of the 250 and 350cc races where a dead heat was declared for the 350cc runner-up spot between Courtney Junk and Conor McGinn. Jack Wilkin edged Joey Dunlop for the 500cc win in which Joey's brother Jim was third with the unlucky William Johnston robbed of a first time success in this race when his chain snapped at the final bend when leading.

Joey Dunlop and Jack Wilkin

A treble during the McClay scramble left Laurence Spence clear favourite to retain the Ulster scramble championship.

Storming through clouds of dust at Craigantlet Suzuki mounted Spence won the feature race from Davy Crockard and Stephen Russell the same result as the Grade 'A' race while in the U-21 championship race Russell followed Spence home.

There was a tragedy at Skerries road races during practice when one of Ulster's best known and popular competitors Joe Lindsay, the 1975 Manx Grand Prix winner, lost his life in an accident.

Robert Wilkinson finished 10th equal in the overall standings at the 500cc British MX Grand Prix at Farleigh Castle.

Wilkinson then returned to Ulster but failed by a point to win the Tuca Tile International motocross at Whitehead; victory going to Midlander Vaughn Semmens, who had a first and two seconds compared to Wilkinson's first, second and third.

Tom Herron was bang on form at the 14-mile Nurburgring Circuit scene of the West German Grand Prix finishing third behind the Kawasaki's of South African Kork Ballington and Australian Greg Hansford and taking fifth in the 350cc event.

Joey Dunlop sailed the Armoy Armada into battle at the Southern 100 and left his Dromara Destroyer rivals licking their wounds as the 'wee man' from Armoy raced to a hat trick in the Solo Championship and unlimited solo races before switching from his Rea Yamahas to Hector Neill's Suzuki that Ivor Greenwood won on at the Killinchy to win the solo consolation race.

The Dromara men did not leave empty handed, as their lead rider Ray McCullough completed a 250/350cc double ably backed up by near neighbour Trevor Steele.

McCullough won the 250cc race, but only after breaking the lap record by a second and a half to shake off the persistent Bob Jackson with Steele third then in the 350cc race Steele hounded McCullough throughout, so much so that the lap record went by the board seven times finally going to McCullough 5.6secs under the old mark, the speed upped to 95.14mph.

Fresh from his Southern 100 success Dunlop ran into bitter disappointment at Kirkistown when he was sensationally waved off the grid prior to the start of the feature race.

The reason – Belfast and District officials said the race was by invitation only and that Dunlop had turned the promoting club down some weeks previous.

Dunlop, however, had then had a change of heart and left his machines in England before flying back to Ulster especially for the Kirkistown meeting where he was to ride borrowed machines.

Booing could be heard from the Dunlop supporters, as the B&D officials met twice and stuck by their guns, the race going ahead without him.

Dunlop was given the all-clear to ride in the other events and compensated with a fine 500cc victory on board the Neill Suzuki.

Noel Hudson took his OW31 Yamaha to an unchallenged 'King of Kirkistown' victory during the Munster Simms sponsored meeting also winning the 750cc race with ease before crashing out of the 250cc race at the hairpin suffering ankle and elbow injuries.

Courtney Junk did the 250/350 double while Graham Young won the Embassy race sweeping to a six second victory over Dunlop.

A Crown Prince race was won by John Johnston from Dundrod, who had to work hard to stay ahead of Richard Hewitt, with Davy Wood third and Peter

Herron, Tom's brother, fourth.

Graham Young at Kirkistown

Three major motocross events held over a sun-kissed July Holiday weekend and with tremendous crowds attending saw Robert Wilkinson (Maico) win three races at the Ards Club Terence McKeag meeting at Clandyboye on Thursday, miss the Friday meeting at Donard Park, then return to action on Saturday over a new course at Ballynahinch to score another treble.

At Donard Park Pete Mathia, Stephen Russell and Jimmy Aird took a leg each in the Class 1 races with Russell also winning the U-21 championship race from Kirk Robinson, Laurence Spence and John Lewis.

Tom Herron stood on the rostrum at Imatra having finished third in the Finnish 350cc Grand Prix, but eighth was the best he could manage in the 250cc battle. The best British privateer of 1977 now looked forward to his home Grand Prix at Silverstone.

Courtney Junk set a new absolute record of 97.63mph for the Temple 100 circuit on his way to victory in the 350cc race in which Joey Dunlop was relegated to second with Steven Cull third.

Courtney Junk at Temple

Cull won the 500cc race on the much sought after Hector Neill owned 500cc Suzuki that Dunlop had ridden at the TT and on which Ivor Greenwood beat Tom Herron at the Killinchy150.

Dunlop rode to a 250cc / 750cc double,

while Ray McCullough, making his first Ulster appearance since his North West 200 crash, had a disastrous day around the course where he failed to register a win for the first time in fifteen years, retiring from both the 250 and 350cc races with broken crankshafts.

The British Grand Prix was a frustrating day for Tom Herron despite being named John Player Man of the Meeting for three second places in the TT F1, 250 and 350cc Grand Prix races.

In the TT F1 race John Cowie dived under the Mocheck Honda of Herron on the last corner to win by two hundredths of a second with Mike Hailwood only a few yards behind them and then in the Grand Prix races Kawasaki power ended his dreams of that elusive GP victory.

Mervyn Robinson at Mid Antrim

Man on form Courtney Junk smashed the Mid Antrim 150 lap record with a speed of 91.52mph on his way to a 34sec victory over Trevor Steele in the 350cc race in which Conor McGinn was third.

A thunderstorm prior to the 250cc race saw a course inspection by Clerk of the Course Tom Steele, Junk and Ray McCullough, who gave the race the go ahead albeit shortened by two laps.

McCullough mastered the difficult conditions best winning from Trevor Steele after Junk fell uninjured while challenging for the lead.

John Williams at the Hairpin during UGP

The Ulster Grand Prix was a black day for racing following the death of John Williams in the Royal Victoria Hospital hours after crashing at Wheelers Corner on the sixth lap of the 1000cc race while chasing Tom Herron, having earlier in the day won the 500cc race. Williams was transferred to hospital with a suspected broken shoulder and not thought to be in any danger, however later that evening he passed away with what a Belfast pathologist described at

Tom Herron winning 250 UGP 1978

the post mortem as, 'acute heart failure, the result of extensive internal bleeding combined with existing disease in one blood vessel supplying the heart.'

It was a bad weekend for the UGP as Jeremy Montgomery Swann was killed when he crashed from his 500cc Suzuki approaching Budore during Thursday afternoon practice.

Triumph and tragedy walk hand in hand in motorcycle racing and Herron, a great friend of Williams, had scored a brilliant treble at the same meeting.

Herron won the 250cc race where he beat South African Jon Ekerold into second, the F1 race where he the lead from Mocheck Honda team mate Tony Rutter on the fifth lap going further and further ahead as the race progressed and that ill-fated 1000cc race where he overhauled leader Williams with a record lap of 118.84mph to win from Rutter.

Ekerold rode to a magnificent 350cc win heading home Graham Waring and Steve Tonkin, with Herron, saving his Yamaha for the following week's West German Grand Prix, a non-starter.

In front of a reported 30,000 spectators Mick Boddice and Charlie Birks won the sidecar race having been under early pressure from Jock Taylor and Jamie Neil, who dropped out with gearbox problems.

Diesel, oil, nails and broken glass strewn on the course forced officials to abandon Fore Road Races in Co Westmeath following earlier objections from residents to the meeting taking place. The vandalism came overnight following the completion of practice the previous evening.

Tom Herron followed up his UGP hat trick with a rostrum for third position in the 250cc West German Grand Prix around the 14.2 mile Nurburgring Circuit then taking fifth in the 350cc race.

Herron was in fourth and fifth places in the 250 and 350cc championship tables following these results.

There was no stopping Bob Wright (CCM) in Ulster scrambles registering his sixth win from six starts in the province to win the Tommy Stewart Memorial Trophy at Downpatrick in appalling conditions.

In the mud bath Wright finished first, second and third to take the overall victory ahead of Jimmy Aird and Robert Wilkinson.

A week later Laurence Spence arrived late and then in the first race was involved in a huge first lap pile up, but it did not stop him winning the Bobby Whyte Memorial Trophy scramble near Londonderry.

He only just made it to the line for the NI Dealers U-21 race, but after taking four laps to familiarise himself with the course he stormed past leader Kirk Robinson to win by half a minute.

In the main race most of the field went sprawling as they all tried to get through a small gap in the hedge and Spence was down in twelfth position at the end of lap one.

He quickly made up ground and when leader David Johnston went out at half distance Spence was the easy winner from Robinson.

Tom Herron's final Grand Prix races of 1978 were a disappointment retiring with a broken rear brake from the 250cc Czech Grand Prix and battling through to eighth in the 350cc after a poor start.

The long trip to the Yugoslavia went unrewarded when he crashed out of the 250cc race at Rijeka when dicing for a podium in the final Grand Prix of the season

In the final classifications Herron finished fifth in the 350cc championship and sixth in the 250cc standings after what had been for him an unlucky and unrewarding season.

Bob Wright was again in unbeatable form winning the John Donnelly for the third time in a row as his rivals fell by the wayside.

Since he first won the Donnelly two years ago Wright won all seven of his Ulster starts.

Dave Watson suffered clutch problems and had a crash, Robert Wilkinson had his Maico seize and Andy Roberton had a faulty brake on his Montesa.

Joey Dunlop forgot to bring back the Wills Embassy Trophy he had won in 1977 when he left home for Kirkistown in a hurry, but it didn't matter as he retained the trophy pocketing £215 for his best short circuit pay day to date, however it was close at the end of 15-laps.

Dunlop and Graham Young diced for the lead after Noel Hudson stalled at the start, but once underway Hudson made up 24 places in the first four laps to be in sixth position. Setting the fastest lap of 90.05mph Hudson took second from Young with four laps to go chasing hard after Dunlop, who held onto the lead to win by 50-yards.

A week later at Aghadowey Dunlop turned the Hillsborough Club Sunflower Champion race into an anti-climax leading from start to finish winning handsomely from Young and Jackie Hughes.

Conor McGinn had a good week being uncatchable in the 350cc race at Kirkistown to register his first Ulster short circuit success repeating the feat to score his first Aghadowey win bursting through to thwart early leaders Courtney Junk and Hughes.

David Watson (Maico) clinched the British U-18 MX Championship, but the final round at Ladies Mile, near Petersfield in Hampshire was disappointing for the young Ulster rider, now based in England.

He was forced to retire from the first race with a puncture and then came a 'mighty purler' on the first lap of the second race.

Stephen Russell finished second in both races to end the championship in third position.

Sensation of the Race of the Year at Mallory Park was Tom Herron, who led the race during the opening stages, then dropped back to third three laps from the end of the race before a rear wheel puncture on his 750cc Yamaha forced him out.

Herron had the consolation of finishing third in both the 500cc Shellsport and Brut Superbike races.

Closer to home Joey Dunlop rode to three victories during the North Armagh Race of Aces meeting at Kirkistown where Cullybackey rider Donny Robinson scored his first ever victory in the 350cc race.

Into the winter trials season and Colin Bell, back home after quitting the international trial circuit to concentrate on his studies as an architect, scored his second successive Irish championship win in the Shaw Cup event losing fifteen marks fewer than runner-up Ian Davidson (26 – 41).

The rumour mill linked Tom Herron to a ride with the Suzuki GB squad for 1979. Herron finished his season with third and eighth place results in the Gauloises Powerbike and Brut Superbike races at Brands Hatch.

Herron was announced as the first winner of the Enkalon Irish Motorcyclist of the Year Award presented to the competitor who received most votes from a nationwide public vote, the first of its kind for motorcycling.

Tom and wife Andrea were at the function in the Enkalon Sports and Social Club for the first presentation of an award that is still presented 35-years on.

Tom and Andrea Herron

Word filtered through from the FIM Congress in Poland that the Ulster Grand Prix was to be included alongside the TT to determine the F1, F2 and F3 world champions in 1979, elevating the Ulster back to world championship status for the first time in eight years.

Fighting flu Colin Bell battled his way to a convincing win of the 22nd Irish Experts Trial at the Batt Estate, Rostrevor, Co. Down, an event that attracted 25 starters.

"I have been in bed for three days and probably shouldn't have been here at all," Bell said, *"had it been any other event I would have stayed at home."*

Bell had twenty one marks to spare over Dublin rider Derek Burton (107-128) after four laps of 12 observed sections, many of which had to be altered following torrential overnight rain.

Ireland's FIM delegate Billy McMaster won a certificate of commendation for his services to motorcycling in the province at the new British Airways Tourism Endeavour Awards for Northern Ireland, in particular for helping to restore the Ulster Grand Prix to world championship status in 1979.

*John
Shepard
on KTM*

*Charlie Smylie
observed by the
ever present and
much respected
Gillie Iveston*

*Relaxing at Tandragee 100
(left) Mervyn Robinson and
Joey Dunlop (below) Brian
Reid and Jim Dunlop*

*Mick Grant
chatting
with Ray
McCullough's
mechanic,
Hubert Gibson*

*Ray McCullough, Dennis
McBride, Maurice McBride,
Tom Herron and Stephen
McBride on Bike at
official Opening of Denis's
shop in Newtownards*

Con Law

Sam McClements

Ernie Coates

Richard Hewitt

Brian Hewitt

St Angelo Start

Lowry Burton / Marty Murphy

NW200 Start

*Davy Lowry (74), .
George Farlow (82)
and Jimmy Heath
(80) at St. Angelo*

*Brian Reid (9) and Jim
Dunlop (8) at Bell's
Crossroads, Tandragee*

*Joey Dunlop and Noel
Hudson in the air over
Cloughwater Bridge
at Mid Antrim 150*

*Jackie
Hughes*

Tom Herron's Suzuki and Yamaha being taken to scruitineering at NW200 by mechanic Peter Kelly

Con Law

David Wood

Bill Simpson

*Michael Campbell
(36) John Giffen
(33) in 250cc race
at Tandragee*

Steven Cull

John McDowell

John Newbold

Con Law

remembers... racing at the Manx

Born and brought up in the townland of Tyanee, Portglenone, when Con finished school at Rainey Endowed, Magherafelt. he worked at the Michelin Tyre Company in Ballymena.

However getting time off for his first love – motorbike racing – was a problem so when the Michelin factory at Mallusk shut he applied for redundancy and went racing fulltime with Joe Millar in 1983 but a serious accident at end of season Brands Hatch meeting in October that year effectively ended his full-time career.

After a period working on motorbikes Con worked for Lees Sawmills, Magherafelt for five years before embarking on the Maid of Antrim project, which is another story which continues today.

The seventies was a great time to go racing, but if you asked me how I got involved I'm not sure I could give you a straight forward answer.

In later years when my father died, we found an old photograph in his wallet taken when I was about eleven at the North West 200. We'd gone for a day out – a big occasion as my father didn't really have an interest in racing– and I don't remember much about it other than Dick Creith winning a race and me loving the action but perhaps from that moment I was hooked.

My newfound enthusiasm was to have limited outlet for a while seeing as round the area where I grew up, I don't remember anyone even having a road bike let alone going racing.

However the spark of interest aroused in me wasn't to be put out and I began to make my way to a few events cadging lifts from an uncle on my mother's side who followed the motorbike racing and my cousin Jim from Portglenone who would have done a bit of marshaling.

Although Jim had a younger brother around my age that I could knock around with, the older two didn't always want a couple of youngsters hanging about with them so at times I had to make other arrangements.

My brother Danny and I had more than a few great days when we would thumb our way to Maghaberry to watch the short circuit racing there and even further afield – not something many would do today. I remember on one such occasion when I was fourteen, thumbing a lift to Carrowdore for the road race. Given that I had no idea where Carrowdore was this might seem like a somewhat risky enterprise but I had a plan…

Mickey Laverty at Kirkistown

I had seen a signpost for Carrowdore on my way to Kirkistown one day, so I knew the general direction and I reckoned if I got there I would be able to get a lift home by locating Mickey Laverty from Toome who'd give me a lift back to Randalstown.

The first part of the plan worked fine but then things came off the rails when Mickey fell off and ended up in Newtownards Hospital with a broken collar bone! The day was saved when Bill Henderson, an accomplished rider on his two air-cooled Yamsel's, took over the driving of Mickey's van and I got that lift home.

Watching others was fun but I wanted a part of the action for myself and by my mid teens had procured an old moto-crosser for round the fields near home. By the time I was old enough for a licence I'd got a job in Michelin at Ballymena and, needing transport to get to work, I ended up buying a 350cc Yamaha road bike from Jimmy Johnston (an ex-racer from Glarryford).

With my new found freedom I went to as many races as I could, initially as a spectator without much thought about competing but as I watched the lesser known riders in the 'C' group (in those days it was races for A, B and C groups before Heats 1, 2 and 3 were introduced) I started to think 'maybe I'll give that a go'.

Initially I fancied a 200cc Bultaco like Mickey's, but they were very hard to get a hold off so I looked around at alternatives including a 50cc CR110 Honda.

At the time I could have bought it for £160 but on a wage of £11 a week it was expensive for me and anyhow I didn't want to race in the 50cc class. My da said "tell you what to do, buy the bike, don't race it, and keep it one day it'll be worth a fortune." But while I agreed with my da, I wanted to compete and didn't take his advice. Given that today the value of a CR110 in good nick is around £32,000 the phrase 'young and stupid' comes to mind!

I eventually bought a 250cc Greeves Silverstone from Raymond Campbell which was past its best when we got it – well tired – but Maghaberry Easter Saturday 1973 there I was on the starting line –I wasn't a threat to anybody on the grid but I just enjoyed being there.

It soon became obvious if I wanted to progress I needed something not so long in the tooth and the Greeves was soon replaced with a well worn, ex-Ray McCullough Yamsel which in due course was followed by various Yamahas–don't get me wrong I enjoyed the old Greeves and while we didn't always finish, the crack was mighty.

I say we, because, although I rode it, the bike was put in a trailer on the back of my da's car and Danny always went with us. My da, Barney, always told me he didn't want me to race, but he would always be there if I got injured. However he soon got involved and got to know other riders and supporters in the paddock (it was common that a van would come to the meetings with one competitor

and maybe four or five friends on board) it became a social scene for him.

Despite this, my racing was always a concern for my parents to an extent I perhaps only understood later and I always remember coming home from races to find my mother standing at the door just to make sure I had returned safely.

Picture of Portglenone Supporters Club with me (on bike 15), father Barney (back, 5th from left) and brother Danny (back, 8th from left)

Racing motorbikes affected our lives in other respects and in many ways I led a completely different lifestyle to many of my workmates as I scrimped and saved to go racing.

At that time there was nobody supplying parts, so you had to know somebody with something similar and I remember Willie Johnston coming to our house for Krober parts, Sugar Hanna (Raymond Hanna from Tandragee) for bits for a TD2 and on the other side of the coin, me going to people looking bits and pieces to keep my own wheels turning.

I met a lot of people through racing at that time who have gone on to be good friends – the likes of Jackie Hughes, Ray McCullough, Donny Robinson, Martin Barr, John Smyth, Raymond Campbell and Ivan Houston to name but a few.

Racing was swings and roundabouts, some days you came home feeling brilliant after a sunny day at the Temple or Tandragee, others you came home deflated after breaking down or riding below your expectation.

My first road race win came at Tandragee in 1978 in the 500cc class – Ivor Greenwood, Jack Wilkin, Mervyn Robinson and Billy Guthrie were all involved.

Billy was a great engineer and a great TT rider in fact I can picture him yet on parts of the Island where to this day nobody could match that boy. He may have been prone to losing time in the slow parts, but in places like the Black Dub and Ninth Milestone, boys a dear was he spectacularly fast!

As for myself and the mountain circuit, it was Joe Lindsay who kept telling me that I would love the place and it would suit me. I kept telling him no harm

Mervyn Robinson (12) leads Jack Wilkin (2) and myself (6) at Kirkistown

to him or anybody else but it was too ambitious, cost too much, I would need a better and stronger set up and a better bike – basically I wouldn't be good enough.

His retort was 'Do you want to win the race? What would you be happy with? Would you be happy lapping at 90mph?' I said I would and he replied 'I'll take you round at 90mph on the first night of practice riding the middle of the road.'

I thought 'God Almighty' maybe I'll take a look, so rather than enter the race I went to the TT as a spectator in 1976 to see this place I'd never been before. I stayed in a Mrs McGuinness's up in Hutchinson Square, Douglas along with Sam McClements, Jim Scott and a great guy called Malcolm Wheeler, now Classic Racer Editor, with whom I am still a good friend.

Norman Dunn's guest house was just down the road where Joey Dunlop stayed and I would go down to his garage, give a bit of a hand where needed and, when anyone was going for a drive round the circuit in a car or van, hitch a ride and told to sit in the back, shut up and listen to get the place into my head.

Enthused by the whole setup, I went to see about a Manx entry but was told I was too late. This was early June and a Friday; the day the entry had to be in, although I entered immediately, the organizers did not get it to Monday morning – too late.

Although I didn't make it that year, I went back the next accompanied by Jim Dunlop who got a lift in my van. The bike I was riding at that time I had bought from Ian McGregor, a TZ 250A who was sponsored by Manxman Randall Cowell of Glen Cowell Racing who had bought him a new bike.

It was the done thing then that when the Irish boat arrived any newcomers would be met and shown to garages, race control, where to get fuel and accommodation and when we arrived Randall was there to meet us and show us round.

The next day we met up again to go for the first of many laps. Randall had raced both tarmac and motocross, was a travelling marshal and knew the TT circuit inside out. On the way round he listened to you and asked leading questions to find out what you knew or didn't about the circuit. He taught me how to learn the 37¾ miles by getting out and spending time on it concentrating initially on the dangerous sections in and around Glen Helen by getting out and walking them yard by yard.

His teaching proved exemplary as I took the best newcomers award in the 250cc Lightweight Manx Grand Prix finishing in tenth position, the race won by Dave Hickman father of today's fastest TT newcomer Peter Hickman.

At the time I thought that at the speeds we were going at in the middle orders you were safe – it was the people who were winning were risking an awful lot – but that year there were seven riders killed including my good friend Ivan Houston and for the first time I realized that ordinary people could get hurt or killed as well as the guys on the limit at the front.

The dangers of what we were doing was rammed home a year later when Joe Lindsay, who had been instrumental in getting me to the Manx, was killed in an accident at Skerries.

It had started to rain a bit just before the start and Joe had put a blue rain suit on while I'd been talking to him just as the final call for practice was announced. We headed out on what should have been just a shake down for the main event but, as fate would have it, on the fast run down through Shady Lane into the right hand bend before the Hairpin (Skerries was right hand in then) Joe crashed and found a stone pillar covered in ivy that nobody knew was there. When I came along people were waving us down, but I could not get slowed quickly enough and went through catching sight of what I thought were one-piece blue leathers. Finally getting the bike stopped, I remember throwing it in the hedge and running back to help whoever it was and the shock hitting me –"Oh Jeez it's Joe."

I took that very bad for some time afterwards and thought hard about what was I going to do here? I'd always had my heroes who risked life and limb to be at the front and I thought that I was too sensible to do that, but then I realized that when the red racing mist comes down we're all on our limits and that's what gives us the

My good friend Joe Lindsay whose death hit me very hard

buzz! Having thought it out in my head, I realized that this is not a new disease, it had always been there and if you wanted the rewards you just had to go on.

The Manx in 1977 was a good year for me – I went with my own bike, knew it inside out, had a good spares kit to refresh it during practice and I was well pleased with the outcome.

In the winter of that year Randall had invited Ginger (Seamus McDonnell my mechanic) and I over to various club dinners, an excuse to put in more miles around the circuit as well as enjoy the hospitality.

Randall had sponsored Ian McGregor for years and wanted to win a Manx Grand Prix but, a road traffic accident with a horse forced Ian into early retirement and, with him out of the picture, Randall decided to help me with a bike instead.

In 1978 the bike went well at home, but when we went to the Manx no matter what I did, it seized every time we went out. McGregor and Brian Reid were there and they said I was pushing myself too hard, stripping and rebuilding crankshafts, cylinders time after time, but we persevered and eventually got the thing to run and were going well in the Lightweight race until a second lap puncture, after picking up a big nail, saw me retire at Ballaugh Bridge.

Come 1979 we were more organised, no break downs and every time I went out in practice I was able to refine the bike.

On race day, bad weather caused a delay which worked in our favour. For the race I had the option of two different fuel tanks, my own wee tank which was small and light but only held enough fuel for two laps or one I had borrowed from Jim Finlay which, being larger, would let me run for three laps. As the race was originally over four laps, I planned to use my own wee tank but this plan was quickly revised when, with the weather delay, the race was shortened to three laps and we quickly fitted the big tank so I could do the whole distance without refuelling.

I had only one official signalling point, but as the race went on other people round the course started signalling to me that I was winning. I wasn't sure to believe them or not and my only thought was to hope the bike would just keep going to the chequered flag. The bike, a dead standard TZ250 Yamaha, was a good one and brought me home to my first victory on the mountain course at a race average of just over 100mph.

I had a Manx sponsor and between visits to the TT in June, Southern 100 in July, Manx in August / September plus various winter trips had been over to the Island every month for two years making a lot of good friends in the Isle of Man so to finally get the race win under my belt was absolutely brilliant.

On my way to winning the Junior Manx Grand Prix

It still brings a smile to my face to remember the tradition at the prize giving where they carry you on what is basically a wheel barrow without the wheel onto the stage while your mates try to tip you out of it. A brilliant moment and one I'll never forget, the pinnacle of my career at that time and something I never ever imagined when I started out racing in 1973 on that Greeves Silverstone.

After my Manx victory it was an unwritten rule then that Manx winners do the decent thing and move on to the TT and this I did with the same bikes in 1980, that story is for another day with Randall cutting back his involvement and me hooking up with Joe Millar in a partnership that would see me win two Lightweight TT's back to back.

You know every dog has their day as they say and motorcycle racing is the same – the late sixties and early seventies saw the likes of Billy McCosh, Wilfie Herron, Len Ireland and Dick Creith all brilliant riders coming to an end of their involvement handing the reins over to a new generation like Ray McCullough, Mervyn Robinson, Joey Dunlop, Billy Guthrie, Jackie Hughes, Courtney Junk, Ian McGregor and many, many more who, before giving way to a new generation of riders in turn, made the seventies possibly one of the best ever decades to be involved in the sport – the racing and the craic were mighty!

On my boat, The Maid of Antrim with fellow racers and friends John Burrows, Roger Marshall, Danny Law, Dr Fred McSorley, Robert Dunlop, Brian Reid, Ray McCullough, Len Ireland, Jim Dunlop, Robert Britton and Trevor Ferguson

1979

Margaret Thatcher elected as Prime Minister following 'Winter of Discontent' – 15 killed in Fastnet yacht race – First J D Wetherspoon pub opened – 'The Hitchhiker's Guide to the Galaxy' published. Art Garfunkel tops UK charts with 'Bright Eyes' and Pink Floyd release 'The Wall' – Pint of milk was 15p but not for long with infation at 17%!

Former works Honda rider Tommy Robb, who won the 1973 125cc TT and collected 29 TT replicas, announced he was making a racing comeback at 44-years of age riding a 250cc Yamaha for Appleby Glade boss Dave Orton.

John Newbold in more familiar competition!

In the Coleraine Club 'Super Stars' contest John Newbold emerged the clear winner having managed 73 press-ups per minute and 80 squat thrusts per minute – he also won the long jump, hockey goals and roller skating sections, not bad for a motorcycle racer at a time when fitness was not a number one priority!

Junior motorcycle sport in Ulster was booming with almost 400 licence holders participating mainly in scrambles and grass tracks.

Raymond Davison scored his second successive Enduro win in seven days when he won the Coleraine Club Causeway Cup event at Cushendall held over three laps of a snow covered 16-mile forest course that featured eight speed tests. Davison (Bultaco) had eight minutes to spare over Scottish visitor Peter Reid with the top six completed by Hughie Simpson, George McCann, Bryson Perry and Winston Buchanan.

Former road racers Billy McCosh and world champion Ralph Bryans had their own private battle for eighth, won by the Ballymena man.

Ian Davison (Montesa) didn't have to break sweat when he scored a comparatively easy win in the Ards Club Sandown Trial at a new venue in Glenoe, Co. Antrim.

Davison scored 16 fewer penalties than runner-up Tom McBride whose brother Davy was third.

A name to become familiar with all trial supporters, Harold Crawford, topped the schoolboy competitors.

After four laps of twelve snow covered sections Colin Bell won the Slemish Cup Trial, his fourth win in five rounds of the Irish Trials championship.

A triple tie between Henry O'Kelly, Trevor Callaghan and Billy Wightman on 34 marks lost

Harold Crawford

each after the Larkin Cup Trial was settled by the tie break.

When the three rider's last lap scores were compared it was Dubliner O'Kelly declared the winner, his first Ulster success, having lost just five marks on the last lap to Callaghan's seven and Wightman's twelve penalties.

The world trial championship commenced with the Hurst Cup at Clandyboye Estate where four different makes of machine filled the first four positions – 1st Rob Shepherd (Honda) 79 marks lost, 2nd John Reynolds (Suzuki) 84, 3rd Martin Lampkin (Bultaco) 95 and 4th Malcolm Rathmell (Montesa) 96.5.

Top Ulster rider was Colin Bell in eighteenth position.

Plans were drawn up for a special match race series to take place on the Isle of Man to celebrate Millennium Celtic week where six man teams from the Celtic nations were invited to take part, the races to be held on the 3-mile Jurby Airfield Circuit where the winners received a full size replica of the Manx Sword of State. This was of course the fore runner of the Celtic Match Race series that was ran at various venues in Scotland, Ireland, Wales and the Isle of Man over the next decade.

It was the Laurence Spence show during the Ayton Trophy Motocross the second round of the Irish Championship at Ballyculter, near Strangford.

Stephen Russell

In scintillating form riding his Cotton EMC Spence scored three wins from three starts taking both championship races and the feature event followed home on each occasion by the Suzuki of Stephen Russell.

Joey Dunlop could not improve on his 1978 eighth position in the Daytona 250cc race by finishing twelfth this time around. Dunlop did not even get to start the main 200-mile race, as his brand new 750cc Rea Yamaha broke a crank during morning warm-up.

Fellow Ulster riders Ernie Coates and Jackie Hughes rode their 350cc Yamaha's to 31st and 48th respectively, Hughes having been in the high twenties before a broken gear lever slowed his progress.

Now a fully fledged factory 500cc Suzuki rider in the World Championship Grand Prix scene with Texaco Heron Suzuki Tom Herron made his debut for the team at the opening round in Venezuela where he qualified second on the grid.

Herron rode to 2nd, 3rd and 4th position finishes during the Daily Mail 500cc race and World of Sport International Superbike races at Donington Park

Herron finished third overall in the MCN/Duckhams superbike event at Cadwell Park taking his 500cc Texaco Herron Suzuki to fourth position in both 12-lap races, backing those results up with a third in the 500cc race.

He then made his debut for the British Team in the Transatlantic Match Races (an event that was the backbone of British racing at the time where the best of the UK took on the best Americans over Easter weekend at Brands Hatch, Mallory Park and Oulton Park) riding a 653cc Suzuki for the first time.

Herron's Transatlantic debut was short lived however, as after finishing third in the first match race at Brands Hatch he lost the front at Westfield in race two dicing for a podium. Despite borrowing Barry Sheene's helmet for the following Shellsport 500cc race in which he finished second further checks revealed a broken bone in a hand ruling him out of further participation at Mallory and Oulton Park.

In a preview for Easter Monday races at Kirkistown in All Ireland Racing Magazine advised,

'Get there early, as this is the best attended short circuit meeting of the season. Oh and by the way to make matters worse diversion signs from Greyabbey to Kirkistown will be in place, as Kirkubbin will be closed to through traffic from 10am.'

Incidentally the cost of hiring Kirkistown for 1979 had jumped 150% stunning the circuit main motorcycle promoters, the Belfast and District Club.

Rises were quoted in MCN as: Easter Monday hire in 1978, £1000 rising in 1979 to £2500. The July meeting in 1978 was £500 rising to £1500 in 1979.

The B&D were quoted, *'If owners, the 500 Motor Club' stick to what we believe are exorbitant hire charges, racing at the Co Down track looks bleak.'*

Thirty four years on and the B&D are still the main promoters of motorcycle meetings at Kirkistown.

The opening round of the 1979 Embassy Championship at St Angelo saw a shock winner in George Farlow on his Team Castrol Yamaha.

A bout of flu saw Noel Hudson a non-starter while pre-race favourite Jackie Hughes led until two laps from home when Farlow pounced to steal the show ahead of Hughes, Steven Cull and Con Law.

Farlow doubled up by leading home Jim Dunlop and Jack Wilkin in the 500cc

George Farlow

race while Joey Dunlop scooped the 250cc honours from Hudson and Law.

Donny Robinson was the 350cc winner, Richard Nesbitt took the 200cc honours, Cull was the 750cc race winner and Lowry Burton with Marty Murphy in the chair was the sidecar victor also in Team Castrol colours, the driving force behind Team Castrol being Davy Wood.

Two second place finishes was enough to give Laurence Spence the overall victory of the Henderson Trophy held over a new course at Greyabbey where a dry fuel tank robbed Steve Harrison of victory in race one in which Scot Willie Simpson beat Spence by five seconds.

Stephen Russell won leg two from Spence and Simpson; second enough to give Spence the feature race trophy to add to his 500cc Ulster Championship race win over Russell although these positions were reversed when it came to the 250cc championship race.

Noted performances in a Mid Antrim Club Junior Motocross came from young stars of the future – Paul Chambers and Dwayne McCracken second and third in the cadet class, David Tougher and Philip Neill third and fifth in the Junior class while William Burgees won the intermediate class from Julian Patterson.

Tom Herron's injured left hand sustained in his Brands Hatch spill continued to improve with full movement almost returned, as his excellent Austrian Grand Prix performance indicated – fourth behind Kenny Roberts, Virginio Ferrari and Wil Hartog putting him second in the championship.

The second round of the Embassy championship looked a sure fire win for Jackie Hughes riding the ex-Tom Herron OW31 Yamaha only for the machine to seize on the final lap at the hairpin handing victory to a surprised Donny Robinson.

Hughes had the

Enkalon Trophy winner Jackie Hughes with young fan Paschal Corrigan

consolation of winning the third running of the 15-lap Enkalon Trophy Race, leading throughout.

Stephen Russell was a triple winner at the Bobby Whyte Memorial and Ulster championship motocross meeting at Magilligan where he was followed home each time by Laurence Spence, despite Spence being reported as, 'riding against doctors orders having suffered dizzy spells the previous day.'

Tom Herron forced out of West German Grand Prix when his Texaco Heron Suzuki spluttered to a halt with reported crankshaft problems when in fifth position, but followed this retirement with third in the Italian Grand Prix at Imola.

Do you remember the first published names for the Golden Jubilee North West 200 Match Races? If your memory needed jogging it was in the red corner Tom Herron, Ray McCullough, Joey Dunlop, Steven Cull, Billy Guthrie, Graham Young, Noel Hudson, Jackie Hughes, Con Law, Frank Kennedy, Alex George, John Woodley, Denis Ireland, Warren Willing, Jeff Sayle, Gerhard Vogt and American John Long while in the black corner it was Tony Rutter, Mick Grant, John Newbold, Steve Parrish, Ron Haslam, Roger Marshall, Dave Potter, Kevin Stowe, Neil Tuxworth, Bill Smith, George Fogarty, Derek Chatterton, Alan Jackson, John Weedon, Ian Richards, Chris Guy and Derek Huxley.

Wet roads greeted competitors for the Tandragee 100, Ulster's opening road race of the season, where there were six different winners of the six races.

Scoring his eighth successive win over the Co Armagh circuit Ray McCullough won the 250cc race, brothers-in-law Joey Dunlop and Mervyn Robinson kept the Armoy Armada flags flying with their respective wins of the 350 and 500cc races – Dunlop winning at a canter while the 352cc Yamaha of 'Robo' saw off the 500cc Suzuki's of Billy Guthrie and Frank Kennedy.

Steven Cull ruled the roost in the Unlimited class, Richard Hewitt zipped past Richard Nesbitt to claim the 200cc encounter with Lowry Burton and Marty Murphy edged out the Coates brothers Wallace and Ernie in the sidecar.

A week later at the Cookstown 100 Joey Dunlop produced the tonic required prior to the North West 200 taking the Man of the Meeting Award with two wins and a second, Dunlop won the 350 and 500cc races, but had to settle for second in the 250 event

coming from eighth at the end of lap one closing down, but unable to catch Ray McCullough.

In a pre-TT diary slot in MCN on the Wednesday prior to the North West 200 Tom Herron wrote,

'What can I say! An injury just before the North West and TT was the last thing I needed and now I'm fighting for fitness so that I appear at my two most important meetings of the year. With practice starting this evening it is a tall order for me to be in the saddle, but I'm determined to do it subject to what the specialist says. I've broken my right thumb, right at the knuckle. It would not have been so bad if it had happened to my clutch hand, as I would have been able to manage a bit better. The crash happened on the last lap of the last training session at Jarama (Spanish Grand Prix) on one of the fastest sections of the course. I felt the rear go and the tyre trying real hard to hang on, but I just had to let the machine go and follow it into the catch fencing. It's so frustrating. One thing in my favour is that the Coleraine – Portrush – Portstewart Triangle is not the most strenuous of circuits, unless you are having a real ding-dong battle with someone.'

In that MCN the headline article was;

In search of the 130mph lap!

The following week the headline was;

Black Saturday – Ulster tragedies as Herron dies.

Tom Herron, the 30-year old Ulster rider, who joined the works Suzuki team at the start of this season after several seasons as one of the world's leading privateers is dead.

He died in Coleraine Hospital on Saturday night after crashing heavily at Juniper Hill on the last lap of the 1000cc race, the final race of the day.

Tom Herron on the fateful day

Brian Hamilton

The Golden Jubilee North West 200 was marred by several high speed crashes one of which claimed the life of Scottish rider Brian Hamilton, who crashed at Black Hill on the first lap of the 350cc race.

A three-rider pile up on one of the fastest parts of the course on the first lap of the opening Match Race close to the University entrance saw Kevin Stowe and Frank Kennedy critically injured and Australian Warren Willing suffering a badly broken leg.

Kennedy died in hospital some months later while Stowe and Willing never raced again.

Brothers Roy and Mick Jefferies also crashed approaching Black Hill, Roy receiving head injuries and a broken leg, his brother escaped with cuts and bruises.

In another major incident former North West lap record holder Mick Grant lost control and crashed heavily whilst braking for York Corner suffering pelvic injuries

Of course racing had continued throughout the day and should have been not only remembered as the events 50th Anniversary, but also for Joey Dunlop's first North West 200 victories taking the chequered flag in the opening Match Race leading the Herron selection to a 193 – 119 points victory and final Morans North West 200 feature superbike race, Tony Rutter's 350/500cc double, Bob Jackson's first and only North West victory in the 250cc race and the appearance of Mike Hailwood as guest of Honour for the day.

However all that was overshadowed by headlines about the deaths, especially Herron's and the serious accidents.

The funeral service for Thomas William (Tom) Herron took place in Leitrim Presbyterian Church, Castlewellan on Monday 28th May, conducted by Rev. James Johnstone, BA, BD and attended by a huge turn-out of mourners including many of his racing rivals.

Later in the year (November) North West 200 Race Secretary Billy Nutt announced that for 1980 the North West 200 course would not include the Shell Hill Bridge section with riders turning sharp

Mike Hailwood

left from Station Road (University Corner) and travel to 'Magic Roundabout' taken anti-clockwise – the first course change since 1973.

Two weeks after the tragic North West the TT was in full swing with new sensation Kiwi Graeme Crosby (Moriwaki Kawasaki) from a starting number of 46 race through to finish an incredible fourth in the F1 race on his Mountain Course debut behind a trio of Honda's Alex George, Charlie Williams and Ron Haslam.

Joey Dunlop's six cylinder Benelli lasted two laps before a valve seat came away from the cylinder head and bent a valve on the Agrati entered machine leaving Ernie Coates as best local in 28th position on his Suzuki.

Mike Hailwood in his second comeback year won his 14th TT and become the first rider to win the Senior Race on a works 500cc Suzuki setting new race and class lap records in the process – Steven Cull was the top local rider in eleventh position.

In the Classic TT Hailwood lost out on victory in his swan-song appearance by 3.4secs to Scotsman Alex George, a race in which Joey Dunlop finished sixth.

It was quoted in the book '80 Years of the TT' published in 1987 that *"Hailwood's 14 wins is a total that is unlikely to be broken."* We now know different of course with Joey Dunlop holding the record at 26 TT victories.

In what was a disappointing year for local riders at the TT Sam McClements was best in the 250cc Lightweight race in 17th position, Joey Dunlop was 13th of 19 finishers in the F2 race again riding a Benelli while Tommy Robb was best in the F3 event on a 250cc Suzuki with the Coates brothers Wallace and Ernie completing both sidecar races in 19th and 18th positions for tenth position overall.

In addition to his racing successes, Ernie Coates gained an entry in the Guinness Book of Records for achieving the unique distinction of riding in every race session both solo and sidecar during the '79 TT.

Ernie Coates made the Guiness Book of Records

Motocross Switch – Rob Wilkinson quit Cotton-EMX after failing to secure a single point in the British Championship while at home Dennis McBride

Wallace and Ernie Coates

(former Irish champion) had secured the services of Ulster's top scramblers Stan Chambers and Wallace Seawright to ride 400cc Moto Villa machines for the remainder of the season hoping to challenge the established Maico, Suzuki and Cotton-EMX machines.

Former British U-18 champion Dave Watson quit Montesa and would finish the season riding a Suzuki.

Laurence Spence clinched the Irish Scrambles championship for the third successive season since leaving the schoolboy ranks following a hat trick at the Ards Club McClay Memorial event at Craigantlet.

Notably a motorcycle scramble due to be held by the Banbridge Club was reportedly cancelled at the last minute by the farmer who owned the property. The reason given – although the field to be used was fit for racing, the way in was water-logged!

Just three weeks after his North West 200 double Joey Dunlop landed a unique treble at a record shattering Killinchy 150 at Dundrod – the first ever three-timer in the twenty three year history of the event.

In the 1000cc race Dunlop set a Killinchy lap record of 118.74mph dicing with Ron Haslam, who eventually crashed out at the Hairpin sustaining an ankle injury. In the 350cc race Ian Richards and Dunlop locked horns resulting in a near photo-finish that saw the Rea Yamaha a bike length ahead at the chequered flag.

Riding Sam Taggart's Yamaha Dunlop quickly opened up a 200 yard advantage over the chasing pack speeding to a 250cc race win.

Trevor Steele won the 125cc race riding an exotic 125cc Morbidelli from the Honda of David Wood, while Lowry Burton and Marty Murphy were victorious in the sidecar event.

Dunlop continued on his merry winning way securing five wins from five starts paying scant regard to the patchy wet and dry Aghadowey track the week after the Killinchy.

In rampant form the dynamic 'Gurk' as he was nicknamed outgunned the opposition in the 250, 350, 750, 4th round of the Embassy Championship and the 'Ace of Aghadowey' races while his brother-in-law Mervyn Robinson claimed a win in the 500cc class.

A fierce sidecar race saw the Coates brothers gain the upper hand marginally over the Burton / Murphy duo.

To celebrate their 30th Birthday the Lightweight Club organised a short circuit meeting at a resurfaced and modified Kirkistown and brought top cross-channel competitors Tony Rutter, Derek Chatterton and Derek Huxley to challenge the local aces, but Joey Dunlop proved too hot a handful for the visitors scoring four wins to make it 14 wins in four meetings in five weeks. He only lost out on a clean sweep at the meeting when Donny Robinson ran away with the 350cc race.

Mid July saw Kevin Stowe, one of the riders seriously injured at the North West 200, on the mend and likely to be returning to England in a few weeks.

Described by doctors as a walking miracle Stowe fully regained his sight and could now hold a normal conversation while he surprised everyone when he left his wheelchair and walked 20 yards for the first time since the accident.

Chasing his first Southern 100 Solo Championship success Joey Dunlop was thwarted by two seconds by George Fogarty after fifty miles of flat-out action.

Dunlop was forced to ride his 350cc Yamaha in the race having smashed his 750cc Yamaha in a spectacular moment earlier when he shot through a conveniently open Ballanorris Farm Gate into a corn field at over 90mph. This bend on the Billown Circuit has been named Joey's Gate ever since.

The Armoy Ace still managed a treble at the meeting winning the 250 and 350cc races on his Yamaha's and the Millenium Solo Race riding Hector Neill's RG 500 Suzuki.

The first Irish Motocross Grand Prix at Deerpark, Slane, Co Meath was hampered by dust problems, which tried the riders' patience during the 125cc World Championship round.

A combination of warm sunshine and a light breeze left the ground powder dry with the steep slopes preventing easy access for water trucks.

Belgian Harry Everts, father of future King of Motocross Stefan Everts, won both legs of the event to clinch the 1979 125cc World Motocross Championship.

Rhodesian born (now Zimbabwe) Jackie Hughes was crowned Munster Simms King of Kirkistown beating off the challenge of Joey Dunlop, just returned from the Southern 100.

In the Crown Prince race Richard Hewitt just held off the strong challenge from Paul Cranston, yes the same Paul Cranston still racing today over thirty years later!

George McCann missed out on a gold Medal by one minute after 14-hours of hard riding in the Welsh 2-day Trial, comfortably taking a Silver along with MCUI team mates Winston Buchanan and Davy Mills.

The damp, sandy Markelo Track in Holland was not to the Ulster riders liking in the 500cc Motocross Grand Prix – Laurence Spence retired from the first moto when his front brake became clogged with sand and seized, the young rider going on to bring up the rear in Moto 2.

Fellow countryman Rob Wilkinson (Hewitt Maico) managed 22nd in Moto 1 and one place ahead of Cotton-EMX rider Spence on their second outing.

Both fared better at Namur in Belgium with Spence 10th and 11th in the two races with Wilkinson 15th and 16th.

The 48th running of the Temple 100, the oldest road race outside of the TT, saw a terrific 200cc battle between Richard Hewitt and Richard Nesbitt going right to the wire with Nesbitt waiting until the last corner (Rectory Corner) on the last lap before snatching the lead from race favourite Hewitt and beating him to the short run to the chequered flag.

Noel Hudson was the start to finish winner of both the 350 and 500cc races while finishing second, having had to battle through from nineteenth position, to Ray McCullough in the 250cc race.

For McCullough this was his nineteenth Temple victory in as many years while Jackie Hughes scored his first ever Irish road race win in the 750cc class.

A month later writing in Motorcycle Racing Magazine celebrated journalist the late John Brown wrote of his experiences at the Temple 100,

> "Nothing can compare to this circuit. 45 riders per race starting in groups of 15 at thirty second intervals in the interests of safety. The 5½ mile circuit a frightening mixture of high-speed jumps, bumpy straights and sharp corners that would seem impossible to get a road bike around let alone a race-bred 750cc Yamaha. No more than 10 foot wide in places the circuit is trackside furniture lined with telegraph poles, stone walls, barbed wire fencing and grass covered stone walls. Riders paid a £4 entry fee that just about covered insurance, for the first time a travelling Doctor was introduced – Dr Bob Richardson who quipped, 'It has been said that the Temple is the only circuit where you get thorns from the hedges in both knees at the same time , if you stick them out,"

Donny Robinson

A strong Ulster contingent travelled overnight from the Temple to East Fortune in Scotland and scored a 1-2-3 in the 350cc race with Graham Young winning from Ernie Coates and George Farlow while Donny Robinson and Young finished second and third after a race long battle with the winner, local star, Bill Simpson father to TT and North West 200 winner Ian.

It was announced that five past and present world champions would be in Ballynahinch for a Tom Herron Tribute evening – Kenny Roberts, Barry Sheene, Mike Hailwood, Kork Ballington, Takazumi Katayama (nicknamed Zooming Taxi), Mick Grant, Ron Haslam, Charlie Williams, Steve Parrish, Eddie Roberts, John Dodds and Steve Ellis attended.

On home territory at the Mid Antrim 150 Joey Dunlop was in record breaking form on his way to a flying double – the outright lap record extended to 95.15mph as the Armoy star won a cliff hanging unlimited encounter, getting the better of

Jackie Hughes on the final lap.

It was another close call in the 350cc race with Steven Cull less than 3 secs behind the Rea Yamaha while Con Law got the better of Rob Britton in the 500cc race in another close finish.

Ray McCullough won the 250cc race from

Robert Britton

rising star Donny Robinson – with this victory McCullough had won every 250cc race in the 70s at the Mid Antrim bar one, the 1975 victory going to Ian McGregor.

Two well-known English visitors Bob Jackson and Phil 'Mez' Mellor acquitted themselves well around the tricky 6-mile Rathkenny Circuit; Mellor second to Richard Hewitt in the 200cc race while in the 250cc encounter Jackson was fourth and Mellor fifth.

Quote from Coroner Robin Wray at the inquests into the deaths of Tom Herron and Brian Hamilton at the North West 200 compared them to Battle of Britain and Normandy Landings with their courage and bravery saying, *"If they had not been racing, then they would have found something else to do, just as dangerous."*

Graham Young and Joey Dunlop finished 14th and 15th in the 350cc race during the British Grand Prix at Silverstone with Young 15th in the 250cc race.

On the same weekend in August Roger Harvey (Maico) easily won the Tommy Stewart Trophy and both Irish Scrambles Championship races during the Knock Club event at Downpatrick with rising Ulster star Stephen Russell (Suzuki) second each time.

Further afield in Luxembourg Laurence Spence claimed two ninth place finishes in the 500cc

Roger Harvey was a frequent visitor to local meetings

Grand Prix and was presented with a £250 cheque for being the best newcomer in the GP using Pirelli Tyres. Robert Wilkinson finished 13th and 15th.

The Thirty Club ran their first ever Ulster Vintage meeting at Kirkistown where 23-year old English visitor Steve Linsdell (father of Olie) was a double winner riding a Royal Enfield – however he was no match for Sam McClements on the Ryan Norton when they clashed.

In modern races at the meeting Donny Robinson won the 250 and 350cc races with Arnie Hill on his 700cc Yamaha taking the unlimited victory.

Jimmy Walker reporting in the Ireland Saturday Night (The Pink) from the 50th Anniversary Ulster Grand Prix wrote, *"Ron Haslam, the rope thin road racer smashed the Dundrod lap record by almost 3mph to become the new F1 World Champion winning before 50,000 spectators, who basked in sun and high speeds during today's UGP."*

That new record was 116.15mph.

Walker also wrote, *"Cullybackey's Donny Robinson became the new local hero when he scored an incredible victory in the 350cc class, which he led from start to finish."*

Not only was this Robinson's first ever UGP win, but also his first win on any road circuit and it was obtained on a machine provided for him at the last minute by Haslam's sponsor Mal Carter.

In a memorable Grand Prix Ray McCullough won an epic 250cc encounter by overhauling Bob Jackson on the final bend to win by half a bike length with Aussie Graeme McGregor third and Robinson an impressive fourth.

Joey Dunlop sent the crowd wild piloting Hector Neill's RG500 Suzuki.

All the odds were stacked against him, as he had to start from the fifth row of the grid, apparently not having completed sufficient qualifying laps due to a crash in practice necessitating a trip to hospital for a finger x-ray. Eleventh at the end of the opening lap Dunlop seemed well out of it as Denis Ireland, John Woodley, Tony Rutter and John Newbold set the pace.

With six laps to go

L-R: Donny Robinson, Sponsor Mal Carter and Alan Carter, later to become Robinson's team mate at Mitsui Yamaha

Dunlop was up to fifth and, urged on by the enthusiastic home crowd began to claw back the leader's advantage until, with two laps remaining, the word from Cochranstown was that Dunlop was ahead from where he went on to win by eight seconds.

Having beaten the latest 1979 models with his two year old machine, a naturally delighted Neill joked, *"After this they will be looking me to work for Suzuki"* – history shows that Hector was bang on the money as he and his son Philip went on to run Suzuki's British Championship and International Road Racing campaigns for many years, winning races and championships at both levels.

Alan Jackson won the F2 race and with it his third world championship while Australian Barry Smith, who had apparently retired from European racing ten years previous and last rode at the UGP in the 1969 50cc race, returned to win the F3 race and world championship.

Commercial sponsorship for the UGP was a record £10,000 plus an expected UGP Supporters Club donation of twice that amount helped towards what was a truly epic Ulster Grand Prix to end the decade on a high after all the events trials and tribulations.

After his surprise UGP 350cc victory MCN reported that Donny Robinson was to retain the Pharoah Yamaha for the Manx Grand Prix where he was also to ride Mervyn Turtle's 250cc Yamaha, the bike he rode to fourth position at the Ulster.

Hector Neill's UGP winning 500cc Suzuki was to be ridden at the Manx by Ronnie Russell, but he ruled himself out after he thumped the bank exiting Hillberry at 120mph during second practice suffering arm and leg injuries.

Four Irish riders were inside the top ten of the Lightweight 250cc Manx practice – Conor McGinn, Con Law, Robinson and Rob Britton.

Joey Dunlop finished a creditable 9th in the 350cc race during the French Grand Prix at Le Mans.

Stan Chambers (Husqvarna) won three races during the Ulster Championship Campbell Donaghy Memorial scramble at Magilligan, but when it came to the main event David Johnston (Maico) following an early tussle with Alan Magee (Maico) ran out the comfortable winner.

Portglenone rider Con Law (Glen Cowell Yamaha) joined the Manx Grand Prix record busters when he hoisted the 250cc Lightweight lap record to 102.51mph as he raced to victory by 56.6secs from Dubliner Conor McGinn, who also finished second in the 350cc Junior Manx.

Law, Martin Barr (9th) and Raymond Campbell (12th) won the Lightweight Team Award for the Mid Antrim Club.

Steven Cull on 750 Suzuki pictured here at the Temple 100

Law returned home to win the 250cc race at the Carrowdore 100 leading from start to finish in what was reported as the events worst weather in 20 years.

Steven Cull raced to a 350 /750cc double; the smaller victory after a thriller between Cull, Graeme Young, Law and Martin Barr when they were never more than a few lengths apart throughout.

Brian Reid won the 125cc race on a Morbidelli, Richard Hewitt the 200cc class and George Farlow led the 500cc race all the way.

It was announced that there would be no new 350cc Yamaha's for 1980 as the factory concentrated their development emphasis on the 500cc class and a refined 250cc machine.

Not good news for those fighting to save the 350cc world championship and an announcement that would eventually filter down to national racing in the future.

Robert Dunlop and Don Carlisle

Report in MCN stated that five competitors, three marshals and a spectator all had to have hospital treatment following a series of accidents at an Aghadowey meeting.

The name of Robert Dunlop crept onto the leader board at this meeting when the 'Micro' as he was quickly christened by his fans finished third on his Kreidler behind Don Carlisle (MZ) and John Borne (Suzuki) in the 50cc race.

Steven Cull collected the Wills Embassy Championship after a titanic scrap with Graeme Young and George Farlow.

Belgian Andre Vromans on his first to the John Donnelly International scramble won two of the three legs and finished third in the last one to claim overall victory. Best of the locals was Rob Wilkinson in fifth overall with 3rd, 9th and 6th place results.

Tom McBride

From top Harold Crawford and Colin Perry

The Ulster Trials series began at Spelga Dam and defending champion Tom McBride won the Lightweight Club event losing six penalty marks, two fewer than runner-up Brian McAllister.

The top three schoolboys at this event were Colin Perry, Harold Crawford and Raymond Davison – all three going on to participate at higher levels.

Joey Dunlop finished a brilliant ninth in the World F750 round at Hockenheim in Germany scoring two points the week after winning a non-championship international 750cc race in Austria.

Dunlop returned home for the Embassy final at Kirkistown, one of the first short circuit meetings to be televised. It was his first home outing since the UGP, however it was not a happy home-coming as gearbox gremlins side-lined his 350 effort, a puncture just before the start ruled him out of the 750cc race, he was not allowed to start the Embassy final not having competed in the final qualifying round and then in the 250cc race he could only manage a lowly eighth position. To rub salt in the wounds his sponsor John Rea had his request for a licence to ride in the one-off sponsors' charity race refused.

It was Steven Cull's day winning the Embassy race after a sensational dice with Graham Young, making the winning pass three laps from home. Cull completed a hat trick by winning the unlimited and 350cc races.

Young looked to have the 350cc race under control, but Cull made rapid ground onto his back wheel after a poor start with the pressure telling as Young slid off at the hairpin with four laps to go handing Cull a clear run to the chequered flag.

Alan Irwin

A shock 350cc winner at the two Aghadowey end of season meetings was 22-year old Alan Irwin riding Donny Robinson's Yamaha. In the final 350cc race of the season he beat George Farlow and Joey Dunlop into second and third places.

One of Ireland's top road racers Reg Armstrong was killed in a car accident on the 24th November.

He first rode at Skerries in 1947, was second in the Senior Manx a year later and then joined the AJS factory team until 1952 when he joined Geoff Duke on works Norton's winning the Senior TT and finished second in the Junior TT.

Duke and Armstrong then switched to Gilera where Armstrong was a treble world championship runner-up before his retirement in 1956.

Colin Bell (Bultaco) dropped 81 marks over a tough sixteen sections tackled three times to win the Terry Hill Trophy Trial at Saintfield, the fifth round of the Irish Championship.

Derek Burton, who finished second some 19 marks adrift at the Temple Club event, hit back a week later to win the Irish Experts Trial held at the 'Vee' Co Tipperary. Only three Ulster riders made the long journey south including Bell who had to be satisfied with second six marks behind Burton.

MCN in December 1979 had a report that told how, 'world class racing' could well be on the way back to Ulster in the not too distant future if a blueprint to have a purpose built track in the memory of Tom Herron was given the go-ahead. Estimated cost of building the circuit, understood to be adjacent to the Maze

Horse Race Course, £3million!

Like a number of other proposed ventures – adjacent to Ballymena Showgrounds, Benvarden Lion Park, Nutts Corner expansion, Kilroot etc. – none have ever got off the drawing board. Incidentally the cost would now have arguably become tenfold what it would have been in 1979.

Willie Stewart and Davy Gault

'Mud glorious mud' did not prevent Stephen Pyper from winning the Lightweight Club Autumn Trophy Trial (it was held in mid-December), his task made easier with the retirement of halfway leader Lance Owens on the third and last lap of ten sections at Dunmurry.

Six sidecar crews entered, but no one got near the Bultaco combination of Davy McBride / Jim McCrea who lost only 5 marks twenty less than second place duo Willie Williamson / Billy Wightman.

Mervyn Robinson
and Rob Britton at
Metropole NW200

Peter Herron at
Mid-Antrim 150

Tom Herron
NW200

Graham Young
& Noel Hudson
rounding Metroploe

Harold
Crawford

Pete Cartwright

Robert
Davison

*Donny
Robinson at
NW200*

*Denis
Todd*

*Brian
Reid*

Jackie Hughes

Ian McIntosh

remembers Ulster Scots Racing...

Born in Perth Ian's father, a police inspector, took him to many a race meeting, but when Ian wanted to race as an U-18 his father, knowing the risks, wasn't so keen.

He first visited Ireland when the company he served his time with in Perth sent him to install machinery in the Lurgan area where, after attending the Tandragee races and watching spell-bound, he was hooked on road racing.

Ian moved to N. Ireland to work for the Michelin Tyre Company, in Ballymena met his wife Iris and over forty years later is still here, obviously not racing any more but still enjoying the craic of the race paddocks.

In the mid 1950s, as a wee boy, my father and brother-in-law took me to a motor cycle race meeting at Errol Aerodrome, an ex-WW2 airfield between Perth and Dundee, where for the first time I saw motorbike racing and witnessed riders of the calibre of Bob McIntyre, Alistair King, Ewan Haldane, Terry Shepherd, Gordon Bell to name but a few.

In those days there was no TV coverage of racing – and even if there was we didn't have a TV – and only limited radio and cinema newsreel coverage of major events so I had no idea what I was going to see that day but the noise – mainly 4 stroke singles, the smell of Castrol R, the speed, excitement, the look of the machines and riders meant from that day on I have been a motor cycle racing fanatic!

When I got a bit older I went to the Errol races regularly on my own, where I had the privilege of meeting my hero Bob McIntyre and Alistair King which as an eleven year old was very special! A chance encounter with a man who turned out to be Bob's uncle ended up with me being introduced to him and spending the day in the pits with them. That evening was the highlight of my young life when I was given a lift by Bob McIntyre and his future wife Joyce in his Bedford van, complete with race bikes in the back, the few miles from the circuit up to Errol village where my Father ran a hotel. Now that was one very special day!

Other circuits I visited in those days were Charterhall, Gask, Beveridge Park Kirkcaldy and on one occasion a long trip to Silverstone to see the Hutchinson 100 meeting. I just lived looking forward to the next meeting I could get to and avidly followed racing in the motor cycle magazines.

By the time I was sixteen I wanted to get a road bike of my own but my ex-policeman father had seen too many motor cycle tragedies and said if I would wait a year he would help me buy a car instead, an offer too good to turn down and one which, in hindsight, probably kept me alive!

Of course runs out on friends' bikes still took place which kept the desire alive and I was keen to try racing although, as in those days race entries for under eighteens had to have a parental signature, that had to be put on hold for a couple of years until I was old enough to enter on my own.

At the time my brother-in-law worked with a bloke called Jimmy McCabe from Kennoway in Fife who had a little 204cc Ducati sleeved down to 200cc for that class and I got the chance to try this out a few times at practice days at Errol and Gask airfield just outside Perth although I fell off first day out!

In those days the circuits in Scotland were becoming fewer and it was a long jaunt to the circuits in England so the races were few and far between but we did a few meetings in Scotland and the North of England, starting with a meeting at Crimmond, a wide bumpy ex-airfield near Peterhead

It was on the way to that race meeting, in a transport café outside Forfar, I first met the late Colin Keith who became a real good friend and he and his sponsor Norman Lindsay would stay with Iris and I on many occasions when he raced in Ireland.

This sort of cameraderie is at the core of motorcycle sport and I quickly got to know and make friends with many of my fellow competitors including some who might be described as "diamonds in the rough".

One such was Alex George who I met when he was parked next to us at Gask one day and we got chatting.

In those Days Alex would have had a tendency towards the odd bad word or two and it never occurred to us that a friend's young son, who Jimmy McCabe had brought along, was recording our conversation on his portable tape recorder without thinking. All was well until, at home a few days later, his mother heard the recording and informed him that if that was the company he was keeping at motor cycling then he was not getting back – we never saw him again!

At that first race at Crimmond I remember being out round the course and talking to Alex's father while watching the 250 race. Alex was going real good but was up against the early Yamahas and was struggling on the Ducati. His dad turned and said that he didn't realise Alex was so good and was going to have to buy him a Yamaha – not too many Dad's like that.

My first experience of Northern Ireland came about when the company I was serving my apprenticeship at in Perth got a contract to install a grain drying and animal feed plant at the Ormeau Bakeries home farm just outside Magheralin. I was one of the team who went on that job and I had my first and very enjoyable introduction to the Province. We stayed in Lurgan for about six weeks, enjoying the craic in the pubs, going to dances and seeing all the showbands in places like the Banbridge Bridge Ballroom and the Flamingo in Ballymena. I also became aware of the enthusiasm for motor cycle racing in the country and the existence of proper road races which made a big impact with this aspiring racer.

After my apprenticeship I worked as a trainee toolmaker at Timex in Dundee for a year or so before moving to Michelin in Stoke on Trent. During the time training and working in Stoke I was able to go watch racing at Aintree, Oulton, Mallory, Croft, Darley Moor etc., but I still wanted to try and have a go again myself, especially on the roads.

When I heard Michelin were opening a new factory at Ballymena it sounded an ideal opportunity and I moved to Ballymena late 1969, initially on a temporary basis for a few months and then full time from mid 1970.

John McDowell at St Angelo

I was at a Mid Antrim trial at Slemish one day and was introduced to the late John McDowell, a great character and a good friend, who had a 1961 7R AJS for sale and I ended up the proud owner.

My initial plan was to enter the Temple 100 in August but following a chat with Jimmy Johnson in John's garage one evening I took his advice and postponed my debut until the Mid Antrim a couple of weeks later.

Although I went on to ride at and really enjoy the Temple from 1971 onwards, when John, Jimmy and I went to watch in 1970 the wisdom of Jimmy's advice that it might not be a good event for a beginner became apparent. I watched as Raymond McCullough, Tom Herron, Dennis Gallagher, Gerry Mateer, Cecil Crawford, Billy McCosh, Len Ireland, Ian McGregor and especially Billy Guthrie landed off the jumps on the back wheel while cranked over – it scared the hell out of me!

Suitably chastened, I headed off with the 7R to the Mid Antrim for my first proper road race on the long Rathkenny circuit which went nearly to Broughshane at that time.

To learn the circuit Jimmy took me round it a couple of nights before the race in his MK2 Jag in the dark – I'm sure he got round quicker in the car than I did on the 7R and scared the life out of me in the process!

For the race itself Billy McCosh loaned me a set of leathers for the day that had been Malcolm Templeton's and were a wee bit short for me making my eyes water. Maybe I could use that as an excuse for my lowly finish in the race but in truth my objective for the day was just to get round and complete my first Irish road race!

Last or first I was smitten and for the next 18 years, for 14 of which I did not miss a single road race in N. Ireland. I traversed the length and breadth of the country to race between the houses, hedges, ditches and walls of the Irish and Manx countryside – so much for my initial plan of staying for only a couple of years.

Me at the NW200 1978

Back then Con Law and Jack Agnew were also working in Michelin and had started racing as well which was good. The racing, the roads, the people, the craic and the fact that most of the circuits were within about two hours from home, with plenty of pubs along the way, meant that for every reason to go back home that arose, two or three reasons to stay would pop up. Of course I met and married Iris which sealed the matter and here I still am today.

Road racing in N I has always been unique, but the racing during the seventies and eighties was a particularly special time with the likes of the Armoy Armada and the Dromara Destroyers battling it out over the unique racing circuits we have! I have met so many really nice people and made so many friends in racing here, but sadly have also lost a great many along the way, such is the nature of motor cycle racing.

For my own part I was not in it for the glory, just for the fun and the thrills and maybe that's why I never had any serious accidents or maybe I was just lucky – but one way or another I wouldn't want to have missed a minute of my time in the sport.

Epilogue

Thus we come to the end of an era dominated by Ray McCullough but also saw the emergence of Joey Dunlop, who would go on to become the master of the eighties and beyond.

Young chargers Dave Watson, Laurence Spence and Stephen Russell were coming along to challenge Norwood, Crockard and McBride on the local motocross scene before all three set out on the world Grand Prix trail in the eighties

The emergence of the Japanese two-stroke machines ruled the sport in all classes as we left the seventies, a dominance that was to prevail well into the future.

Events throughout the seventies were organised and run mostly by amateur, but enthusiastic and respected clubs and officials; a situation that did not change with the same speed as the sport was changing in the decades ahead.

Technology was moving along at a fast rate with lap times decreasing as tyre development, chassis design, engine power, stopping power and road surfaces all progressed – however circuit safety was still a long way behind the progress of machinery from the seventies through the eighties.

The sport itself had changed dramatically through the seventies as top names shied away from pure road racing and the likes of the TT and Ulster Grand Prix lost world championship status, which many thought would see the demise of these famous events.

What was to emerge were new Formula 1, 2 and 3 world championships that had their detractors, but turned out to be a lifeline to the two international events with new names coming to the fore with Joey Dunlop making the F1 series his own into the eighties.

The Embassy Championship – supported by Imperial Tobacco whose support of motorcycling in Ulster spanned four decades before Government Legislation scuppered their involvement – would continue as the main short circuit series in Ulster well into the next decade before a national short circuit championship would be launched with riders of the caliber of Mark Farmer, Gary Cowan, Robert Dunlop, Johnny Rea, Alan Patterson, Geoff McConnell, Ricky Wilson and a young charger named Phillip McCallen muscle their way into the results challenging the likes of Brian Reid, Alan Irwin, Steven Cull, Sam McClements, Paul Cranston, Con Law and his cousin Gene McDonnell – and yes all were as comfortable riding short circuits as they were riding the roads i.e. they could race and win on both.

Rider and event sponsors became more prominent in the sport with Rea Racing being followed by Millar Transport, Starplan, Francis Neill, Brian Coll, Team Wood, Enkalon Club, East West Transport and many, many more who were to lift the sport to another level.

In the years since, generations of fearless and daring young men plus the occasional young woman took to the roads and tracks (in many cases following in family footsteps) to fulfil their dreams and love of a sport that brings thrills, exhilaration, deep satisfaction and firm friendships yet can be sullied with uncertainty, sadness and grief, a formula that has went hand and hand with motorcycle racing and other sports since the invention of the wheel.

I hope you have enjoyed the surface scratch into the seventies within these pages with many memories aroused of who and what happened, where and when it happened with the prospect that you the reader can say, "I was there when that happened."

If so then I will have fulfilled the expectation of what was envisaged when the idea of this book was first mooted – we're all in it *Just for the Thrill*.

Dear Reader,

I hope you have enjoyed this publication from Ballyhay Books, an imprint of Laurel Cottage Ltd. We publish an eclectic mix of books ranging from personal memoirs to authoritative books on local history, from sport to poultry, from photographs to fiction and from music to marine interests – but all with a distinctly local flavour.

To see details of these books, as well as the beautifully illustrated books of our sister imprint Cottage Publications, why not visit our website **www.cottage-publications.com** or contact us on +44 (0)28 9188 8033.

Timothy & Johnson

BALLYHAY BOOKS